THE THURSDAY SHOP

The Thursday Shop

an antique dealer's diary

Anne Summers

Kineton · The Roundwood Press
1969

First published in 1969 by
The Roundwood Press (Publishers) Limited
Kineton, Warwick

Set in 'Monotype' Bell, series 341, and printed by
Gordon Norwood at The Roundwood Press, Kineton,
in the County of Warwick
and bound by Henry Brooks at Oxford.

Made and Printed in Great Britain

For 'My Quiet Girl'

1

MY DIARY is rather like a home-made cake, into which I have flung, grated, whipped, and stirred everything I can think of. Now, if you will open the oven (or the book if you are determined to be literal) I will lift it out and cut you a slice. It is full of real happenings, happenings in our village and in our family, but mostly about my small business which adjoins our cottage.

First of all I must rename my husband, the children, and the village. I can't have people coming up to me on Market Day or at Auction Sales and asking, 'Are you the woman who wrote "The Thursday Shop?"' I said that this diary would never get sorted out or rewritten unless I broke a leg or something, but I'm tired of waiting to go into hospital so instead I will retreat to the apple-room on a closing day sometimes and choose a few pages.

Each time I had a baby I never had the right name ready, now I am ready. My son shall be Gordon and my daughter, who is five years younger, shall be Angela. This was a name I rather liked originally, but she was born hungry, and if I had suggested that, or anything else cherubic, I think my nurse would have thrown her at me. After three days and nights of listening to her solo, Nurse's 'patience was exhausted' as Hitler is so fond of saying. My husband shall be John, our village Penny Priors, and the county can remain, as it will always be, leafy Warwickshire. You know who Anne Summers is, I, me, I, and there is an 'e' on the end of Anne. You may have guessed that I keep an antique shop and I certainly do, and 'custymuds,' as a small niece calls my patrons, keep exclaiming,

'What fun!'

It certainly is fun, and hard work too, but that is also great fun — if you happen to like it. But I do sometimes wonder how some of them would react if they came home to find a load of furniture dumped outside on their footpath in the rain, or a pile of firewood on their lawn, which was what the railway lorry delivered one day — all that was left of a beautiful moulded chest-of-drawers which I had bought in Wales.

I'm going to start at the beginning by saying that we all think we have some gift or talent and I think I was born with a good memory. I remember once trying to convince my mother that I could remember lying in my cradle, (mind you it was a large one). I gave her so many details as to where it was and various happenings I witnessed from it that she had to believe me, and to this day I can see the shape of its hood and the plait of wicker-work round its edge. My elder brother had used this before me and two younger brothers were to follow. I like to think that the first thing I held was the antique silver rattle with its little bells and ivory handle which appears in some of the family photographs; but the first plaything I *really* remember was my mother's lovely turquoise and pearl bracelet which she quietly put into my hands as I sat on my little red hassock in the bottom of the pew on Sunday mornings, and my first antique possession was the family coral necklace which I have since passed on to Angela.

When I was twelve years old I had a form-mate who lived next door to the Sale Yard at the West Gate in Warwick and we used to haunt the place. The sale was a regular Saturday afternoon affair and we were attracted by the pens of puppies, rabbits and poultry. One day I bid for two enormous cabbages; they were knocked down to me for threepence. But how was I to cycle home with them? A piece of raffia solved my difficulties and I hung them on either side of my handlebars. All went well until I was speeding down the steep Smith Street; it was then that the raffia parted and the cabbages rolled away in opposite directions. When I did reach home, my mother was not impressed with my bargain — and I was late for tea. My second venture was no more successful; I bought a hen that never laid an egg and, looking back, I think she may well have been my first antique as she died a natural death some weeks later.

In my art student days I became a sales addict, and began to attend regularly a sale-room. This was a weekly treat I squeezed in between the afternoon and evening sessions on a Friday. The people there interested me as much as the furniture

2

and I often wished we had some of them to pose for us at College. I could soon price things to a shilling or two, and never once made a bad buy as having no money I never bid for anything. After three years I took my finals and then followed marriage and motherhood. Ten years later came the outbreak of war. It was then we moved to Penny Priors and for some weeks we did not know that the half-timbered building alongside the cottage went with the property. I well remember our landlady coming to tea and asking if I let the children play in the shop.

'Oh!' I said, 'was that included?', and she replied

'Didn't I give you the key?' and opening her crocodile handbag she took it off her key ring. We could hardly wait for her to go. The shop was long and narrow and full of rubbish, old tin trunks, mouldy advertisements and damp Seidlitz powders. The old ledgers there gave us readymade insight into our new neighbours' tastes and finances. Through the years the shop had been a cow-shed, a carpenter's shop and a village store. I began to have ideas about it and wrote away for leaflets about growing mushrooms in pans, rearing chickens in brooders and even considered opening a baby crèche.

I must close my diary for to-day and I haven't said anything yet about antiques and dealing or ghosts and grub-holes, but it's all there in my diary — if I can read my own writing.

❦ 2 ❧

LAST TIME I wrote how pleased I was to find out that the shop alongside went with our cottage. Urged on by wartime leaflets I dug the neglected garden and planted it with neat rows of early peas, French beans, beetroot, carrots and cabbage lettuce. I stuck the illustrated packets on little sticks and told the seeds to keep their eyes on the pictures and to do their best.

Each time I straightened my back I took a long look at the shop and my mind was one big query; — what should I do with it? One day when I was feeling particularly energetic I turned it out and threw the old ledgers and junk on to the garden bonfire and hauled the old tin trunks into an outhouse to use for fowl-corn and meal.

One spring day before I had come to any conclusion Mrs Clancey and I had a day out. There was to be an auction sale at a cottage less than two miles away. She said I was to be ready at ten o'clock. I was up early and flew around; gave the children their breakfast, got Gordon off to school, fed the fowls, washed up, made the beds, laid the table for tea and packed a picnic lunch and filled the thermos with soup for Angela. Mrs Clancey insisted on pushing the perambulator and I enjoyed swinging my arms.

I had about eight pounds housekeeping in my purse and rather to my surprise I began bidding for everything I liked and succeeded in buying a few lots. Mrs Clancey was highly amused and asked me what I was up to. I heard myself replying, 'I'm buying stock!' That is how it really started.

After tea Mrs Clancey brought in her knitting and 'baby sat' while Gordon and I took the empty pram to collect the goods. We set off at a spanking pace, Gordon pushing this time. As soon as we were out of sight I raced with him down the hill. We were soon loaded up and on our way home. We had packed the china and glass in newspaper in the bottom of the pram and surmounted the load with an old spinning wheel which slowly revolved as we bowled along.

After Gordon had gone to bed I unpacked my 'pantechnicon,' putting everything on the shop floor except the spinning wheel which I put in the shop window with a little notice propped up against it, saying 'Opening shortly.' But I didn't. It was the first year of the war. I could not settle to anything. Disaster followed disaster, Dunkirk, the fall of France, terrible losses at sea; invasion seemed imminent. Gas masks were issued, more leaflets and warnings, and orders to stay in our homes whatever happened. This latter instruction was, of course, to leave our roads clear for our forces to move and repel the invader. Signposts were pulled up and church bells silenced. As the harvest began to ripen, the battle of Britain began in the summer skies. On Sundays, the War Memorial of the Great War looked down upon us and its golden sword hung there like the sword of Damocles, and we wondered,

'How many men *this* time? How many years *this* time?'

The children hadn't a care in the world. We picnicked on the little island, we paddled below the weir and we swam in the mill-pond. We gleaned, we blackberried, we went wooding with the pram. But after they were asleep it was different. Darkness descended and the silence was broken only by the sound of convoys grinding along the Roman Road and planes throbbing across the night sky. Tragedy had already struck our family — my brother in the R.N.V.R. was lost at sea.

After the first sale when I bought the spinning wheel out of housekeeping money, I withdrew my savings and opened a banking account. Most weeks I added a few things to my stock. Sometimes I walked with Angela in the pram to a Saleyard Sale and sometimes got Mr Bede to take us in his taxi to an open air sale at a farm or a cottage. There I would sit Angela on top of a chest-of-drawers in the garden and stand with my arms around her. She would watch the auctioneer's play with his little hammer with grey-eyed wonder, but when she had got her bearings she would want to get down and make friends with all the dogs there.

Only the planes above in the blue sky reminded us that we were at war with Germany — it was like waking to a nightmare.

'Now what will you bid me for this wall-map of the British Isles?' called the auctioneer. 'A shilling, Sir? Is that all? Everything Hitler wants for a shilling — going, going, gone!'

'Now come along my friends, you will have to bid quicker than that, Joe Wilkins here wants to get back to the milking and we all know he's waiting for the churns at the end of the sale.'

'Lot 202, any offers for the coal-box and contents? Winter's coming!'

'Lot 280, mangle and stand. Five shillings I'm offered. Red Hat! Green Hat! Red Hat! Green Hat! — Green Hat has it at 15/-!'

The bees droned across the summer flowers and the scent of the phlox drifted across us. I found an old wicker chair and Angel spread-eagled across my knee was having her nap. I looked at the sleeping pink face with the black lashes in strange contrast to her soft fair hair and I thought, 'I'm going to remember her like this!'

At four o'clock the children breaking loose from school raced down the lane to join us before the fun was over. They pushed like lambs among the flock locating their own mothers and then, satisfied, ran off as lambs do to some little knoll and played and gambolled. Angel waked to this world of children and quickly toddled off. A big girl took her hand and tried to mother her, but she shook herself free and tagged along independently.

Angela usually has her mid-day sleep in her big pram and I shall certainly not part with it until things are better. The war news is dreadful, there is no other word for it. Each time I polish the pram I think of those thousands of refugee women on the dusty roads of France with *their* prams and pushcarts. Could it happen here and where should we go? Each time I have these thoughts I remember friends in a sheltered green valley below Cader Idris in the Welsh mountains. There are great stone barns there and mountain streams full of rainbow trout.

The very permanence of the Church and the building itself which overshadows us, is a perpetual comfort. One shakes a duster from a window, it is there. One mows the lawn, it is just behind or just before us. As we wait for the jug to be filled at the Glebe Farm dairy, it is at our side. Frightened women for almost a thousand years have knelt on that very spot, in fear of death, invasions and the enemy. In ancient times they used to take refuge there, pulling up ramps like drawbridges, for there were no doors on ground level then. Cut deep in the pew back in front of me are the letters A.M. These seem to be full of promise and to me mean that glorious word 'morning.'

WELL, I AM A SHOPKEEPER, and Penny Priors now has two shops. I opened my antique shop on Saturday, October the twelfth 1940 at nine a.m. Several villagers were waiting for the door to open. They had got tired of seeing the notice about 'opening shortly.' and were curious to see my stock. Pretty antique cups and saucers sold like hot cakes, and so did a mountain of old blue and white willow pattern plates and tureens piled high on an old spinet. An unknown dealer bought all my wheelback chairs and an old Credence table. Another dealer advised me to fix up some shelves or racks on the walls for setting out my stock and he said 'never sell the spinning wheel in the window, it is as good as a shop sign.'

At noon, after three busy hours, I closed the door, till the following Saturday morning. I had not 'sold out,' but the shop looked as if a bomb had struck it! There were thirty-seven pounds in the till, which was not the sort that 'pinged' but a lovely old rivetted *sucrier*. I folded the notes (I had no cheques that first morning), and put them into a purse-like old cigar case which Mrs Clancey had given me.

That was my first day; the following Saturdays followed a similar pattern. I would buy during the week, usually getting to one of the local sales, and on Friday evenings after the children were in bed, I would set to work with the beeswax and my dusters, giving everything a good rub up, and set out my stock.

There are only three ways of buying stock :-
(1) at Auction Sales (2) from other Dealers and (3) Privately. Many dealers never go to Auction Sales, they think it is a waste of time.

I must confess I much prefer buying to selling, and I love turning out the shop and working on the furniture. When people were looking in the window I used to hope they would go away, but I soon got over this phase and sometimes talked so much that the poor souls had a job to get away from me.

It is funny how unfussy people are these days, for no one expects anything to be wrapped up or wants a receipt. The war news is so grave and everyone looks anxious. People seem kinder, and to value things that really matter, and glad to find someone who has time to listen.

Shortly after opening, I had the chance of buying several hundred yards of short remnants at 1/- a yard. They were ends of rolls or slightly faulty pieces of furnishing fabrics. There were beautiful printed linens, glazed sprigged chintzes, delicate percales and flowery cretonnes of the finest quality. These proved a great attraction and brightened up the scene too. Customers kept coming back for more, for curtains, aprons, house-coats and bed-spreads. I took my sewing-machine into the shop and hemmed scores of little curtains, while the customers explored the shop, dived into books, and discussed the war news.

Angela loved to help and sat close by me in her great-grandfather's little antique chair, busily cutting out Teddy-bear's trousers and dolls' cradle covers, from the offcuts and snippets. When customers were choosing fabrics and were undecided, she would forget her shyness and hold up lengths against her shoulder and say slowly,

'*This* is pretty 'terial.'

If I had a surplus of any garden produce, that would go into the shop too. Bunches of parsley and mint were free, and so were lettuces . . . I once made the mistake of planting the whole packet in one go. I had quite two hundred ready all at once, for my outlay of threepence. I sold eggs at twopence each. A neighbour brought in quantities of windfall apples and baskets of greengages too. Mrs Willows from the Crossroads, some-times had some honeycombs for sale, some 'wasp customers' discovered these and pierced the cellophane covers, so we had to clear a glazed jewellery cabinet, and put the honeycombs in that, out of harm's way.

That first year, just opening on Saturday mornings, I took £700, the following year £1,400, and doubled again the third year. These figures were takings; that is to say 'sales,' *not* profits. After this Angela started at school, Ruth came to help us and I began to open three days a week and go into it more seriously.

Anyone who starts the most modest little antique business will be amazed how the expenses add up. Here is a little list which are weekly expenses:—

Rent	Rates	Travelling
Lighting (heating)	Carriers	
Tips	Insurance	
Stationery & Postage	Phone	
Cleaning materials	Stains and strippers	

After a few years, with a little help, my expenses rose to over £10 a week, but a woman friend, in London, with an even smaller shop than mine, has to pay £15 a week in rent alone!

Then, as now, furniture has always been my first love, especially chairs. I particularly like the Country Chippendales and wheelbacks, but the finer ones in mahogany and walnut are the best sellers, also fine Georgian wing chairs sell themselves at thirty pounds. The finest one I had in the early days was fifty-eight pounds, and the lady who bought it said that it was finer than the one she had just bought in Cheltenham for £110.

Most dealers will only buy sets of chairs, this means six, and a 'long set' eight or more. The chair frames are usually numbered in Roman numerals, so it is easy to tell when the sets have been split up and divided among the family! It was usual for a set to consist of ten single chairs and two arm dining chairs. My private customers, however, will buy the odd chairs, pairs and threes and fours too, which are the fraction of the price of a set. For example, a neat little mahogany Georgian dining chair might be as little as three pounds, but fifty pounds for the six and seventy five for eight! They go up in leaps and bounds.

As modern furniture disappears from the shops, so the demand for antique and second-hand furniture increases. I continue buying little loads of domestic antique furniture every week — tables, chairs, corner cupboards, chests-of-drawers, coffers, bureaux and firebaskets too. I am wary about buying beds as they take up so much room, but I have a waiting list always for four-poster beds, which are as much sought after round here as country cottages are!

I have so many regular customers that I feel I must keep changing my stock, and how I enjoy my little buying sprees each week! I make a very quick small profit, this pleases my customers and suits me. I rarely have a piece of furniture more than three weeks. and many pieces never get carried in. This way of trading is called 'quick return profits,' or the 'nimble ninepence' method! I turn over my stock nine or ten times a year.

❧ 4 ☙

MRS GLENN, whose family interlocks very happily with mine, comes in most school holidays for a good chat. She is always on the look out for some antique piece for herself or her numerous relatives — she is the youngest of twelve! The other day she exclaimed laughingly,

'You would have loved my Father. He was a sale addict. He would buy the most frightful things and there was always room in our old-fashioned large house for something else. For years a hideous old American organ lived under the front stairs and if a brother was not performing upon it then a sister was. He once bought a life-size white marble figure of a child, a little girl, holding a dove on her breast. I can remember him saying to me, 'Stick up for me Joey if your Mother doesn't like it, you may not like it either, but you love doves, don't you?.'

'His recreation was buying pictures. He would go happily off to a sale, armed with his catalogue saying breezily that he was "just going to have a look at the pictures." As the years went by our old house became a veritable picture gallery; they hung everywhere — on all the walls of all the rooms, the halls, the landings, down the staircases, even in the 'smallest rooms' in the house. Finally, my mother went on strike,' she continued 'She said she would leave him if he bought another one. Needless to say, not many weeks had passed before he was tempted and bought an enormous pair of landscapes in gilt frames. He dare not bring them home after such an ultimatum, but his faithful and understanding carrier said to him "Just bide your time, Sir. I will keep the pictures ready in the van and then the first time the mistress goes out, give me a ring and I will be round with them like a shot. She will never notice them when they are hung."'

'Well the day arrived and my mother set off on foot to visit a friend and to do some shopping too. The plan worked well up to a point, within fifteen minutes the van was at the door and the conspirators were unloading the second picture when a little figure appeared at the far end of the drive — Mother had forgotten her purse, and of course she had to laugh.'

Writing about 'the smallest room' reminds me of what Robert, a young pilot, told me of some of his tricks. His home was a beautifully proportioned Georgian house where his Father frequently had to entertain business acquaintances to luncheon. During the school holidays Robert would be expected to guide the guest down various corridors to his pre-luncheon toilet. He said that the lofty moulded ceiling was rather wasted on the smallest room and that the chain was quite fifteen feet long. On various school outings he had collected a notice from a bus, a train and an aeroplane and rescrewed them on to the inside of the toilet door, they ran as follows :—

MIND YOUR HEAD WHEN RISING FROM THE SEAT
PENALTY FOR IMPROPER USE OF THIS CHAIN £5.
PROPER ADJUSTMENT OF THE BELT MINIMISES
DISCOMFORT WHEN LANDING.

He said the guest's face would be a study when he emerged!

Our pigeons kept getting killed on the main road, the acorns that fall off the great oaks are the attraction. I often collect a basketful, crush them with a stone and throw them on our lawn, but no, they prefer the ones on the king's highway. A food they do fancy which is home grown is our border of stocks. They proceed in single file down one side of it nipping off choice bits, do a smart right turn at the end of the row and proceed down the other side for a second course. They multiply at a surprising rate, they lay two eggs each time which hatch into a male and female . . . hence the expression 'a pigeon pair,' but they repeat the process several times during a good summer. Lately two of our babies have been bereaved and we tried to hand-rear them, holding the beaks open with left finger and thumb and squeezing pulpy bread and milk down with a fountain pen filler. One was quickly reunited in death to its parents, the other progressed after a fashion. At the side of the fire below the cupboard are some little drawers, we pulled one half open, lined it with newspaper and there the little object perched. It turned out to be piebald, and its greasy little feathers stuck up in a little topknot above its hideous little face while below its beak its dribbly bib of wet feathers did nothing to improve the picture. Several neighbours, quite devout ones, exclaimed in sudden horror

'My God, what's that?' and we replied,

'Only a baby vulture we are rearing' and they believed us. In time he became, like the ugly duckling, a very handsome fellow, snow white except for one black quill. We called him Blackpin. On summer days when the front door stands open, he will often strut in with his missus and latest son and daughter, proceed round Angela's high chair picking up odd crumbs and out again. Mrs Muffit our cat, objects to this intrusion but only rumbles in her chest.

A YOUNG DEALER home on leave from the R.A.F. called for me this morning. We went to view a sale up on the hills. The old house is well named The Folly. The architect must have had a really jolly time designing it; most of the rooms are hexagonal and so are the two lodges for good measure. The bathrooms in the little turret with windows in five of the six walls made one feel rather like a shy fish in an aquarium. There was nothing modern however in the great kitchen. An enormous blackleaded range filled one wall, the iron doors of it embossed with thistles, roses and shamrocks. The little flues or chimneys were encircled with bands of polished copper and the whole contraption reminded one of a prize steam engine. A neat elderly maid in spotless cap and apron stood alongside it as if on guard. As we passed her my companion asked roguishly,

'And where is the string that works the whistle?'

On our way home we called on a lady who had written to me to say that she had lots of things to sell as she was moving house. The young gunner and I both armed with wads of notes waited for her to open the door. She led us up to the attics. There were lots of things there that we wanted to buy, but when we tried to do business she was full of excuses, saying,

'Oh yes, the little cradle? I've changed my mind about that, I think a niece may want it. I *was* going to offer you the Georgian commode, but it was a wedding present so I have decided to keep it. But perhaps you would like the little bamboo table? It's a pity it's broken!'

We then sounded her about a little mahogany sewing table. I had a customer who was longing for one. She had said,

'I don't know how to describe it Mrs Summers, but it's about so big and has a little pleated silk udder underneath, you know Mrs Summers?' I knew, and here it was. But no luck again, the vendor, if you could call her that, was keeping it after all. But would we like the magic lantern? Or the curtain poles? We made our way dispiritedly down the stairs. She paused on the landing and offered us the pampas grass in the hand-painted drain pipe and the pickled cabbage coloured jardinière on its sickly stand.

'No, thank you,' but would she like to sell the flower painting in the hall? Well, yes, that was one of the things she had meant to sell when she wrote, but only that morning she had re-membered that her Doctor had always admired it and she was going to give it to him as a parting present.

We found ourselves in the vestibule again. 'No, thank you we really had no sale for giant aspidistras, although they were the finest we had ever seen. We made our way down the drive, carrying three moth-eaten samplers and two maple frames. We had not wanted them but had agreed cheerfully to the price in the attics hoping the sprat would catch a mackerel, but the mackerel had other ideas!

When I got home dear old Mr Forrester was waiting for me and bought a quantity of pictures and all my prints. When he left I felt I could treat myself to a brooch that I had seen in a jeweller's shop in Parsons Street in Banbury. I had resisted it last Friday but had thought about it quite a lot; it was diamond-shaped and made of gold with a border of real half pearls, the centre had a background of plaited hair and on this were the initials, *my* initials A.S. in tiny seed pearls, on the reverse side in a black border were the words A.S. died May 12th 1816 aged 32. I phoned the jewellers and they are keeping it for me.

Lots of mourning rings, lockets and brooches were made in the early part of the nineteenth century although many people think they were a fashion dating from Queen Victoria's widow-hood. Sometimes the hair is not interwoven or plaited but curled round like tiny little ostrich plumes and must have been done with tiny curling irons, and by fairies I should think.

We had an early lunch and John, who was home for the day, decided to walk up with me to the Sale, that I had viewed in the morning. We popped Angela into the big perambulator and Gordon rode alongside. The lots were now laid out in rows on the great lawn by the cedar trees; but the children were far more interested in the local hermit and had eyes for nothing else! He arrived draped in sacks and riding on a bicycle, his long beard and long dark hair and flashing dark eyes made him look like something direct from the Old Testament. Local gossip (hotly denied by bachelors) has it that he had been crossed in love. A kindly farmer lets him live in the corner of a field and there he has a dugout covered with brushwood. There are all sorts of stories in the neighbourhood of his superhuman strength. He keeps body and soul togther by doing some field work and supplements this by posing for his photograph, carefully keeping his face covered with his elbow until he has received his modelling fee. He bid for some pots and pans and an iron kettle, paying the five shillings all in pennies.

Gordon's face was a study while all this was going on; he appeared fascinated too by the long brown toes that protruded from the hermit's boots. I heard John say quietly to him,

'You know Daddy would look like that if Mummy had said "No," when I asked her to marry me.'

The children are in bed now and I am writing up my diary while John is playing his favourite records. Among the books we brought home from the Folly in Angela's pram was an old Court Circular, published on January 26th 1901, recording the death of Queen Victoria. There are pages of flowery language describing her birth, early life, her ascension, happy marriage, early widowhood and long reign. I have copied out a few lines which make a lovely picture; the Queen at twenty-two had just given birth to her second child and at Christmas the Queen wrote in her journal, 'To think that we have two children now, and one who enjoys the sight already (the Christmas tree); it is like a dream.' Prince Albert writing to his father said, 'This is the dear Christmas Eve on which I have so often listened with impatience to your step, which was to convey us to the gift room. To-day I have two children of my own to make gifts to, who, they know not why, are full of happy wonder at the German Christmas tree with its radiant candles.' Her Majesty gives us another sketch of the peaceful 'interior;' 'Albert brought in dearest little Pussy (Princess Victoria), in such a smart, white merino dress, trimmed with blue, which Mamma had given her, and a pretty cap, and placed her on my bed, seating himself next to her, and she was very dear and good; and as my precious invaluable Albert sat there, and our little love between us, I felt quite moved with happiness and gratitude to God.'

THIS MORNING I decided to clean all the windows inside and out, it always seems to make it rain but that couldn't be helped. My char had the copper on in the wash-house down the yard, so I was in charge of the shop and Angela. I had milked Nancy and pegged her out at the side of the road, and the two kids were in the front garden with Angela, so I had tied the gate. She will soon be four and is a picture of a little girl, she has pale gold curls, serious dark grey eyes and black lashes and brows; she still has her baby face and five dimples and her top lip still sticks out as far as her squabby little nose. She was wearing her curly white lamb-skin coat and the kids were, of course, wearing their glossy black and white goat-skin coats. Angel was too busy marshalling her pets to notice me; first she coaxed them over to the gate and then holding up one finger said firmly, 'Wait there.' She then walked purposefully across the little lawn, up the rockery steps (she calls it her little mountain) and turning smartly said loudly 'Now! Come!' Instantly the two kids with three hops and two skips were across the lawn, up the steps and at her side. 'Good!' she said, without a glimmer of a smile, 'Now wait there.' The kids obliged while she marched down 'the mountain,' across the lawn and back to the gate and repeated her orders. Really it was like a circus act — I wished John could have seen her.

Although she talks very well she will not use a word till she has mastered it. You know how toddlers raise their hands and say "All gone,' when a meal is over. Well, not so my daughter, at just two years old she folded her hands in her lap and said 'Finished.' I have often heard her practising words when she has been cleaning her doll's pram. She also makes a thorough job of this, turning it upside down and shaking it violently by the wheels, while the hood is polished with her handkerchief and spit. Once I heard her practising a new word at dead of night; she had made a new friend, a young pilot named Robert. I heard her stirring in her cot and out of the darkness a sleepy little voice said 'Obert, Wobert, Obert, Bobert, *Robert*. Done it!' Silence. Sure enough next day she could say his name! The word which has been her Waterloo is the word 'Yes,' for this she has substituted 'Et.' But Gordon must have taken her in hand and given her a secret lesson, for at breakfast the other morning he said 'Listen, Mum. Angel, do you love me?' and Angela replied without hesitation 'Yes.'

I would always rather have another child here than let mine go away to play, but of course she has to go sometimes and I am beginning to wonder if she is going to have an adventurous life. She has twice been lightly bitten by two of the sweetest of dogs and it might well have been a third time if we had not stopped her gently lifting this dog's eye lid to examine its eye-ball. I left her for a whole day with Mrs Clancey last month and when she returned to me she shot on to my lap, not for the embrace I expected, but to pull my teeth out. Evidently she had watched Mrs Clancey's complete toilet. I felt I had failed her!

16

The other day, to my horror, when she returned from one of her rare outings she said she had seen the pig killed and 'it didn't like it Mummy,' she said 'they pulled its tail.' When she goes to tea at the 'end house,' she loves to climb up the loft stairs and turn round and jump to be caught by one of the big girls there. Their father is the village undertaker and when I found no one in the barn last time, I went through into the workshop looking for her. There was a partly made elm coffin lying across a pair of trestles . . . my Angel was the corpse! She was lying in it beaming with satisfaction while the big girls were putting daisy chains and buttercups in her hair.

The favourite village game without a doubt is 'weddings.' Angela rushes to find me if she hears one approaching. She doesn't want to miss it but is too shy to face the cavalcade as it passes the gate. Of course the girls take it in turns to be the bride, while all the rest are bridesmaids. Some unwary small boy is press-ganged into taking the part of the groom. He is usually woefully short for the rôle and the old top hat rests on his ears but the girls, decked out in old lace curtains with posies and circlets of flowers, look surprisingly beautiful. I pick Angela up and we stand at the little green gate as they pass, and I keep saying 'What a *beautiful* wedding!'

In the afternoon, the weather still being set fair, (despite my window-cleaning activities of the morning) I decided to work on a corner cupboard in the garden. I lifted it out on to the steps and set to work removing the varnish with the edge of a penny. This is a fool-proof way of scraping it, it cannot scratch, and the pressure of the coin leaves a beautiful silken surface. It looks as if days, weeks, months, years of my life are going to be spent removing varnish, or 'muck' as the trade call it! Why *did* people paint it on? To save polishing, of course. But it doesn't look like polish. Well, it shines, doesn't it? Oh, shut up! I don't want to talk to you — I calmed down. Perhaps loving husbands put it on to save their wives drudgery, well perhaps they did. But I would like to choke them all the same. There! I can see the lovely figuring in the wood now, it's only elm or ell-um as they say round here, but it's lovely, like the ripples in the sand and softly golden too. I will beeswax the door before I do the rest, it will encourage me while I gouge the varnish out of the dentil cornice.

Angela waking from her afternoon nap, appears in the doorway carrying her sandals. She wants to help. I find another penny. She fetches her little chair and her hair brush. I brush out her squashed curls and she settles down happily beside me.

'Mummy, why did they varnish it?'

'Because they were silly.'

'Why were they silly, Mummy?'

'Because they didn't use polish.'

'Why didn't they use polish?'

'Because they were sil — perhaps they hadn't any bees to make the beeswax.'

'Why do bees make beeswax?'

'They need it for their homes, darling.'

'Do they polish their hives, Mummy?'

'Well, not exactly, they make little cradles of it.'

'Well! What next!' she exclaimed in Mrs Clancey's voice and was satisfied.

7

AFTER THREE YEARS OF WAR, toys have practically disappeared from the shops and children nearly always receive books as presents; because of this I am constantly asked for bookcases and bookshelves, and customers sometimes buy old dresser racks for this purpose.

Many young mothers are setting to and making old fashioned peg-dolls, stocking dolls, and home-made golliwogs and transforming shoe boxes or strawberry chip-baskets into little basinettes with frills.

I have a waiting list for old dolls' houses, little prams, rocking-horses and outgrown tricycles, not to mention Miss Muffet's blue Kittens!

Angela 'rides' an old tree trunk under the willow tree which looks more like a prehistoric monster than a horse. Occasionally I do get an old pine rocking-horse; they are reappearing magically from old lofts, attics, and lumber rooms. Our old family charger has vanished; it was stabled in my paternal grandmother's neglected conservatory. Childish memory recalls him as large and white, with flaring nostrils and golden eyes. We four children would all ride him at once, the baby behind the one in the saddle and the other two squatting on the curved platform between the rockers, whilst clinging on to the fetlocks for dear life. When my turn came to be in the saddle my pleasure was considerably dampened by the sickening fear of pitching forward through mossy panes of the greenhouse.

The first rocking-horse I bought was in such fine fettle that I sold it immediately for ten pounds. I am now working on another one from which most of the paint has gone. If you had called on Monday around midnight you would have seen me in my dressing-gown scrubbing at his gesso-like undercoat as I soaked him in my still warm bath water. It is going to take quite a week to dry out. I think I shall wax polish it and not repaint it. I have a pair of tiny stirrups and the saddler has found me an old boxful of brass studs in the shapes of hearts, crescents, stars and suns to decorate the harness. I have some scarlet leather that will make a little padded saddle and two wide scarlet belts for the girth and bridle, but it will still be maneless and tailless. Mrs Clancey said that I should be able to get some horsehair from the local knackers.

'But don't go there if you are squeamish,' she added, 'my brother took a dead ewe there last week and the knacker, who had just skinned a calf, was sitting on a dead horse, holding his bread and cheese in a blood-stained hand and drinking tea from the spout of a tea-pot.'

Not only are the toy shops almost empty but the sweet shops too, as sweets and chocolates are on coupons, children's pocket-money is rather a farce. Yesterday evening Angela and I were turning out the button-box and I was telling her of the wonderful things I could buy for a penny when I was five years old.

'*Forty* aniseed balls! *Twenty* glass marbles! A tiny dolly! *Weren't* you lucky?' she exclaimed.

'Yes,' I went on, 'and sometimes for a little treat we were taken into town and given sixpence each to spend at the Penny Bazaar. Here were boxes of daisy plants, forget-me-nots and pink primroses; also revolving racks of plant seeds in gay packets. I loved Canary Creeper, Virginia Stock and Mignonette. There were also little packets of Japanese pith flowers which swelled and opened before our eyes when we soaked them in cold water. Clay pipes were two a penny and sheets of transfers, and so were pretty balls of shaded knitting wool. Little packets of crayons, chalks and Christmas candles were only priced at a penny and so were little needlework pictures traced ready to embroider. There were also tiny chairs, tables, mirrors and fenders to buy for my doll's house. In the sweet section we were not allowed to buy any green sweets as 'they were poisonous,' or the cheaper varieties at four ounces a penny. Favourites with my brothers were bulls-eyes, barley sugar sticks and Edinburgh rock, but I liked liquorice ribbons — eight yards for a penny.

Angela cannot remember ever seeing a box of chocolates of course. I told her how with one finger we used to feel down the rustling side of the box, to find out of there were a second layer and how we sometimes ate out the inside of a chocolate on the head of a pin to spin it out.

I have lately bought some reproductions of some charming little drawings from Herr A. Hendschel's Skizzenbuch. They are of children playing together, or playing with toys. I am going to copy some of the drawings into my Skizzenbuch, or rather, diary, for the playthings must be antiques by now.

Since writing this, all those years ago, I have heard of a wonderful dolls' museum, that a lady, a Mrs Robinson, has opened at Okens House in Warwick. I hope to take my granddaughter to it, for a day out, when she is a little older. We will take a picnic lunch into the Castle Grounds and share it with the peacocks.

I have caught sight in my diary of a copy I made of one of Angela's childish notes in her inimitable spelling. Fiona wrote the following little note for her Mother when her Father took her into town to catch the post. She is just five and a quarter, and not at school yet.

GUWYN TOTAWN YN THE CR. It is English not Welsh.

8

THERE IS NOTHING about antiques this time. It's all about Mrs Clancey, who is about fifty so only half an antique! She is one of our dearest friends in the village and as her orchard adjoins ours we see each other most days. She appears to be as strong as an Amazon but worries about her health. Mr Clancey has to take her pulse at frequent intervals, and he gives the most roguish wink if he is caught in the act. As soon as he has gone off to work, Mrs Clancey appears with great buckets of pig swill and strides off up the orchard with them. A little later she reappears, this time with a stiff broom and buckets of water; she sweeps her yards, the drive-in and then a bit of the footpath for good measure — the roadman says she ought to get a job on the Council!

Through the years she and I have had friendly rivalry over our poultry. Neither of us had kept any until the war, although we had helped our mothers with theirs before we were married. We each borrowed a broody hen and bought a sitting of eggs, Rhode Light Sussex cross; these are ideal for beginners as the pullet chicks are brown like father and the cockerel chicks are white or yellow like mother. Mrs Clancey's hen hatched the twelve eggs and there were ten pullets and two cockerels. Real beginners luck! My hen produced ten chickens, six pullets and four cockerels; so Mrs Clancey won the first round. However, at Christmas my fattened cockerels weighed nearly a pound more than hers, although she kept jerking the balance to make it less. Second round to me! My next move was to buy some goose eggs secretly and to set them four at a time as each of my hens went broody, but before the first lot hatched, Mrs Clancey called me round to see one of her hens proudly parading a brood of guinea-fowl chicks. Round three to her! The following week she came round to admire my first goslings; I sent some of these to market and they made such a ridiculous price that it was mentioned in the local press. I now felt I was slightly ahead, but my pride went before a fall; one of her hens hatched a turkey egg that she had found in a ditch on the way home from Church. I jokingly said that I would inform the police, for it did not need a Sherlock Holmes to guess to whom it belonged. I was now a poor second. We did equally well with our ducks; we both had Aylesbury and Indian Runners; the former are the large white ones like Jemima Puddleduck and the Runners are the sprightly almost vertical brown ones! When we had our first one for Sunday dinner, I felt rather proud of our war-time spread. The duck was stuffed with home-grown sage and onions, the home-grown vegetables were Arran Pilot new potatoes and Little Marvel garden peas; these were followed by home-grown gooseberries in the pie. Angela now five wanted to say 'Grace;' but she got a little confused once she started and the familiar grace was rendered as follows:—

'Thank You for the world so sweet
Thank you for the *birds* we *eat* . . . Good morning.'

There was a sequel to our poultry rearing venture. The following spring Mrs Clancey squeezed her now well-grown turkey-hen into the basket on her bicycle handlebars, and cycled miles to get her mated. In due course she laid and produced a brood. By this time I felt completely routed, but the fates were kind. A customer, whose hobby is doing up large neglected houses and gardens, asked me to tea to see her latest acquisition. I admired everything — her baby, her paintings and her home. I was then walked around the grounds and shown her pens of peacocks which she bred as a hobby. I bided my time. A week later she called again and asked the price of a panelled oak door and I laughingly replied,

'A pair of young peacocks.'

'All right,' she said, 'you shall have them.'! I could hardly wait to see Mrs Clancey's face. Before I could say anything, I had to take her pulse. She was in low spirits and said that she did not appear to have one. I've never managed to locate it either, but I looked motherly and reassuring, and said,

'Well, it's strong and steady now, old dear!' (may I be forgiven): I then broke the news about the peacocks. She wouldn't believe me at first and then reached down two port glasses and a bottle. She said we must celebrate with some raspberry wine which she had made from some bottled fruit which had gone wrong. We settled down to a good gossip, but I had hardly had a sip before Ruth called for me and said that I was wanted.

'Drink it up first, dear,' urged Mrs Clancey. I gulped it down, it was delicious — but there were after-effects. The customer who was waiting wanted to see some rugs. I only had one, an old Persian. I held it up to display it but to my astonishment I found that my left leg had shrunk and would not touch the floor; I stretched it hard but no, it was about two inches too short. I kept my balance by resting my left elbow on a convenient mahogany pedestal, and assumed a carefree air which I was far from feeling.

I wish I could say that Mrs Clancey then found an ostrich or a stork, but it wouldn't be true and I was unable to take delivery of my peacocks after all. They needed pens and the wire netting was unobtainable. If they were unrestrained they would make havoc of our neighbours' gardens, and John and I felt the pony was enough of a liability.

OTHER THINGS besides food, clothes and luxuries have disappeared after three years of war. Tramps for instance and horses, while young men are only seen at farm sales. The only tramp who ever calls is Nococoa and he is as regular as the phases of the moon. He got this name for himself by refusing cocoa on one occasion when we were out of tea. His usual routine is to present his tea-can, mumble something, and then perch on the garden wall till he is hailed. He then settles down on the footpath, his back pressed against the back of the chimney breast, the little patch warmed by the fire. There he enjoys his brew and anything else we rustle up for him. Angel, now five, likes to stand and watch him. One day he asked her how the hens were laying, and in a clear little voice I heard her reply,

'Not very well, only china ones we can't eat' and when he asked her about a strange pinky artichoke-like plant she said,

'We don't know what it |is, but it came from Uncle Tom's, so it must be something very choice!' I heard him mutter something about 'a funny little cuss.'

Everything has changed, the few private cars have their wings painted white to show up in the blackout and others have balloons of gas on their roofs. Great convoys of army vehicles keep passing south, but when there is a raid in the Midlands, fire tenders keep slipping through northwards in the night.

The cottage seems very quiet to-night. The children have been asleep for hours. I have caught up with the ironing and done the evacuee's too. Her baby is very near and her legs are swollen. Last night there were eleven souls sleeping under the roof — counting the shop roof too. A record! The two children and myself, the expectant mother and her toddler, and six strangers who had come out into the country to get a good night's rest away from the sirens, the bombs and the gunfire. They made themselves as comfortable as they could in the shop. We filled their rubber bottles, made tea, and they draped themselves in their own travelling rugs and odd curtains and old Persian rugs they found there. By morning several had moved out out on to the grass verge which they found softer than the shop floor. Last Saturday John was here for the weekend : we were very late getting to bed and as I opened our bedroom window I saw a chink of light through Mrs Webb's blackout.

'Mrs Webb hasn't gone to bed, John, she must be ill. She always goes about nine o'clock.'

'Shall I go ?' came John's sleepy voice from the bed.

'No, a man's voice might frighten her, I'll go' I said getting into my walking shoes and a coat. I was there in two minutes and tapped gently on her window calling out at the same time

'Are you all right my dear ?'

'Why yes, that's Mrs Summers, isn't it ? What are you doing up at this time ?'

'That's what I have come to ask you.'

'Why what time is it ?'

'Half past midnight!'

'Good Heavens, I thought it was six in the morning!' came her voice 'I've misread the clock.'

'You'd better undress again.'

'Not I, I'm going to stay up now. I'm not going to get my corsets on twice for old Hitler,' and I could hear her defiantly stirring her cup of tea and knew she meant it. So I wished her good-morning and left.

Anything funny these days seems twice as funny, and anything sad seems twice as sad.

When I was ironing this week I had the best laugh I have had for months. I had to put the iron up on its rest and weep with laughing. On the radio a Quiz was being broadcast and two First Aid Teams were competing. One of the questions was 'What would you do if you found a casualty bleeding profusely from the head?'

'I would send for a doctor quickly,' came the reply.

'Yes, and what else?'

'I would apply a pad of lint and bandage the head.'

'And if the bleeding continued?'

'I would bandage more tightly.'

'And if the bleeding still persisted?' pressed the examiner.

'I would apply a tourniquet to the casualty's neck' came the desperate answer.

Another little incident which kept me chuckling all morning was a little note sent up to me by the retired school-mistress at Church Cottage. Like us she lives under a thatched roof and she had read somewhere that if a bomb landed on a thatched roof it would slip off and not pierce it as the cant of the roof was so steep. While a friend of hers, another old lady, said she thought all the fuss about invasion was silly, all that needed to be done was to 'put a trail of gunpowder round the edge of England, and put a match to it if we saw them coming.'

⊰{ 10 }⊱

So MANY OF THE THINGS we dread, never happen, while others are quite bearable when they do. I had hoped I would never have to see Jane Tudor leave her home; she loved every stone, or rather mellow brick of Heritage Farm. She had gone there as a bride five years ago and her child was born there. But now it is sold, and I have offered to help on the day of the move. I am to accompany her down that beautiful meadow drive — for the last time!

'Is there anything else upstairs?'

'Nothing at all,' came the answer.

But I pretended not to hear and ran upstairs for a last look. It was true, there was nothing left. Nothing left but memories! The curtainless windows let in a flood of silvery spring sunshine, the diamond panes threw a tracery of shadows on the bare boards and the sprigged paper. The attics are empty and scrubbed clean. Here Jane kept her incubators, here she filled baskets with bronze chickens to carry down to the foster-mothers.

Through the stairs window, the farm-yard looks strangely empty; most of the stock is sold and the poultry ready crated. The silence is intense; it is strange not to hear old Savage bellowing in the bull-pen but he has gone and will never kill anyone now, though he did his best, one terrible day.

I go into the guest-room where John and I have been welcomed so many times. I put my head where my pillow used to lie and take a last look at the poplars cresting Old Pastures. I remember the deep baying of their Newfoundland, the alarm calls of Jane's geese and the soft whistlings of her goslings in the hen-coops below the window. I open the nursery door, no serious brown-eyed little girl there now, doing her gymnastics in her pink cot. Her pets and toys and cats are crated too.

The dining-room is ready for another wife to arrange her

furniture and hang her curtains; only a match is needed to set the logs ablaze and the shadows dancing. This room is strangely silent too, no measured 'tick tock' of the grandfather clock, no voices, no laughter, no music. A last look in the old kitchen! What fun we had bathing our babies there, what peace we knew, feeding them there. What convenient hanging places those bright knobs on the range had been for little sleeping suits and warm towels!

They are calling for me, for I am supposed to be helping. The daphne mezereum is still in bloom, the primulas make a patch of purple, and the daffodils are opening under the pear trees. The two furniture vans lead the way, followed by a cattle truck transporting the two mares, with old George in the back. He is to wave his spotted handkerchief if Blossom or Flower crowd him; the driver is to keep a look out for this in his mirror. Jane and I follow in the two-seater. I avoid looking at her. We have not gone a hundred yards before some rugs slip on to the mares. George is frantically waving his distress signal. We accompany his shouts with tootings on the horn. The three drivers all accelerate. George loses his head and tries to save his life by swarming up Blossom's tail! We pass through the drive gates in convulsions of laughter.

I SOMETIMES WONDER if I love my family as much as I profess! It's so *simply lovely* when they have all gone in the morning; John first and then the two children and I pour out my second cuppa. Dear Mrs Muffit sits against my foot and purrs and we smile at each other. Then I read my letters and slit open any catalogues, firmly putting on one side those advertising sales on my opening days. Yes, there is one for next Tuesday, at the old Mill near Littleford. Why, that place has been unoccupied since the beginning of the war! The catalogue starts with the maids' bedrooms, washstands, iron bedsteads, cane-seated chairs. Ah! this is better in the attics, archer's bows and arrows, croquet set, rugs, leather hat-boxes — these make delightful waste paper boxes, I have seen them lined with old maps and varnished inside. I read on — towel rails, cricket bats, antique baby's cradle. What is an antique baby? Three tin trunks and contents — I must look in them — pictures, frames, fenders, antique lady's sewing table. Mother of the antique baby, perhaps? Now down to the bedrooms, the furnishing old-fashioned but not old, Edwardian and heavy Vic. The brass inlaid chairs sound like Regency, I hope thay have sabre legs; I must see if the two in Bedroom 5 match the pairs in bedrooms 6 & 7 — a set perhaps. Just what the new Doctor at Appleton wants to go with his Regency dining table. I will try for the wheelback chairs in the kitchen too for they sell like hot cakes, and the wire flower-baskets in the greenhouse and the firebaskets in the stable. The other pieces sound immense and I must not spend more than £60 this week unless Mrs Jay pays up, the wretch! I will skim through the list again and mark the lots. It will be nine in a few minutes, yes, there is the gate — Ruth is here to help me. She is getting really interested in the trade, I will be able to leave her in charge when she is older, then everything will have to be clearly priced, or marked sold or RESERVED. She is going to meet heaps of interesting people, even if she does live in a quiet village. Mrs Muffit has gone to welcome her and here she comes like a breath of sunshine.

Later the same day. We turned out the shop to-day. The worse it is, the more Ruth enjoys it and she says 'it makes her feel better!' Mrs Jay called, settled up and bought a picture that I thought would be here when I was dead and gone. This evening after a long drought there has been a tremendous thunderstorm, torrential rain and great rivers of lightning down the sky. I do not know whether my offspring or the ducklings enjoyed it most. This was the first rain the brood had seen and I wish you could have seen them. Have you ever seen wee black and yellow Muscovy ducklings? They are like those common little pansies that cottagers love, only highly animated. Well, the six of them set off in single file on a cross country run, zigzagging across the lawn in the downpour. They discovered miniature water-falls deluging off the great peony leaves and you could almost hear the leader say 'Come on, fellows, it's better still over here.' The children had their own game. Gordon gave Angela a walking stick for a gun, stuck it out of the window and said,

'When I shout "Fire, mate!" you shout "Bang!"' Of course he knew by the lightning when to give the signal and there never was a more obedient little gunner. Her little throat must be skinned to-night.

Angela too is getting interested in the trade. One of her great delights is to explore the contents of a piece bought as 'Bureau and Contents' or 'Chest-of-drawers and Contents.' I give her a drawer at a time and she sits on a minute stool and 'sorts' as she calls it on to a tray. Although she is only five, she fans fans, if you know what I mean, and opens the tiniest boxes with her minute thumb-nail and rewinds silk on fretted mother-of-pearl stars and ivory bobbins. She is so independent and loves to discover and find out about things for herself. I pretend I don't know, and we find out things together. Gordon, on the other hand, discovers something from the sale that interests him, and settling down, back to front on a chair, he enjoys it whether it is a book, a flute or a telescope.

Bedtime on these happy evenings comes all too soon and to satisfy Angel we have to cover her half explored drawer with a cloth and *promise* not to touch it. An hour later Gordon still with his book, flute or telescope makes his happy way up the wooden hill.

This was all written twenty years ago but the children have not changed a great deal. Angela now has her own small Cottage Antique Shop packed with lovely things; old lace, she has mounted on tissue paper, little boxes she has lined with silk velvet, tiny objects of silver, ivory, jade and bronze; collections of Victorian card boxes, antique buckles, antique tortoiseshell combs, beautiful old lamps and antique jewellery. People are always asking, 'Where does she find it all?' and I remember those little hands and the bureaux and contents and the secret drawers. And if you want to know about Gordon he is still the reader of the family and the musician.

❧ 12 ❧

I WAS IN THE PET SHOP this morning buying Mrs Muffit's rations, when to my surprise I saw that the dishes in an occupied canary cage were a pair of exquisite Waterford salts. I asked if I might buy them, and the reply was,

'Yes with pleasure, ninepence each.'

'I will certainly give you more than that.' I replied and produced a ten shilling note.

'We've a drawerful here.' came the cheery reply.

'My!' I thought, this is too good to be true. It was! The drawer was jerked open and some multiple stores' ones were displayed to my view. Really! Even a canary could have told the difference!

Mrs Muffit, our blue Persian, was given to us by a lady who was leaving the district. The baker brought her over in his van from the next village. Her bed awaited her. It was an antique mahogany music Canterbury with the divisions missing. We had aired an old velvet cushion. I lifted her gently from the sack. She looked ruffled and distressed. Her golden eyes were hauntingly beautiful. We buttered her paws and gave her a saucer of milk — she shewed no inclination to wander and sprang back gladly into her bed and settled down. The children were told to leave her alone, and when I locked up and took a last look at her at midnight she was giving little grunts in her sleep. Next morning, I knew the reason why, curled close against her were two lovely tabby Persian kittens.

For the next seven years she kept us in kittens — all the blue ones were promised before they were born. Angela appointed herself lady-in-waiting to the queen. She handled the babies, sometimes weighing them on the letter balance (they doubled their birth weight in five days) and recording their progress. When they were about three weeks old, she would dress them in her dolls' matinee coats and little bonnets; their long grey fur would be brushed down on to their shoulders and back view they looked like prematurely old babies.

Through the years we must have used up every name we could think of — Silver, Misty, Grey, Smoky, and Pussy Willow, were favourites. After tea, Angela will often get out the leather pouffe and saddle up a couple of kittens. One saddle is a miniature high pomelled Turkish one (from a sale, of course) and the other is of scarlet calf and sheepskin that she had made herself like a numnah. The top of the pouffe is the Circus Ring and there the little dears are put through their paces, Angela using the loop of her crop to sit them up and guide them. Really it is enough to make a cat smile, but Mrs Muffit will ignore the whole performance and come on my knee and look the other way. When they are unsaddled and brushed and kissed, they are made to lie on her lap on their backs with their four little legs in the air — a friend calls this position 'Summers trained!' Mrs Muffit in her detached way is devoted to us, she will follow us at night to other houses in the village and even wait sitting in the snow. After Evensong, she is often waiting for us in the porch and will run before us home, zig-zagging across our path with her lovely tail aloft. One fellow worshipper exclaimed

'She is more like a Christian than a cat!'

Gordon has now started at the Grammar School and settled down very happily there. Poor Angela has started at a private one and wishes that 'schools had never been invented.' She finds it as difficult as Gordon finds it easy. She is as pale as a candle on Monday mornings and I have to tell her a story all the way to school to keep her courage up. When Gordon went for his oral examination for entrance to the Grammar School, he was asked what he intended to be when he was a man. To our surprise, and doubtless the Examiner's too, he replied that he was going to join the Canadian Mounted Police. When asked the reason why, he replied,

'For two reasons, I like riding, and I believe in people behaving themselves.'

Really I think Angela should have been born into a Romany family. She is an outdoor child, so good with the ponies and to see her putting her dolls' washing on the bushes to dry — well, she does it to the manner born!

Last autumn I was standing with her in my arms on the green when a cavalcade of gipsy caravans passed through. One horse was being led by a strong young fellow while his beautiful dark wife stood in the open doorway. We smiled at each other, and reaching up she tore a trail of hops from above her head and coming down the caravan steps with the grace of a ballerina she put it in my hand. It made my day. It was so lovely and un-expected!

Angela said to me

'She liked you, Mummy.'

'Yes' I replied 'and I liked her, darling.' The hops, amber coloured now and paper dry, still hang on the beam above the fireplace.

I had my first American customer to-day. Although he was in mufti, I should imagine he is over here with the Forces. He had heard that I had a harp for sale. Yes, it was true and there it was, stringless but beautifully gilded with elegant rams' heads. Yes, he would take it. Had I any others? No, sorry, but London customers had said there was a shop packed with them there. Would I let him have the 'ad-ress?' Yes, I felt sure I could get it and would post it to him. He settled for the harp and said he would collect it in a taxi in the afternoon. He arrived in the middle of a cloudburst. While he took cover inside the shop the driver and I eased the harp into the taxi, the American then found he could not get in. So we tried again getting our friend in first and framing him in the stringless harp. His pale rubbery face could not have looked less seraphlike. The taximan gave me a dazzling blue-eyed wink. But our ally was not amused!

⅍ 13 ⅍

I TRY TO LEAVE THE WAR and the weather out of my journal.
I found the beginning of another diary, when I was turning out
Gordon's cupboard; it was headed 'Outstanding Events of the
War,' the only entry was 'M. Laval flew to Paris. He flew back
again.' I'm glad it was still-born. I only listen to the war news
after the children are in bed, and I mean to spare Gordon the
nightmares and fears I knew at the same age, just twenty-five
years before. Little did my mother know that my nightmares
sprang from reading my brother's weekly, 'The Scout,' which
spared us little of the Huns' devilments.

Everything has a deeper meaning these days, our letters,
our farewells, our thoughts. No woman sings about her house-
work, only in church. As we sing the Benedictus, how well the
verses shape our prayers and the Londoners' fears, as they
crouch in their shelters:—

'That we being delivered out of the hands of our enemies
might serve Him without fear:

'To give light to them that sit in darkness and in the shadow
of death: and to guide our feet into the way of peace.'

As for the eighteenth Psalm, it could be about our fighter-
pilots. I am copying out a few odd verses here, starting at the
tenth verse:—

'He came upon the wings of the wind: He made darkness
his secret place: with dark water and thick clouds to cover
him.

'He sent out his arrows and scattered them: he cast forth
lightnings and destroyed them.

'He shall send down from on high to fetch me: he shall
take me out of many waters.

'It is God, that girdeth me with strength of war:

'He teaches mine hands to fight: and mine arms shall
break even a bow of steel.

'I will follow upon mine enemies, and overtake them: neither will I turn again till I have destroyed them.

'Thou hast girded me with strength into the battle: thou shalt throw down mine enemies under me.'

A training plane has crashed near the Roman Road, and eight young lives have ended. Another, a bomber, has failed to clear the hills and again all were lost. A more fortunate young pilot came down into a tree on the valley-side of a friend's farm; they saw a light shining in their dark valley and went to investigate; he was only shaken, and was soon at their fireside, being restored to life and laughter.

One young pilot is the hero of all our village boys. Someone says his name is Eagles and anyway, he could not have a better one! Often for an hour or more, high above us in the summer blue, he spins and loops and climbs. Only lately have I found the following poem written by another fighter-pilot, who gave his life at nineteen. He had scribbled the lines on the back of a letter to his parents. His name was John Magee.

> Oh, I have slipped the surly bonds of earth,
> And danced the skies on laughter-silvered wings;
> Sunward I've climbed and joined the tumbling mirth
> Of sun-split clouds — and done a hundred things
> You have not dreamed of — wheeled and soared and swung
> High in the sunlit silence. Hov'ring there,
> I've chased the shouting wind along and flung
> My eager craft through footless halls of air.
> Up, up the long delirious burning blue
> I've toppped the wind-swept height with easy grace,
> Where never lark, or even eagle, flew;
> And, while with silent, lifting mind I've trod
> The high untrespassed sanctity of space,
> Put out my hand, and touched the face of God.

We have a pilot's wife and babies sharing our home. Her husband has gone overseas and she came to us a few weeks before the birth of her second babe, to have it in our cottage hospital. That was three months ago and the poor man has still received no mail from her, not even the cable announcing the birth!

It was she who told me, that the jelly baby sweets in our

Post Office, had been rechristened 'Evacuees.' So I told her that I had written in my diary, 'we now have water beetles in the soft water tank, minute shrimps in the well-water and evacuees in our beds!' She is shortly moving into one of a pair of empty lodge cottages and her cousin with her family is having the other. She is a dear girl and, as we are both so fond of children and home-life, we get on famously together. I get the meals and she clears and washes up. At night we take turns with the ironing and talk. She is like no-one else I know, in that she is rather plain by daylight, with pale eyes, and mousy hair, but in the firelight, as the room darkens, she becomes slowly beautiful. The head is beautifully placed on her long neck, the gracious moulding of her brow and cheeks are revealed and deep shadows conceal her eyes. She looks like a gentle Madonna, as she sits there, suckling her babe.

The next customer from the States was unmistakeable, he was one of five, all youthful and in uniform.

'Say, Lady, would it be O.K. if I tried your horn on the sidewalk?' he enquired.

'Certainly' I replied and he and his confederates trooped outside with the old copper coach-horn.

The blast that followed might have been the last trump! I expected our old friends in the Churchyard to sit up at least, but they were not deceived and our five allies trooped into the shop again, replaced the horn on its hooks and left remarking that 'there was a note missing.'

For years we have meant to take the children up the Church tower and on Sunday we got the key from the sexton and made the effort, after Sunday dinner and all.

The steps were deep and dark and dusty. Gordon led the way, then Angela with me on her tail and John brought up the rear. Penny Priors with its winding river, its two mills and two farms lay beneath us like a toy village. The tiny circular stacks stood neatly below us and Mr Lancer's minute white hens were scratching about in the farmyard. Old Mrs Miller had, rather surprisingly, a line of washing in her back yard. Old Hawkins was pushing greenstuff into his rabbit hutches and a dozen shorthorns were strolling down the green towards the milking sheds. We saw Poacher London's old dog ford the river to go hunting in Sir John's woods; a troup of children were petting the mare in the Rectory Field and someone, under a newspaper, was fishing by the weir.

This weir, or rather the pool below it was our favourite place for a paddle or a swim on a summer evening; as often as not a child's face would appear at the window as we were having tea and inquire,

'Are you going to the pool? Because Daddy says we can come too if Mrs Summers is going?'

Then there would be five sunburnt little backs to run down, my two and the three children from the Manor. As we wended our way home through the deep grasses of the water meadows, I would think, 'this would be Heaven if *only* we were at peace.'

One does not really expect a confidence man to turn up at a village antique shop but I received my first one some two months back. A young man with a week's growth of beard arrived on a bicycle and asked if I had some cheap cottage furniture.

'Yes,' I said 'I am trying to clear out the stable, come and have a look at what there is.'

He decided on some old Welsh chairs, a drop-leaf table, an old chest-of-drawers and two wooden armchairs. He told me that they had had a fire at their cottage at Yesborough and it was having to have a new roof; the neighbours he said had been wonderfully kind and taken them all in. He went on to describe most graphically how he had rescued a little box of his Mother's while the firemen had played their hose around him.

'I reckon my Mam's heart would have broke if she had lost her little box,' he added.

We lashed two of the chairs to his bicycle, he was going to walk the seven miles home with them, and he said he would borrow a farm cart and collect the rest on Saturday, and pay the six pounds for the lot.

'Well,' I thought to myself as he disappeared up the green, 'he may look more like a gooseberry than a man, but his heart's in the right place.'

Saturday came and went but no Gooseberry, no horse and no cart. After six weeks I found myself at an auction sale in the village of Yesborough.

'Tell me,' I said to a couple of local women in flowery aprons 'which is the cottage where there was a fire recently?'

'A fire?' they asked blankly, 'There hasn't been no fire.'

'Well, that's funny,' I replied, 'a young man told me that the roof of his home had fallen in after a fire and that you kind people had given the family shelter while the builders were at work.'

They looked at each other. The penny dropped.

'She must mean young Silversmith,' they whispered to each other. 'Don't let on we told you,' said one 'but it's all lies that you've been told. That's where he lives,' they said and vanished round a corner.

At my second knock a young woman answered the door.

'I have come for the money for my two chairs,' I said.

The door almost closed and some whispering went on.

'I don't think we want them after all,' she said.

'Then I must see what your village policeman says about it,' I said, and walked away slowly and fiddled about the garden gate — and the ten shilling note appeared as if by magic!

The police have been around and warned us that there is a much larger fish doing the rounds. His method is to pay cash for some item which he says he will collect next day. When he arrives, he then 'buys' a valuable piece and 'pays' for this with a cheque. He then departs with his two purchases and only his cheque is ever seen again. The Bank returns this!

⁓{ *14* }⁓

THIS MORNING before the shop opened I cycled a couple of miles to fetch some day-old ducklings from the keeper's house in the woods. The couple are childless, but hardly familyless, if there is such a word! Two setters ran to welcome me, or dismount me, I am not sure which, and everywhere I looked was some feathered or furry creature. How I wished I had Angel with me! A pet jackdaw squawked 'Hello' and three tortoiseshell cats circled me caressing me with their tails and a parrot, who ignored me, preened himself on the handle of the coal scuttle, while a red squirrel half asleep was curled on top of the mangle! If I lived there, I should need just four foster children to complete the picture. There was absolute quietness except for the distant murmur of the weir and the soft cooing of the wood-pigeons. No war there, no traffic, no convoys. Just peace!

We had coffee made with goats' milk in the kitchen. I paid for my ducklings and set off for home with them in the breast pockets of my wind-cheater; I buttoned the flaps down but four yellow heads squeezed out and made remarks. The broody hen who had been on a china egg for a week gave me a fierce reception as I slipped them under her, but an hour later, she had calmed down and was parading them across the lawn.

I have had two 'weepy' mothers in the shop to-day; they had returned their children to school. One said with sobs,

'His last words were "Why did you have me if you didn't want me?"'

Someone wiser than I said that you should judge the school by what the child says about it when it comes home for the holidays, not by its parting remarks! Or volley in this case! Lots of people who call know they will never see me again and get things off their chests — usually troubles of course. I often stand there for an hour listening to an account of a family quarrel, an unfair will, a gruesome operation or, saddest of all, to a tale of a broken marriage. I cannot say how many times a wife has said to me 'If *only* I had been wiser, or older, or kinder, or more understanding.' Some have married again and are reasonably happy — but the magic has gone!

Last week someone came in with a joyful tale. This farmer's wife, who has worked for years like a galley slave, with her own family, countless evacuees and farm work, called in to say 'good-bye.' An aunt of her husband, whom he had only seen twice, had left him a Welsh farm in the Precelly Mountains — lock, stock and barrel.

'I kept thinking of you, Anne,' she said, 'as we went through everything in the house, you would simply love it all and you must come to see us when the war is over. The antique furniture is beeswaxed like satin, the chests are filled with real hand-woven linen marked with the date in tiny red cross-stitch in the corners. The dressers are filled with pewter, and from the hooks hang old lustre jugs, while the kitchen is literally lined with glowing copper pans. There are lovely old four-posters in the great bedrooms and early oak presses serve as wardrobes and snowy white sheep-skins cover the elm floors. Oh, Anne!' she went on, 'it is just like a dream and the children say it is like a Play on the Children's Hour. My kitchen window looks out on to a little paved yard surrounded by a fuschia hedge and from the attics we can see a shining line of sea. It's St. Bride's Bay!'

I rejoiced with her and promised to help her with the move. They are letting their farm-house here furnished for the duration and an older brother is working the land and taking over the lease. Her husband is already at the Welsh farm as the lambing is in full swing there and she will join him as soon as she can find a tenant for here.

A lady has brought back a ring I sold her. It is a large silver one set with tiny turquoises and she has lost a stone and has asked me to get it replaced. I did not tell her that it was the third time it had come back! I bought it some years ago, it was a copy of an Italian ring, it was brand new and I paid purchase tax on it. I sold it as a new ring but this customer soon brought it back, a friend had told her it was an antique ring and she said that other people's jewellery made her feel queer. I refunded the money quite happily. It was a lovely ring. The next time I sold it as a second-hand ring, a copy of an old one, this customer brought it back, she had felt sure that it *was* antique and now had found it was not. Soon it would know its way home! Just say 'Mrs Summers, Penny Priors' and it would come bowling along on its own!

This reminds me of a lady in our village who has a dearly-loved sister in Devon. Every time there is some particularly dreadful war news, she packs her traps and makes a bee-line for Devon, complete with luggage, cat basket and a smoked ham. We tease her about this ham, and say it is the most travelled bit of pig in the United Kingdom. Gordon says that if she doesn't look out, the war will be over before she eats it.

Gordon is now twelve and has gone into long trousers. Clothing is now so difficult that the boys are allowed to wear anything to school as long as it is topped by a school cap. His great delight is his canoe, bought at a sale, of course. He goes off quietly in this canoe of his, by the hour. He knows where there is a kingfisher's nest and countless little moor-hens' nests on their reedy rafts. He talked me into a little expedition in this canoe on Sunday, with strict instructions to move slowly, and to turn carefully. It was a wonderful hour! The high banks were deep in meadow-sweet breathing out its marzipanny smell, and the only sounds the chatter of the water in the shallows and the zoom of an occasional dragon-fly. It was wonderful to be quite alone, unseen, detached, everything beautiful in a world of horror, everything at peace in a world of war. 'I must turn now,' I heard myself say 'move slowly, keep the paddle close in, turn in this deep water, keep calm, and don't wobble.' I am facing upstream now, but drifting downstream, I must start to paddle. Steady, gently, that's the way, quite easy, but it seemed a long way back. A surprised water-rat saw me and dived for safety, a moor-hen called in alarm. I rounded the bend. There were John and the children.

'Clever old Mummy! You did it! You did it! Did you go as far as the weir?'

'Not quite,' I said, not letting on that I had turned for home when I remembered it. I was not up to shooting the rapids at my advanced age.

⚜ *15* ⚜

SOON AFTER I OPENED my shop a friend in the trade gave me some good advice. 'Never, never' she said, 'put closed on your shop door, put GONE TO A SALE or OUT BUYING, OPEN TO-MORROW. This will fetch the bargain-hunters along.' And it certainly does! All sorts of notices get fixed to the door

 BACK IN TEN MINUTES
 GONE TO FEED THE PONIES
 AT THE PHONE-BOX
 OPEN AGAIN THIS AFTERNOON, Etc.

I know a little town antique shop where they tie a notice on every object, (or objet d'art, I think I ought to say) in their shop window. When I am waiting for my bus I read as many as possible and try to memorise the funniest to tell to my family. A silver tray engraved with the initials M.D. may bear a label saying in neat script 'Is there going to be a Silver wedding in your family? What a delightful gift this would be for Mum and Dad!' A silver goblet inscribed with a letter 'B' 'A present for your Godchild perhaps? See it is marked with a B like the biscuit in the jingle.' Really it is a job to keep a straight face, but is one meant to?

It is a seller's market these war-time days, as little or no furniture is being made. Many people who would ordinarily buy new furniture are patronising antique and second-hand shops. Second-hand prices of modern furniture are controlled. At an auction sale if people bid up to the controlled price the auctioneer *has* to knock it down. If a wardrobe, say, is of first class quality and worth much more than the controlled price, perhaps a dozen people will call out this maximum bid, then there is nothing for it but to draw lots, and how that holds up the proceedings. Dealers these days are not allowed to put anything into an auction sale. I suppose if they bought loads in some areas and rushed them to others they could make fortunes overnight. The prices of antiques are not controlled, it would be impossible : for instance a Georgian bow mahogany chest-of-drawers could be worth anything between six and sixty pounds, depending on its quality, its condition, legs, brass furniture, drawer linings, size and patina. Customers tell me that at some of the London house sales as few as six people may turn up. When the siren goes for a raid, the auctioneer may remain fearless on his little rostrum while his audience take cover under the stairs or below a billiard table, and shout their bids or pop an arm out and wave a catalogue.

The scrap-metal dealer driving through the village yesterday sold me a couple of wooden gig wheels and left them leaning against the front wall. I had ideas about building them into the orchard gate, but a few minutes later a local lady pulled up in her trap, borrowed my rule and proceeded to measure them : at this moment Mr Lancer returning from the hunt rode across the green, doffed his bowler, and gave me the most mischievous smile. Later in the day his wife said,

'Ralph reckons you could sell anything! He says I am to

tell you that one day he is going to breed hunters again. He will peg them out on the Green and you shall sell them on commission.'

Customers who are collectors appreciate it when one hides away things for them. One lady buys all my miniature chests-of-drawers, another any doll's house furnishings; another, a woman dealer, all my china cottages and castles, as she has her own private collection; these quaint little objects were used as pastile burners or nightlight holders. I saw a modern version of one the other day — it looked like the mouth of a rabbit-hole with Mrs Rabbit and the Flopsy Bunnies gathered round the light. Another customer collects old candlesnuffers and trays : the snuffers were used for putting out tallow candles and removing the smuts from the wicks. This gentleman says he may write a book about them one day. I asked him if he knew the riddle about a pair of snuffers and he got me to write it out for him. It runs,

Eyes like spectacles
Body like a box
Beak like a blackbird
Smells like a fox.

Another gentleman collects anything he can about Napoleon (Napoleon was laid out on his dining-room table). He inherited it from a great-grandfather or great-uncle, I forget which, who was the Governor of St. Helena when Napoleon died there.

Some customers ask you to get them something unusual or difficult and then a few months later dash in and say 'Any luck ?' My brain does mental gymnastics, they expect *me* to appear from the shadows but I do not know who I shall find, let alone what they want till I have collected my wits.

It is quite funny how one gets asked for the same thing by a dozen people or more and then one finds the reason — they have seen one in a film perhaps. A 'snow storm,' that is to say a miniature scene under a tiny sealed glass dome with tiny loose snowflakes inside, was in demand at one time, and just recently dozens of enquiries for rocking chairs. A doctor in a Radio Talk said they were good for the 'screws' and the 'nerves.' I sold my three in two days and now have a waiting list. So it looks as if it may be some time before I have another to put out on the pavement. The slight breeze there will keep it rocking and we say it is being used by the ghost of Penny Priors.

⌇ 16 ⌇

JOHN WAS GOING TO GIVE ME A LIFT to a sale this morning on his way to town, but when I tried to lock the front door the key would not turn. So I had to let him go and struggle with it. I found one of the old iron hinges had cracked and the door had dropped slightly. I soon had the hasp off and screwed it in a fraction lower and all was well. I went upstairs to wash again but heard footsteps in the garden. A new customer was trying to find me. She chose a lovely antique oak bureau, almost ashen colour. We loaded it into her station wagon and I went up stairs to wash again. Once more the gate squeaked and a rough voice shouted up,

'Anyone at' ome.'

'Yes, coming!' I shouted back. It was a fellow who buys sets of chairs, for board-rooms I think. I had some lumpy Victorian ones and sold him ten, a 6 and a 4 that exactly matched but had different coverings, of course.

'They be a bit "cobby"!' he remarked as we loaded them. I nearly replied 'Ay, they be thaat!' But I held my peace and whispered 'Three cheers they're sold!'

I had taken £64 before 10 a.m. on a closing day!

I wondered how many customers I missed on closing days, as I went up to wash for the fourth time. Still one can only sell a thing once and money isn't everything. Ruth always has tea ready for us all at five o'clock and the shop door is firmly closed and I'm mother for the evening. I also close on all school holidays and devote myself to the family and the home. Even customers who are disappointed are understanding and say they don't blame me?.

Like most dealers I enjoy buying expeditions more than anything, and then perhaps working on the furniture (when I can

48

do it in the garden.) Turning out the shop is also great fun and in fact doing any job without being called away is a treat.

I managed to catch the bus and got to the sale on time. I bought some useful lots, a wonderful Spanish refectory table with fish scales carved along its edges and a perfect Victorian swing cradle with a pointed hood for an 'expectant' customer. I 'phoned the carrier and he had me home by four. We stacked the furniture in the stable ready for polishing next day. Ruth had gone to fetch Angela from school, so I washed and changed and got the tea on. I gathered a bowl of strawberries. We have had either home-produced eggs, raspberries or strawberries for tea every day for five weeks. What a scrumptious change from our wartime rations! Fat is the chief problem, and sugar a good second, but tins of glucose from the chemist are bought for the children. It is surprising what one can do without, if one has to. The children have my sugar of course and I am down to ten stone again, thank goodness! I manage to get Ruth's tea meals and 'elevenses' out of the rations and John's extra meals when he comes at the week-end. Ruth gives her teenager's ration of chocolate powder to Angela as it is too sickly for her. Sometimes on Sunday afternoons Angel gets out her dolls' pastry set and rolls out some chocolate balls for her Daddy.

I once made a Yorkshire pudding without eggs and it was quite nice and yesterday one with eggs, flour and *water*. The result was satisfactory. One day I'm going to put the 'drippingey' tin into the oven, close the door and twenty minutes later say 'Hey Presto,' open the door and lift out a golden Yorkshire pudding.

People in towns are encouraged to eat all sorts of queer things, mutton smoked like bacon and called macon I think; also tinned fish called snoek, which the public has been told barks like a dog when it is dying. That's enough. Don't say any more. I'm not hungry! The first time I queued I got a quarter of liquorice sweets, not favourites of ours, and so now I only queue for buses.

Last week I went to a sale at a mansion. I could remember the place from early childhood. It is in the village where my paternal grandmother was born, grew up and was married. She was one of twenty children (let's hope there were two wives!) A poem was written about the family but alas I never

44

saw a copy. I walked through the great gates, up the mossy
drive and wandered round the neglected grounds that my
brothers and I had longed to explore. The trees and bushes were
all unknown to me — a previous owner had been a botanist
and had collected rare and wonderful species.

I wandered round the house with my catalogue and happened
to meet a very jolly friend, not a dealer. An hour later, we were
together packed like sardines on the great landing while the
auctioneer was selling in one of the magnificent bedrooms.

'What am I offered for this beautiful toilet service' he asked?
'It is a double one and complete!'

My friend kept calling her bids as she could not see the
auctioneer and it was knocked down to her at four guineas.

'Name please Madam?' he called loudly.

'Chambers!' she called back 'Mrs Chambers!'

There was a tiny silence then a roar of laughter, a bigger
pause and a second prolonged roar of laughter.

'That's quite enough, ladies and gentlemen! Let us proceed
with the sale. What am I offered for lot 92?'

❄ 17 ❄

QUEER THINGS HAPPEN to everyone of course, but I think
doctors and dealers have more than their share. Years ago,
with many interruptions, I heard a talk on the radio about queer
happenings; the bit I remember was about a woman who
purchased an old wing arm-chair. This chair was placed in her
sitting-room, through which she had to pass to her kitchen.
Several times, during the first day it was there, she got the
impression that an old man with a white beard was sitting in it.
On looking more closely of course there was no one there. But
when her children raced home from school and joined her in the
kitchen, her little boy said 'Mummy, who is the old gentleman
sitting in your chair?' Now I can't beat that, but I did sell a
chair in the village that walked. It only moved a foot or so when

no one was looking — it was a mystery. Another chair I bought in far away Bristol went to some customers here and the address on the back of their cheque was that of the house from where I had bought it!

I remember one winter's day a neighbour from the next cottage came along to have a chat. She saw I had a shop full of customers so let herself into the cottage and sat by the fire waiting for me. When I joined her she said, 'May I look inside the Bible box under your dresser, dear?' 'Yes, of course,' I replied 'but why?' She replied 'Do you know I believe it once belonged to us when we lived in Yorkshire and my husband glued a deed inside the lid.' It was there, it was the same and had travelled all that way and changed hands at least three times. I should have bought it back if I had been her, thinking it was trying to find me, but she was made of sterner stuff.

Another happening that gave me quite a thrill was on another winter's day. I was in the middle of reading M. H. Tiltman's wonderful book 'Quality Chase' and had just read the description of Mr Joseph Chamberlain's coming into Jonathan Chase's antique shop. It tells how Mr Chamberlain reclined on a sofa there, puffing away at his black cigar and gave advice to the young dealer. Well, at that identical moment my shop bell rang, and in the shop two ladies were waiting for me. One was a titled local lady, a regular customer, who introduced her guest to me — Mrs Chamberlain, a daughter-in-law of Mr Joseph's. They stayed for a while examining everything and Mrs Chamberlain purchased a piece of old glass.

I jot down in my shop diary all the things people ask me to find them, with their names and addresses. There is everything imaginable on this list from a set of Spillikins to an Elizabethan staircase. Both these entries have ticks by them, showing that the missions were accomplished. I can well remember buying my first Elizabethan staircase because I told the next customer who came in all about it. He was a retired builder, he listened quietly and then said, 'Now I come to think of it, I have a very fine old oak staircase. It is in one of my barns and you can have it for £30 if you want it? The old Dowager Countess of Warwick is supposed to have ridden up it on her white pony.' I sold this one very quickly, and it now graces a house that overlooks the English Channel. The Elizabethan one is now in an old manor house which had lost its original staircase and had a poor modern pitch-pine one.

One of my first enquiries was for a royal blue witch ball. The old belief was that a witch entering a house would see her own reflection and be frightened from the home. Being wartime, none of the Czechoslovakian ones are coming into the country and my customer could not afford an antique one, but as luck would have it, I found one the very next day and it was a blue one at the Red Cross Shop in Banbury. The next witch ball I had shortly afterwards was from a grand dealer to whom I had introduced a good customer. This dealer said the ball was not really for sale, but that I should have it as a 'thank you.' He said that he had lately lent it to some young friends whose little boy was dying. They had hung it about his cot and it must have made a wonderland in his familiar nursery. Needless to say I did not pass on this sad story when I sold it.

Now that petrol is so severely rationed one finds a large proportion of one's customers are doctors and specialists who have a good allocation. This leads me to a funny tale after that sad bit. One Doctor, a regular customer, suddenly espied a chamber-pot in blue dragon design that I had discreetly tucked under a love-seat in my shop.

'How much is *that* Mrs Summers?' he asked, pointing.

'25/-, Doctor.'

'Right, I'll take it. One of my patients has a tea-service in that design.'

I tried to look unsurprised and swathed it in tissue paper without comment. But I did wonder. Was he going to give it to her?

This customer has some lovely furniture and a collection of old glass. He asked John and me over one evening to see it. He told us how his mother used to drive in her little trap to country sales in Ireland, and would sometimes buy a trayful of old Waterford glass for a few shillings. Talking of those more leisurely days reminds me of a little red morocco leather casket I once bought. It locked with a tiny brass key and contained three little red leather books embossed in gold and bearing the words Diary, Engagements and Household Accounts. I spent a happy evening delving into them and wish I had not sold them. They appeared to have been kept by a bride, whose husband

47

was a doctor. In the Account Book were the following entries :—

To Basket of Mushrooms	6d
To picking Mulberries	1/-
To stitching girth	9d
To cleaning Lily Pool	4/-
To digging out Jasper	1/-

Her diary was blank so we know nothing of her thoughts but her Engagement Book had daily entries as follows :—

'Drove over with William to see old Benson again he is very ill'

'Drove over to Hollowdell with William. The Webb children have the fever.'

And nearly every Tuesday and Friday she entered,

'Agnes and the boys to tea. Played croquet.'

Did the sun always shine? After ten months the books petered out. Was she too busy? Did she have a child? Did she die? Or did she just get tired of unlocking her little casket? I would love to know. She drove along these lanes, *our* lanes; perhaps trying to keep up with *her* little girl on *her* little fat pony. We shall never know — it was all one hundred years ago.

⁓ *18* ⁓

I WAKED EARLY this morning and heard the dawn chorus. How I used to love it when I was feeding my babies and the world was at peace! The songsters sounded as if they were lined up on every twig! During the lulls I could hear the distant waterfall and the eerie cry of one of Sir John's peacocks. Then a little later I heard the clock at Evenlow across the river strike five, echoed a few seconds later by our own church clock. I know why I waked so early — it was to plan my day. I had a choice of programmes — should I go to the rather important local sale where the many treasures were likely to attract a big crowd and high prices or should I keep the shop open in hopes of selling a lot? This rarely works out as, when there is a sale in the village, people are in a hurry to get there to view it, and in a hurry afterwards to get home to tea, especially if they have missed their lunch. Should I play clever and go to one or both of the other sales in the district and get some bargains? One started at eleven o'clock and the other at two o'clock. I decided to go to the earlier one, view it and stay for an hour or so. When I had planned my campaign, I went to sleep till seven and waked with that wonderful feeling of expectancy as one does in childhood.

I travelled by bus and there *were* tremendous bargains, but not my type of thing. I could have furnished a youth hostel for £50, carpets and all! But once I started buying I had to stay. When the antique pieces came along the prices soared, a Victorian prie-dieu chair £36, a record price I should think! Still I made up a little load and 'phoned Mr Bede, (or Joe as he likes us to call him) to collect me in his taxi. Taxi is rather a grand word for such a vehicle. It looks more prehistoric than antique and his only excuse for buying it is that the number plates bear his initials — J.B. He kept me waiting ages and everyone else had gone, even the porters, by the time he turned up. We lashed two grandfather clocks on to the roof of the car — he hoped they would not scratch it. We packed various pictures, glass and three antique pierced brass fenders inside. He had gallantly padded the front seat for me with a moulting feather cushion and a decrepit tea cosy, but I edged in cautiously as the coil springs were already on nodding acquaintance with my silk stockings. We moved off in a homeward direction. I cannot say we drove off as the body felt it might leave the chassis at any moment. My china rattled in the back, Joe's spanners rattled in the tool-box, one of the tyres thudded and there were other noises that I could not diagnose.

He explained his late arrival by saying,

'Oh yes — I struck something on Goose Hill, a rabbit I think. We will have another good look on the way back.' We found a half grown hare, stone dead. He gave it to me and I promised to jug it and send a basinful along to him. He had some red currant jelly which he would share with us — it was to be a real feast. I also promised to return the skin which he would cure. We certainly don't waste anything these days. We free-wheeled down all the hills and jerked the car in unison at the bottom to make it go as far as possible and save petrol. It was a good thing my Aunt Millicent could not see me, for she would have thought it most unbecoming behaviour for a granddaughter of Mamma's, but I feel it was quite all right for a country dealer.

When we got home Ruth had given the children their tea and was ready to go. Angel helped me unload, Joe and Gordon carried the grandfather clocks on to the lawn and then began fooling about, tossing the clock weights to each other — really some men never grow up.

All shopkeepers, especially newsagents, find themselves being used as information bureaux. I use them myself and ask hurriedly between their twopenny-halfpenny customers,

'Excuse me, is there an antique dealer's or a junk shop here?' Now, when cars stop in Penny Priors, I am always asked to help as the Post Office is tucked round a corner. Unless I am just dishing up a meal or wanting to listen to the Grand National on the Radio, I give of my best. The lesser enquiries such as to bus times, the location of the phone-box, the store, or the garage are quickly dealt with, but inquiries about houses or lodging take longer and information as to the cost of keeping a pony longer still. Just because Angela has one, I am supposed to know all the answers. I have joked about this and said we should have a little form printed something like this:—

Cost of halter-broken pony £15.

Delivery charge £3.

Breaking in £5.

Shoeing 25/-.

As we have a large orchard and only have to buy hay in the winter you might think the expenses end there, but not a bit of it; my list would continue like this:—

Second-hand saddle £6.

Head stall £2.

Bridle £3. 10. 0.

Angela's hard hat 3 guineas.

Riding mackintosh £6 and coupons.

To eating neighbour's three pillow cases 15/-.

To jumping into neighbour's garden frame 30/-.

To killing neighbour's gosling 20/-, (she only tried to play with it!)

To extra fencing £17!!!

Providentially all the neighbours were different ones. Still looking back, it was worth it all, though after all these years my heart still misses a beat when I hear a loose pony go trotting past in the night. We were lucky enough never to need a veterinary surgeon and as for the child herself, she was golden and strong. In fact the Doctor did not know her by sight. I was the only one who ever went to see him, usually a visit every third year I think, and always with some fatal illness quite undisclosed to dear John; I will spare you the details. After the Doctor's reassurance that I should live to be a hundred and a bottle of medicine in some soft pastel shade I returned home cured. A few weeks later the bottle would come in handy for shellac, bleach or turpentine and it was quite an effort to remember what it was for, but it was for something terrible and something mortal.

19

I had never heard of Josh Billings until to-day when a newspaper cutting about him fell out of an old Scrap Book. Like my young daughter, he believed in phonetic spelling. His reason for this was as follows :—

'A man has as much rite to spell a word as it is pronounced, as he has to pronounce it, the way it ain't spelt.'

Practical philosophy was Josh's forte apparently; he would pronounce weighty matters in popular form as the three following sayings of his bear witness :—

'There is some pholks in this world who spend their whole lives a -hunting after righteousness, but karnt find enny time to praktiss it.'

'It kosts a great deal to be wise, but it dont kost enny thing to be happy.'

'I dont kare how much people talk, if they will only say it in a pheu words.'

When I returned from a sale to-day, I found Angela's little

satchel hanging on the door-knocker and this little note peeping out from under the door-mat,

Dere Mummy,

We have got out of scule erle. We have gone to get the poney. Ive arsked the Grene girls to tea. Hope it is orl rite?

Love from Angela

XXX

Yes, of course it is all right. The jam ration's finished, the butter's gone but we can have eggs and margarine toast and there is a cake tin full of flapjacks.

I guess old Josh Billings would have agreed with Omar Khayyam but spelt it 'Better a dinner of herbs where luv is than a stalled ox and haytread.' I have pasted the cutting about him back in the scrap book, and here are two more of his sayings for good measure:—

'Buty that don't make a woman vain, makes her very butiful.'

'Living on hope, is like living on wind, a good way to get phull, but a poor way to get phatt.'

After tea the children watched me take all the broody hens off their eggs, and listened to one sitting that is clipping; they are all goose eggs, so I gave them a soaking in warm water and they laughed to see the eggs jerking about with their stirring contents. A customer has succeeded in rearing a rather weakly gosling; she kept him for the first few days in a little basket in the open warm drawer of her Aga Cooker; he had now rejoined his relatives in her orchard, and not surprisingly has been nicknamed the 'Aga Khan.' I lost all my late hatched turkeys last year: I asked a neighbour if he had ever reared a sickly turkey.

'Indeed I have,' he replied, 'I once fed one on pepper-corns till he decided to fend for himself. By Christmas he had become so aggressive, there was nothing for it but to wring his neck, in self defence, and clap him in the oven!'

If ever I make some complementary remark about a local dealer, an auctioneer or even a horseman, I may get a grudging agreement, but it is almost always followed by, 'You should have known his father . . . worth two of him!' I wonder if this was said of his father? Have we been steadily deteriorating since the Creation? Can some people only see character on older people, I wonder? They certainly say the most outrageous things, like a relative of mine who asked a timid cousin, 'How is your father? I never liked him.' Personally I think children have it for originality every time. Last week I spoke to a little boy on the Green, saying,

'I don't think I know your name?'

'It is Andrew,' he replied, 'he was a friend of Jesus, you know.'

I've said it before, but it made my day.

One of our local auctioneers, who was before my time (one who was reputed to be worth two of his sons) was selling the contents of a local cottage one day, when an old tapestry was discovered in an elm coffer. The auctioneer immediately recognised it as a Barcheston Tapestry.

'We'll have that out,' he said, 'that shall go up to London,' where I believe it made about six hundred pounds.

In Shakespeare's time there was a little community of weavers at Barcheston, which is now a hamlet in the southern most tip of Warwickshire. The original instructor had been a man by name Richard Hyckes; his patron had been William Sheldon Esquire, who had sent him to the Low Countries to learn the craft. The tapestries produced, often spoken of as the Sheldon tapestries, were of the very finest quality and are believed to be the first made in England; previous to this, all tapestries for the great houses had been made on the Continent. It was said that often a year's work went into one tapestry: some of the most important ones are of Midland Counties. Three of these were sold at Sothebys in 1960, and the one of Warwickshire is on view in Warwick Museum. Angela and I have been looking at it to-day. Little towns, churches, bridges and rivers are wonderfully represented, nestling in valleys and among groups of trees; the names of the places are as clear as when they were woven four hundred years ago. The great map is bordered with fruits and flowers and in one corner is a magnificent coat-of-arms.

Some more of these Barcheston tapestries were discovered recently in an old chest in the butler's bedroom at Chastleton House, a historic Elizabethan house near Moreton-in-Marsh in Gloucestershire, while two more of these tapestries are in Birmingham at Aston Hall. Others, long treasured, are on view at the Victoria and Albert, and another can be seen at Sudeley Castle near Winchcombe in Gloucestershire.

Writing of these tapestries reminds me of a mural that has lately been discovered at the east end of the chancel of the Guild Chapel at Stratford-upon-Avon. I have been to see it; on the left, the righteous are being received into everlasting bliss, while on the right the damned are being subjected to the tortures of Belsen.

There are many things I cannot understand, but nothing confounds me more, than how, not a handful, but tens of thousands of men in our time, could have been found to torture, mutilate and burn — not other men in the heat of battle, but the helpless, the weak, the aged, the unborn!

I remember as a child, on a quiet Welsh beach, watching some children at play : they were dark-haired children, the most beautiful I had ever seen. My Mother told me that they were Jews, and that our little Lord Jesus must have looked like them.

I believe I have only had one woman customer from a German prison camp. She must have noticed me looking at the indelible number on her arm. She smiled and said, 'Yes, I was in Auschwitz. I am one of the lucky ones.' She was thin, but golden and fit. I looked into her dark grey eyes. What terrors they must have seen!

Another customer, also a civilian, has been a prisoner in Japanese hands. His wife and young sons have been frequent callers. He had nearly starved to death, and jokingly said that he could give me an unusual recipe for a cake made with dubbin! Another Daddy was brought along proudly by his beautiful wife and little daughter for me to view.

'Guess who this is Mrs Summers?' It was easy, of course, easier for me perhaps than his family, for he had lost five stone in the last five months of the war in a German prison camp. He had been flown home in the May heat; he had worn everything he possessed to plump himself out a bit.

Another beloved father, home after years at sea, was brought along and introduced by his wife and young sons. He greeted me with,

'So *this* is where my wife spends all my hard-earned cash!' But once again the family cheque book was pulled out, and *he* wrote the next cheque on their joint account.

Some small sons are proving rather jealous of their returning fathers, but in the case of this family, the younger son joined his Mother in the kitchen on the first evening and confided, 'I think I am going to like this man, Mummy.'

It is difficult enough for a small boy to adjust himself to a new brother or sister but a baby does sleep most of the time, and this great big noisy man is always talking to Mummy, and showing off and sleeping in her bed too.

I have been sorting the books in my shop to-day and have found a good ending with which to close my journal to-night. It is Thackeray's ending to 'The Virginians.'

'Twelve o'clock! Bless me! So indeed it is. And I close my book and go to my rest with a blessing on those now around me asleep.'

20

IN LIFE ONE FINDS that after years of plain sailing and happiness, several sorrows may come in a row, and then one is out into calm seas again. But there is a family in Penny Priors whose troubles go on and on. Almost all the men-folk have been struck down, the husband died in his forties; one son gave his life in the war while the other son died in an accident after serving all through the war; a son-in-law-to-be was killed in the air; one little grandson drowned and another half-blinded. If this were a book instead of a diary, you would throw it on the fire! Last week we attended the funeral of the last son. The church was full, the Rector read the bit about the widow of Nain (St. Luke vii, II) and we hung our heads and wept.

Some of the funerals here have been almost joyful; the end of a full and happy life here and then the tired body laid in familiar ground, while we sing 'Lord now lettest Thou Thy servant depart in peace' and in winter time the imported flowers have reminded us of springtime and the resurrection.

It is May now and the war has been over for a year. It is

spring. Everything rejoices! Women sing about their house-work again and talk about clothes again. Fashion has reared her fickle head once more, and the 'latest' is called 'the new look.' Square shoulders have gone, mannish hats are no more, skirts are longer and draped, waists are in, and really slim people are tying in little bustles! I have bought a misty blue halo hat, quite a creation : it is ruched with spotted veiling of the same colour and it does something for me! The postwoman said I looked like a bride, and an auctioneer, not recognising me, asked for my name and then exclaimed,

'I shan't know my own wife next!'

John says we must get the children to the sea this year. It was decided that I should go to Newquay in Wales and book up somewhere; he insisted that I travel first-class and have a little rest and relax. As the train wound its gentle way along the Llangollen valley, I sat back alone in my corner seat, gazing out on the soft green banks dotted with toy lambs. The beech trees were breaking into leaf and white keck like Valenciennes lace edged the route. It was strange to do nothing with a clear conscience — I had even left my diary at home. I just sat and thought, or just sat!

Here I am back home again and such a welcome — John with hugs; Gordon with words, and Angela, with looks and a posy of white violets.

While I have been away a lady called who had lived in our cottage when she was a child. 'I'm sure Mrs Summers would like you to come in and see everywhere,' Ruth had said, and she had stayed an hour and had tea with the children. Ruth said she was so jolly and had told them all sorts of tales. She had slept in Angela's room when she was a little girl. One day she said she had gone upstairs with her mother's scissors determined to cut off her own nose, which she felt to be too large and too ugly. She stood by the little window, scissors in hand and had been screwing up her courage, saying to herself, 'It will only hurt one second, one snip and it will be off!' But just at the very moment, her father called her to go a walk and 'as you see,' she added, 'it's still on.' 'And what *was* it like?' I asked with curiosity. 'Quite an ordinary one' Ruth replied.

While I was in Wales of course I had to call on a dealer or two. I bought a fine model of a Chinese junk. John said I ought to suspend it on an iron bracket outside and rename my emporium 'The Old Junk Shop.' I found also a magnificent German coffer, carved outside and inside the lid and decorated also with poker work; the design was of little figures in ruffs, knee breeches or waisted dresses in the Elizabethan style. Yes, I did buy something Welsh in Wales. I found twenty simple antique wood chairs in a barn; the farmer was most helpful: I left labels for him to tie on, and he promised to despatch the chairs by train tied together in pairs. In fact he was too helpful. He must have had a spare gallon of dark varnish knocking around. They arrived heavily painted with the wicked stuff and quite unsaleable! I've pushed them into a shed.

I had meant to turn out the shop this morning, but made the fatal mistake of starting on the bookshelves and books. These are priced at 1/- each with reductions for quantities. Scores of them sell before I have a chance to peep inside but a tiny one marked 'Everybody's Book of Epitaphs—What the Living think of the Dead', caught my eye. It appeared to be the thing to give the cause of death at one time, and here are three of the quaintest:—

Poor Martha Snell! her's gone away
Her would if she could, but her couldn't stay
Her'd two sore legs and a baddish cough,
But her legs it was as carried her off.

Here lies the body of Mary Ann Lowder
She bust while drinking a Seidlitz powder;
Called from this world to her heavenly rest,
She should have waited till it effervesced.

and in a Cheltenham Churchyard

Here lies I and my two daughters
Killed by drinking Cheltenham waters;
If we had stuck to Epsom salts,
We shouldn't be lying in these here vaults.

And here are three about men, which only run to couplets:—

Owen Moore is gone away,
Owin' more than he could pay

Near Oxford is one to a Doctor of Divinity which runs

He died of a quinsy
And was buried at Binsy

Another to a sportsman:—

Here lies the body of William Beck,
He was thrown at a hunt and broke his neck.

As this is an antique dealer's diary, let's have a good old craftsman's epitaph : it is to be seen in Berkeley Churchyard :—

Here lyeth Thomas Peirce, whom no man taught,
Yet he in Iron, Brasse and silver wrought;
He Jacks and Clocks, and watches (with art) made
And mended too, when other work did fade.
Of Berkeley five times Mayer this Artist was,
And yet this Mayer, this Artist, was but Grasse,
When his own Watch was Donne on the last Day,
He that made watches had not made a Key
To wind it up, but Useless it must lie,
Until he Rise A Gaine no more to die.

Deceased the 25th of February 1665. Aetate. S. 77.

I find I am overcharging for this little book . . . it was published in cloth at 6d, in leather, 1/-, and mine is green cloth.

One more epitaph to finish with. A joyful shout from Tailbach Churchyard in South Wales

Hurrah! my boys, at the Parson's face,
For if he'd lived he'd a' buried us all.

Who paid for this one I wonder, his widow? the P.C.C.? or did the stone-mason give his services?

⇜ *21* ⇝

On tuesday, I saw a house going up near Warwick. This is the first new house I have seen since the war, and to our surprise a brand new shining bus appeared in our village this morning and whisked us off to market. Whether the tyres had been blown up too hard or whether the new springs were too stiff I do not know, but we bounced about on the side seats like peas in a tin. Angela sat between me and the old mole-catcher. The latter remarked that 'this yere was as rough as a crossin' on one of they yere Irish cattle boats!' I said that he didn't often patronise the Thursday bus?

'No, not if I can help it!' he returned, 'but I has to get some bait to-day.' Angela gazed up onto his face, or rather into his neck, where a spirited Adam's apple performed surprising gymnastics.

'The little Missy will know me next time, won't 'er?'

'Yes,' I said, 'she knows about you and the moles, and is very interested.'

'Is 'er indeed! Then p'raps 'er would like to hold one of the little gentlemen in velvet?' And plunging his hand into his deep pocket, he drew out a dead mole. Two small brown hands reached out and cradled it for the rest of the journey.

When we had finished our shopping, and a Chelsea bun and a cuppa, there was still time to call in at the builder's yard and try to cover my expenses. We arrived hopefully, as one of his plasterers had called on Monday to say that 'the gaffer had some 'antics' to show you.' There sure enough were three little Georgian maiden-waist fire baskets at a pound a piece and a pretty wrought iron gate (just asking to be set in a Cotswold wall) for a fiver. I settled and he promised to drop them off when he comes to see to the guttering round the Church porch.

When we got home we found that Ruth had been enjoying herself in the shop! She had had a turn-out and 'done' the window. She had draped it with some faded green velvet curtains and polished up a huge copper tea urn as a centre piece; this she had filled with phlox, sweet williams, delphiniums and penstemons — it looked like a Dutch flower painting — lovely! Just before I closed to-night I'm afraid a customer bought it, flowers and all! Ruth's face will be a study when she arrives in the morning.

Several men dealers have told me that I am a very good buyer; really a woman *should* be able to find beautiful home-like pieces. It is easy to tell when a dealer does well with one's pieces — he is soon back for more. Some are quite puzzled why they sell them so quickly and say so. Two or three of them almost leave it to me and say, 'What can I make a profit on?'

I then load them up with perhaps a gateleg, a set of stickbacks, a large mahogany chest-of-drawers with swept feet, a pretty Delft rack and a dinner service. These are all things that young people who are being demobbed and setting up home like. It is a seller's market, of course. There are countless restrictions, vouchers, etc. and although the war is over, even bread has gone on coupons now, with our Labour friends at the helm!

Some people say 'How I wish I could afford antiques!' when really they should say 'I can only afford antiques.' Of course I am not talking about marquetrie 'grandfathers,' Kingwood commodes or yew tree bureaux, just simple good elm, oak, fruit-wood and country-made mahogany pieces. At the moment there is not a single piece in my shop that could be made for the money. I have two magnificent walnut credenzas, with bowed glass ends, lined with velvet and decorated with ormolu beading and swags. They are in mint condition and priced at fifteen and eighteen pounds. They could not be made for a hundred pounds; they are not fashionable in a home, and will probably go into a china shop or a jeweller's for display purposes, but their day will come.

Regency furniture is the vogue now, especially the pieces inlaid with brass. How dealers wish they had bought up quantities before the war — they would have made their fortunes.

Last week was my record week. I took nearly three hundred pounds and I only open four days a week. My Cheltenham Uncle was staying in the village and he was most interested and highly amused by one little incident. Some new customers, driving north, fell in love with a large Chippendale bureau priced at thirty-eight pounds. They had a trailer behind their car, but this was loaded with several sacks of coke . . . what could they do?

'Shall I have the coke off you and credit you with it?' I heard myself say.

'Oh thank you! Would you? This is the slip for it, 27/6d.'

Dear Uncle and the husband manhandled it into our coalhouse: what would the Aunts say? Especially Millicent!

❈ 22 ❈

JOHN IS ALWAYS TELLING ME I'm a clever girl and I wondered
this morning if there might be something in it, for I sold two
stuffed pike, two marble clocks and two what I call 'Albert
Memorials' to the same unsuspecting dealer! Whenever I boast
about anything I wish I hadn't, so I will stop, now, this instant,
before anything happens. I was telling Angela the other day
that if I think anything horrid or unkind about anyone, something immediately happens to me. I burn myself, scald myself,
bite my cheek, stub my toe or crack my head. Angela looked very
grave on receiving my confession and said

'*And* it does to me, Mummy!'

She is a very thoughtful little girl and a champion of lost
causes. I have visions of her working in a lost dogs' home or
nursing in a leper colony. When she was two years old and
Gordon had to have a graze or a cut dressed she would stand
by very close to him, her dark grey eyes full of what we thought
was sympathy — but we were wrong — it was envy! For one
day she cut her chin quite badly and when her tears were dried
she exclaimed triumphantly,

'I've got a poorly place at last!'

She is eight now, gentle and quiet and as I said very thoughtful. The other day there was a talk on the radio about adoption:
she was drawing horses as usual and we did not realise that she
was listening, but at the end of the programme she looked
up and said,

'I don't think I would mind being an orphan — not if you
and Daddy had got me.'

She has confided to me that she means to marry a farmer one
day, but she hasn't seen him yet. While she is training her first
pony, the pony is certainly training her. There are only two
good things to be said about Possum, she comes when she is
called and is beautiful. She is wild, naughty, 'mischiefful' as they

say round here, and far too fond of walking about on her hind legs for my liking.

Angel was very subdued the other evening and I asked her, 'What is it, darling?' and she replied,

'Sometimes I think Possum doesn't like me, Mummy.'

'Of *course* she does, pet. She wouldn't come trotting up to you if she didn't.'

'I'm afraid she comes for her sugar for one thing, and she can't very well kick me out of the field unless she comes up close, can she?'

'Keep on petting her, grooming her and leading her around. She will soon realise you are her best friend.'

'And there's something else, Mummy, Mr Lancer says you are no rider till you've had six spills!'

Only a couple of days later I saw a spirited sketch of Possum in her drawing book and underneath she had printed the words 'MARCH 4th 1946 POSSUM BUCKED ME OF FURST TIME.'

I congratulated her and she said gravely,
'I think I was wrong. I think she does like me. She stood still looked sorry and waited for me to get on again.'

As I have said, Gordon's great delight is his canoe. He takes this quietly down the river between the deep banks of mead-sweet — rather wonderfully he doesn't want to kill, shoot or catch anything! He still 'packs' a mouth-organ and loves to whistle and sing; he is never happier than when he is helping on the farm. His favourite view is of a golden harvest field.

One day last year I took him into town and got him a new suit with some of John's coupons. We had quite a respectable luncheon, in the afternoon we saw the film 'Desert Victory,' We then had a nice tea and went to the recreation ground until our bus was due. On the way home he said,

'Thanks, Mum . . . very generous of you, but I would rather have been helping on the farm and leading Blossom.'

To-day I bought a bunch of daffodils and filled our Lalique glass bowl which was a wedding present. It is a signed one and smoky blue, the design is of mistletoe in relief. This is the seventeenth spring that I have filled it with daffs and, thank God, we are at peace again. Whenever the children say,

'I've broken something. I'm so sorry' I reply,

'*Not* the Lalique bowl?' and when they say 'No,' I say, 'Tell me. I can bear it.'

I don't believe in hiding beautiful things away. I've persuaded a number of women customers to get out their best silver and glass and china and enjoy it. They all do their own washing up these days, and they get a double pleasure, first seeing it and using it, and then washing and drying it. When I was a school girl I talked my mother into getting out her best porcelain tea service for daily use. It was an adorable Limoges one, the design was of natural May blossom, there were tiny sprays inside the cups too and the handles were of gold leaf. This had been a wedding present from an Aunt May most appropriate!

When I buy some trays of china or porcelain at a sale or great piles of decorative plates I put them straight into the kitchen and then have a session of what I call 'washing up de luxe!' Everything looks so much lovelier when it is softly gleaming. I get the tiny bottle brush round the dusty encrusted flowers and round the curls and the tiny hands of the little figures. Then I price them and put them on trays to carry into the shop. Anything not perfect I mark A.F. which means 'as found.' It took me five years to discover what this stood for, but at last the penny dropped! During the war some unexpected guests arrived. I quickly fetched some extra cups from the shop. I couldn't have given them too good a wash as to my horror I saw the price label still adhering to the bottom of one, as a decidedly odd relative sipped her tea — the label read 1/- CRACKED. Gordon intercepted my fixed gaze. The humour of the situation was too much for him and he hurriedly left the table choking under cover of his serviette!

23

AT TEA ONE DAY, Angela told us that they had to do a drawing of a junk shop at school, she paused,

'Yes, darling?' I said, feeling there was more to come.

'Well, Miss Brighton said *mine* was the best.'

'Jolly good,' remarked big brother.

'What did you do, darling?' from me again.

'Well, Mummy, I thought of everything in your shop and I drew everything I could remember, even the parrot cage, till there wasn't *any* room left on the paper.'

The parrot cage, not an antique, was really a special order and I was lucky enough to get one quite quickly. It was in the shop awaiting collection on this particular Saturday afternoon I am telling about, when dear old Mr Willows from the cross roads came in, and he told me and a shop full of customers the following yarn. Years ago when he was a young man he had been digging in his garden, when a sea-gull dropped dead at his feet. He glanced upwards and saw a falcon against the blue sky. He fetched a riddle from the tool-shed, and set it up with a stick and a line, and put the dead gull underneath. He then got on with his digging, keeping a watchful eye on the riddle and sure enough within a few minutes the falcon was down and at the gull. He jerked the line, the riddle fell and he had the bird captive. He then brought out an old parrot-cage he had, and drawing on some hedging gloves, he managed to get the falcon and the dead gull into the cage and carried it into the house. The next day in his local paper he saw a reward offered for a lost falcon. He replied by post and the following day a gentleman with his groom and falconer drove up in a high two-wheeled trap and claimed the bird. The falconer donned a leather glove and opened the cage door. The falcon immediately took up position on his wrist and was then hooded with a scarlet cap surmounted by a tiny feather. The reward was a golden sovereign. Mr Willows was very curious about some white pencil-like rods in the bottom of the cage. The falconer explained that they were the compressed ribs of the gull's feathers that the falcon had disgorged.

After Mr Willows had left, a lady customer turned to me and said,

'My husband and I love to come out to see you on a Saturday. It is more like a salon than a shop.'

This was rather gratifying after Angel's drawing of my junk shop; so while I am blowing my own trumpet I will give another little toot which may amuse. A Swedish buyer called last week and chose some dessert services, and said he would get some cigarettes while I was packing them up. When he returned he said,

'This is a beautiful village!'

'Yes' I said, 'and the lilacs will soon be in bloom. You should see it then.'

'Have you a horse-pond?' he asked.

'A pool for ducks, do you mean?'

'No, to you married? A horse-pond?'

'Oh, a husband!'

'Yes, a horse-pond?'

'Yes, I have the best of husbands and children too.'

He paused thoughtfully, and said sadly, (I like to think)

'Then that is a pity, for you are a charming lady and I am a nice boy.'

My Aunt Millicent looked quite shocked when I told her this story; still *she* might even be shocked if she saw my hand being kissed! It certainly spoils it for me when it smells of beeswax and turps at these gallant moments. This Aunt however perked up considerably when she found I had some titled customers. I really let it out accidentally for we had been discussing politics and she suddenly said that she had the greatest admiration for Lord Mills: I added that I had too, and that he was one of my most delightful customers. Lady Mills collects old Worcester porcelain if decorated in coloured sea-shell designs. I once found her a little tea-pot stand like this and when she came for it, I asked her if she had added to her collection lately. She said she had been most fortunate in finding a tea-service. Sir Percy had wanted some cigarettes and had pulled up and parked their car outside a little cobbler's shop in a side street and there in the window all among the offcuts of leather was this exquisite porcelain. The cobbler had been asked to sell it by a customer. It was like a dream!

I shall not forget my first titled customer and I sometimes smile about it even now. He arrived on a bicycle and in my brilliant way I had him summed up in three minutes.

'Yes' I thought to myself, 'an elderly recluse, a bachelor, a book worm.' I lashed his purchases, some books, on to his bicycle carrier and advised him to be careful as he joined the Roman Road. Next day I had a post-card from him saying he collected old porcelain mugs. Across the card was printed his name and address — he was Admiral Sir Walter Cowan. No man alive had more decorations and only last year he had been with the 'Desert Rats' in Africa; he was a man of steel without fear and as fearless in war as in the hunting-field. No recluse indeed — he was also a widower with a daughter. In fact he was a legend in his lifetime!

24

You will have noticed inside your auction sale catalogue particulars of Conditions of Sale and one paragraph reads 'Messrs. Dot & Dash Ltd., are not responsible for the correct description, genuineness, authenticity or any fault or defect in any lot, and make no warranty whatever.' Can you imagine yourself dealing at any shop that had a notice like that in its window? The answer to it is of course that you have to use your own judgment, and you are the loser if you make a blunder; also you may have a wasted day travelling to a sale to buy an incorrectly described lot. I did exactly this, travelling sixty odd miles to buy a baby's antique walnut high chair; it was neither antique nor walnut. It was beech.

You may not believe me, but there are lots of auctioneers who cannot even tell oak from mahogany, let alone oak from elm or mahogany from rosewood. Some days each week, they sell farm machinery, and one wonders if they can tell a horse from a cow or a sheep from a pig, but perhaps their drovers prompt them! An auctioneer may ask his audience's assistance at a furniture sale. One day I was just going to pipe up, when a dealer standing by me, whispered,

'Don't tell him a thing!' I could see his point!

One local auctioneer shouts at the top of his voice and positively yells,

'Quick! Quick!' after each rise in the bidding. It is earsplitting and one farmer friend remarked,

'It is enough to make a man get up and strike his Grandmother!'

Another auctioneer raises the bidding like this.

'Is it six? is it six? is it seven? is it seven? is it seven? is it eight? is it eight? is it eight?' One day a wag shouted out,

'It will be if you don't get a move on!'

A customer who goes to the top London Sales was highly amused the other day, when a valuable lot was won by a Mr Cohen and the auctioneer graciously leaned forward and asked him to spell it! This reminds me but in a different way of a very charming elderly auctioneer who believes in cracking up his goods and remaining unruffled under all conditions. He sells in a large saleroom and he is always patient with his unappreciative and plebeian audience. Anything good he praises up to the skies, but if anything is revolting, say a broken-down old bed, he will say,

'Now is any lady or gentleman here expecting in-laws? I can give a written guarantee with this bed that they will not stay more than one night, and there is a good possibility of their leaving before midnight!' When a damaged chest-of-drawers is held up, someone may call out,

'One of the legs is off!'

'Oh! is that so!' he replies, 'thank you for pointing it out. Now here, ladies and gentlemen, is a use for some of those books you never read, just wedge it up and it will be different from your neighbours.' A grub-eaten old gateleg table will be apologised for like this,

'This ladies and gentlemen is genuine — nearly three hundred years old — some gentleman has unkindly pointed out that it has worm in its legs and, with respect, I think it is highly probable that he too may be afflicted in the same manner, when he reaches such an advanced age.' Needless to say the rate of sale here is very slow, about forty lots an hour! A large proportion of the audience never appear to bid or smile or speak; they just sit and smoke and swig tea. Perhaps they come for a tax-free entertainment or is it just for a good sit down?

One of our country auctioneers sells at the rate of one hundred and twenty lots an hour. Everything is set out in the open in a great circle or in rows and the auctioneer 'walks' the sale with his clerk. This auctioneer gets surprisingly good prices as one has to bid quickly or lose the lot, but on the other hand one may get bargains, if one keeps on one's toes.

Dealers soon sum up an auctioneer and heartily dislike the ones who 'trot' the bidding — that is, take imaginary bids and run up the prices. Naturally this fraternity often get landed with unsold lots and may approach one after the sale saying,

'I believe you were in the bidding at £6 each for the Stuart chairs? The purchaser has changed his mind, would you like them at your price. Let me see that would be £36, would it not?'

'My price is now £20 for the lot. I have had second thoughts too, like your *client*.' It is surprising how often this works, and the auctioneer books them to you, wondering if you are cuter than you look, or just short of cash.

A dear old dealer I used to know had his own way with customers. His prices were most reasonable and if he asked £5 for anything and the customer offered £4 would reply,

'No, the price is £6.'

'But you said £5.'

'Yes I know,' would reply my friend, 'You put the price down so I have put it up, and that's the price to *you*!' Like me, this dealer sold old things that were not always antiques, but had some age about them and were beautiful. I said to him one day,

'What do you say when people ask you "Is it really old?" and he replied, 'I just glower at them, and say "What's it matter?"'

One of my customers, a woman doctor once said to me,

'Mrs Summers, you can mix everything that is beautiful.'

Her own home, made from a Cotswold stone barn is a perfect example of this. It is furnished with antique furniture but has modern fitted carpets, modern fabrics for curtains and some delightful modern pictures. The deep window sills continue round the walls as bookshelves and also contain old porcelain and modern coloured glass for inspired flower arrangements. The garden, once the old rickyard, is so fertile that it resembles an illustrated seed catalogue.

Talking about this garden reminds me of another, also belonging to a lady. Her garden blooms the year round and I once remarked about this to which she replied.

'But it's so easy! You keep a little garden diary, you visit your local nurseries every month and make notes of what is in bloom, you ask when things should be transplanted and place your order there and then. Perhaps I should add that this lady has plenty of time and plenty of money.

❧ 25 ❧

THE SNOW PLOUGHS have kept the road open through Penny Priors, but the Roman Road is blocked and great cornices of snow hang high above us. We've literally seen rabbits jumping over the telegraph wires there; John says he will be able to tell his grandchildren about this one day and you can imagine their incredulous little faces and round eyes if he does not mention the snowdrifts and they picture the rabbits doing it from a standing start.

Some time back I bought a real Russian sledge: what a strange thing to find in a Warwickshire loft. I could have sold it the day it was delivered to me, but somehow we got very fond of it and the buxom mermaid on its prow. The children would rock themselves in it, and for a year or more it has lived at the top of the orchard under the old Blenheim tree, but this Swiss weather must have tempted some of the village lads for it now lies deep in a snow-drift at the foot of the Millways. Judging by its tracks up and down the hill they had had a royal time!

Yesterday I called on Mrs Webb. I brought her back a couple of bloaters from market and remembered that she liked hard roes. She is our oldest inhabitant or oldest but one and it is rather funny to hear two females arguing over such an issue. I told her about conditions outside as she is housebound. I told her how the ice had cracked on the river and been tossed in great blocks across the road by the bridge. She told me about the worst winter she remembered. She couldn't remember which year but it was before the turn of the century. The London coach, a four-in-hand had passed safely by the village but did not arrive at its destination eight miles away at Stratford. Riders set out from there when it was overdue and to their amazement saw a whip sticking out of a snow-drift in what we call the Dip — a hundred yards beyond the village. Mercifully men and horses were saved alive.

After breakfast this morning I put a heater in the shop and began to give it a good tidy up. I soon heard a quiet little tap at the door. It was my younger Goddaughter, Caroline. It is lovely to have a little one getting under my feet again now that my two are away at school. I shall not make an antique dealer of Caroline for if ever a child were born to be an actress, it is she.

'Good morning Auntie, I am a lady . . .' she began.

'Good morning Madam,' I replied, 'would you care to look round or were you looking for anything in particular?'

'No, nothing in 'ticular. What a charming shop! May I ask the price of this box?'

'Three Guineas,' I replied.

'How very reasonable and may I ask the price of this fan?'

'Thirty shillings, Madam,' I replied.

'Thank you, I will take them both,' she replied.

A car door crashed shut outside and a prosperous dealer bounded in.

'Good morning Mrs Summers. Is this your little girl?'

'No, she is my Goddaughter Caroline.'

'Hallo, Caroline! Are you helping?'

'Yes,' replied Caroline in a whisper, and was a shy little girl again.

I asked him something that had been puzzling me for a long time.

'Why do we always sell the things we have just bought?'
'You know surely!' he exclaimed.
'No, I really don't, you tell me why.'
'Why because we are so enthusiastic about them.'

Oh! I thought after he had gone, I can turn on a bit of enthusiasm to order. I soon had a chance of putting it to the test. A customer admired a Sheraton knife box that I had had for months. I tilted it till it caught the light and said how lovely it would be for a sewing or stationery box and suggested lining it with silk and, opening a drawer, I fished out a lovely little remnant of azure blue brocade. Yes, the material could be a makeweight — heigh presto! It was sold and off it went swathed in tissue paper. Next customer please!

Of course some things sell themselves. I once bought an eight foot high antique Dutch walnut grandfather clock case without a hood. It was carved and had a little bottle glass window through which the pendulum boss must once have shown. The cabinet-maker fixed little shelves inside and filled in the top. I then offered it as a cocktail cupboard. It was tucked in the darkest corner of the shop. One day a lady was considering it as a present for her husband's birthday. I fetched a flashlight for her to examine it. I had forgotten that there were letters entwined in the carving. They were her husband's initials and that did it! I have written about lots of lucky little breaks but there are countless enquiries for things I haven't got. Only yesterday a gentleman enquired for a really fine mahogany four poster and a choice antique oak bureau. I had both but in the opposite woods. No sale!

I usually start turning out the shop at the front and that's a mistake — in a back corner to-day I found an old red lamp. I remember buying it quite two years ago. The old duck at this particular junk shop said she had something lovely for me and I must wait while she found it, and there it was at last under a seal-skin coat, thirty-two antimacassars and three framed mottoes! Hideous! But I couldn't disappoint her and it was only 10/-: I hooked it on to a beam remarking aloud 'You will be here when I am dead and gone.'

'Do you mean me, Auntie?' piped up Caroline.

'No, darling pet, I'm talking to this horrid old lamp.' I sold it an hour later and went into the cottage to fetch a box thinking

to myself, customers cannot buy things that are hidden away.
When I got back Caroline had made friends with the customer
and was telling her that 'Auntie thought it was horwid!'

⊰ *26* ⊱

GORDON WAS SIXTEEN in the spring and is now six feet three
inches tall but we think he has stopped growing upwards and is
now growing sideways. On the strength of this assumption,
John has been measured for a tweed suit, a Harris tweed, in
russet brown. For years all his clothing coupons have been
needed for Gordon's school and sports clothes and John has
finished up by going to business in some of his son's outgrown,
but almost new, shoes!

I have been thinking about Gordon all evening. Countless
other mothers must have been thinking about their firstborn
children and first confinements this evening, for a Royal Birth
is imminent and my diary is open ready. It seems such a short
time ago that Princess Elizabeth herself was born, and we were
looking at photographs of her in her cradle, and in her Mother's
arms, and then as a curly-headed toddler wearing her coral
necklace.

The good news has come to us over the Radio. Her Royal
Highness Princess Elizabeth has been safely delivered of a
Prince. In the old days, I suppose, we would not have heard
until a London coach passed through the village next day, and
here am I, recording it in my diary, within an hour!

I can just remember the death of this little Prince's great
great grandfather, Edward VII. My mother took me down to
the village, near where we lived, and said 'Nearly everyone
will be wearing black, because the king is dead.' A year or so
later, my mother was in the village again with my grandmother
when King George V drove by in an open car and she said
'Grannie and I were *so* surprised! He raised his hat, just to us!
There was no one else near.'

72

'And what did you and Grannie do? Curtsey?'

'No, we bowed.' This was another game to play in the nursery! Come on, you can be king. I'll be Grannie, you'll need a hat, silly, go and get one from the hall. Help turn the table over for the car. What a useful old nursery table it was, long and narrow and very sturdy. Sometimes it was a house, often a tent, and once, once only, a four-poster bed for the two little princes in the tower — my mother rescued her offspring in time! My mother much preferred boys to girls but, after one son, she had me, to please my father who wanted a daughter, and then reverted to her favourite pattern.

Earlier this evening Angela had been studying an old 'Who's Who' and looking up some of my more famous customers.

'If you get into Who's Who, what will you say for your hobbies, Angela?'

'Breaking in horses and drawing, I expect. I know what you ought to put, Mummy — minding other people's babies and swilling the drains!' I believe she's right. When the water butts are brimming full, I put on my Wellingtons, seize a couple of buckets and the bass broom and dash gallons of water down the yards and really enjoy myself. As for babies, I had not realised how many we had had, till the Sexton went by the other day as I was settling one down in its pram.

''Scuse me Mam,' he said, 'but you and Mr Summers 'av 'em pretty fast, if you don't mind me saying so.' That started John and me counting up and it's true. We have had eleven in nine years, some of them four or five times, evacuees, nieces, nephews and Godchildren! Angel quite likes them, especially after a day or two, they grow on her. Gordon finds the younger ones quite repulsive. He feels guilty about this and says he is going to look at them more and harden himself up. He says he intends to marry, have a family and lead a normal existence. I think he would like them better if they were covered with fur as he thinks new-born kittens are wonderful.

Lots of customers who come in asking for something so unlikely that they must know it is a thousand to one that I haven't got it. Still it is a pleasant change from those everlasting worn-out words, 'May I browse?' One longs to say, 'Certainly, there is some delicious white clover on the Green.' One regular customer came in last year, and said, 'I'm going to ask for the impossible Mrs Summers, but if you should ever find some Regency door plates or door knobs, will you please remember me?'

I gave what I like to think was an enigmatic little smile and said 'I won't be a minute,' and disappeared into the cottage. I returned with a white cardboard box and let him open it himself. Inside were the most glorious ormulu door knobs and finger plates to match, in open basketwork embellished with musical instruments, lyres, flutes and I don't know what. I had seen them in a local jeweller's window, bought them for 50/-, popped them in a drawer and forgotten all about them. They later appeared in photographs of this gentleman's house illustrating an article in one of the glossy magazines.

This sort of business gives one the open sesame into countless interesting and beautiful houses. I shall never forget one of the first I ever visited, or rather attended, as there was an auction sale of surplus furniture there. It was about three miles away across the river. I set off on shanks' pony with Angela in her pram and a packed lunch. The house belonged to a wealthy American family, and their secretary told me that they had bought the wonderful wallpaper which adorned the drawing room, in Paris. It was hand-printed and each piece was different, as it formed, right round the room, a mural of the American Wars of Independence. There were illustrations of skirmishes, landings on rocky coasts, harbour scenes, etc. all in soft pastel tones of greys, greens and blues, except for the uniforms of the soldiers of course; and it was printed on a thick matt paper. The doors of the room were also papered and the door knobs were of glass, so nothing broke the mural except the windows and the fireplace. The doors were quite hard to find.

I was lucky enough to get two spare rolls of this wonderful paper for six shillings. It just asked to go into a boy's room, so I papered one wall of Gordon's bedroom, the wall facing him, as he lay in bed. The scene showed a natural rocky span, like a slender bridge across a great canyon, with a mounted patrol of soldiers wending its way along the valley below. It really opened up the room and gave a marvellous feeling of distance and space. He loved it.

❦ 27 ❦

Mᴀʀᴄʜ 17th saw the first butterfly of the summer this morning, a brimstone, that is apart from the silly little juggins of a tortoiseshell, which keeps fluttering out from behind beams, when I am dusting, and which I keep reposting in the dark warm corner behind the radio set.

To-day I have had a real working day and loved it. All the customers have had a 'serve yourself' day and enjoyed it too, I think. I had to have a collection of chairs ready by four o'clock for a carrier calling to take them to a warehouse in Liverpool, on their way to Canada, for a woman dealer there. Although Victorian furniture is not popular in England, there is a steady demand for it overseas. Some dealers tell me they even have an outlet for immense Victorian mahogany sideboards which only make about fifty shillings at auction, huge dining tables, the sort with a leg at each corner and long sets of Victorian crown back and balloon back chairs with their lumpy old front legs! They ship them to Australia, where they go to sheep-farmers and other buyers, who have plenty of space, and entertain in the good old-fashioned way.

I set the thirty odd chairs out in rows on the lawn as I polished them. They all had cabriole legs but some of the grandfather and grandmother chairs had lost their upholstery.

This Canadian buyer once wrote to ask me if I could find her an old stage-coach; Ruth turned up for work as I was reading the letter, and I jokingly said to her,

'Do you know anyone with a stage-coach for sale, Ruth?' She hesitated a moment and then replied,

'Well, yes, I certainly know where there *is* one, on a farm where I often go. But I do not know if they would sell it. It has been there for years and years. We used to play all over it when we were children.'

I followed this up, but it was one of my wild goose chases.

The rims of the wheels had sunk into the ground and the spokes were rotting; it really needed restoring where it stood. It was beautifully made with folding steps, and little storage compartments inside the seats, all lined with soft leather and the little blinds to the windows still worked. In fact it was just like the ones we see in Western films. Probably my customer wanted it for a Ciné Company.

One of the loveliest sights to be seen in Oxford these days is a four-in-hand, driven in daily from Woodstock ten miles away. Long may it flourish! There appear to be two different teams, beautifully matched; their gleaming backs and brave heads stand high above the surrounding cars and the dauntless driver, believe it or not, is a young woman!

Another dauntless lady sometimes rides over from the next village, to exercise a young stallion, one she hunts and has bred herself. She never dismounts here, so I go out on to the Green to speak to her and carry out anything for her inspection. The fine fellow arches his neck, shows the whites of his eyes and is glad to be away again.

The other day among a collection of books from an auction sale, I found a little booklet written some fifty years ago by a London porcelain dealer who had the Royal Coat of Arms above his door. He called his short story, which only runs to twelve pages, 'My Greatest Asset.' It is written in the first person but he does not state if it is fact or fiction. He tells how on a View Day at a furniture sale in a Wiltshire country town, he discovers something in the secret drawer of an antique walnut bureau bookcase. The 'something' is a small wooden box, tied up with green ribbon under which is tucked a visiting card and, written on it in pencil, are the words, 'This box contains my greatest asset. George Lambert Nov. 3rd 1874.'

He quickly replaced the box in its hiding place and began to work himself up into a state of great excitement. He knew that Mr Lambert had lived to a great age, was well endowed and had been an eccentric. To condense the twelve pages into a few lines, he visited his Bank Manager about an overdraft and decided to stake his all, some £800 if necessary to purchase the bureau. But he won it for £100 and in a fever of excitement excorted it home, walking alongside the odd job-man and his handcart. In the privacy of his own hall, he opened the secret drawer again, and with shaking hands opened the little box. Wrapped in tissue paper were an upper and lower set of dentures, accompanied by a little note which read,

'I have lived to 97 through carefully masticating my food. Had it not been for these wonderful teeth, I might have died years ago of starvation. George Lambert.'

❈{ 28 }❈

WHEN I MAKE A JOURNEY BY BUS, I always try to travel on top at the front. The things one sees in builders' yards and scrap merchants' dumps are surprising, though often not for sale of course. A list of things found like this would fill pages of my diary. Some of the latest discoveries have been eighteenth century maiden waist fireplaces, carved barge boards, (these are the carved or pierced boards sometimes seen under the eaves of old buildings) weather vanes, iron gates and lots of stone troughs or 'trooffes' as we call them in Warwickshire, and staddlestones, those mushroom like stones on which ricks used to be built, to keep the grain from the rats.

Customers often ask me,

'How can you bear to sell these things? Don't you hate to part with them?' The answer is,

'No,' for two reasons. I don't think of the things in the shop as mine, though they are all paid for, thank Heaven, and secondly I am always wanting some cash to buy some other lovely things that I know about.

When I was a little girl, my Mother read to me an old book called 'Eyes and no Eyes,' and this trade certainly teaches one to use one's optics! If you think for instance that your Chippendale 'diner' has an exceptionally large seat, you look to see if there is any sign of arms having been removed. If you find a bit of veneer missing off an old walnut piece, you look to see if the remaining veneer is as thick as a penny, which means that it is hand-cut and old. You pull out the drawer of a Jacobean chest-of-drawers to see if it runs on grooves at the sides instead of runners underneath; you tilt a chair to see if the back edges of the back legs have been worn away by countless dragging back from the table, and so on. People ask almost daily, 'How can you tell if it is really old?' and, to a man, I say the same way that you can tell if a woman is in her twenties or forties — her shape, her colouring, her skin — and I could say—and her legs : but I just say, 'and everything you know. Your eye is trained,' and it's true. Any antique dealer of some years' experience will look across a room at a piece and know it is right; if a doubt creeps in, he examines it closely and it is always wrong or restored. The word 'piece' reminds me of a Doctor customer's story. He had been attending an old countrywoman who had passed away. He and her son stood quietly at the foot of her bed, the son gazing at his mother's face and the Doctor gazing admiringly at a Chippendale chair at her bedside. After a pause the Doctor remarked,

'What a fine old piece!'

'Ah, 'er were that !' joined in the son with feeling, 'A proper wonder!'

A farmer's wife has lately brought in a clockwork picture, It is an oil painting on a wooden panel, of a village scene. The clock in the church tower works, and is wound up from the front like an ordinary clock. The frame is deep which leaves room for a swinging pendulum and the weight behind. She did not know what price to ask me, or I to pay her, so we have put a price ticket on it of £10 and we shall see. This picture was sold with some surplus furniture from a mansion nearby, from one of the real old Warwickshire families. I have written this on a paper and glued it on the back. How often we wish that artists had done this — their name, the subject and the date. I have never seen a clockwork picture before but when my mother was a little girl she visited an old lady who had a clockwork picture of a storm at sea, and a ship in extremis. This was wound up for my mother as a treat. The old lady said she blamed it for giving her three sons a calling for the sea, as they were brought up in the middle of Warwickshire. When I was a little girl, my Grandmother's musical box would be wound up sometimes for my delight. It had enamelled butterflies on silver rods which rose and fell, striking silver bells and, if I was left in the drawing-room, I would softly close the door and hop and skip about between the little tables to the music.

On the mantlepiece were two old glass paper-weights and the glazed Victorian credenza was filled with Spode and flower decorated Rockingham porcelain, and on the front edges of the shelves were miniature cups and saucers, tiny copper pots and kettles and a wee robin. I never saw this cabinet opened and little girls in those days never touched a thing. My elder brother, however, was a law unto himself and once got out Grandfather's lawn-mower on a Sunday (of all days) and hared off down the lawn with it. There was a terrific *schemozzle*!

When I was ten years old my widowed Grandmother left this house. Until then we had had tea there every Sunday of our lives, with Mary in the kitchen when we were small and then later with the Grandparents, Aunts and Uncle in the dining-room. I always sat next to my Grandmother and I sensed as a child can that she was gentle, kind and good. I can only remember my Uncle ever speaking to me at table, when he would occasionally ask me how to spell a word, and the word always had a double meaning, such as quay or key. I didn't know which he meant and was too shy to ask, so I slowly turned puce and hung my head. I tease *him* these days! My Aunt Millicent once asked me to read a letter aloud that I had received. Since I was too shy to start with the words 'Dear Anne' I followed the previous formula — turned puce and drooped! They must have thought I was missing in the upper storey.

Although it is more than thirty years since I stepped through my Grandmother's french windows into the garden I can remember it as well as yesterday. First the mossy smell and the ferns by the window, then the trim little rose garden with its small beds edged with scallopy tiles and the moss roses that I loved, the long flower border, the caterpillars on the nasturtiums, the rhododendrons at the far end of the lawn with the yellowing grass cuttings underneath them; then the shady side of the garden and the great syringa. The summery smell of it all and the neat little tool-shed housing the infamous mower.

My Grandmother's only pet was a magnificent blue Persian cat. My three brothers and I longed to play with him but he did not reciprocate our sentiments. When Prinny heard us at the gate he was over the wall like greased lightning, or under my Grandmother's eiderdown if his retreat was cut off. There he would lie doggo under our hats and coats until we departed. When we grew up, three out of the four of us owned blue Persians, doubtless to appease our childhood frustrations! Our own Mrs Muffit has populated the village and the district, and we always have a waiting list for her blue kittens. My Cheltenham Uncle says she should have a stone erected to her on the village green, bearing the same epitaph as that of Sir Christopher Wren in St. Paul's, the simple words — 'Look around you.'

29

ANGELA IS GETTING more and more interested in the antique trade. Before she went to bed to-night, she had half-an-hour on my knee and was asking question after question.

'Mummy, what is the funniest thing you ever bought?'

'Do you mean queer?'

'Yes, I do,' she replied.

'Well, I once bought a smuggler's kettle. It looked like a rather ordinary tin kettle but the top half of it unhinged and there inside was a squat glass bottle with a cork. If the excisemen called to search, this old tin kettle sitting on the hob would look perfectly innocent, and if friends called, the brandy inside would be pleasantly warm to drink!' I sold this to the Smugglers Museum at Polperro in Cornwall, so perhaps you will see it there one day, pet. The Museum is in the cellars of an old smuggler's house and full of the most interesting things which are very well displayed.

'Mummy, what is the loveliest thing you ever saw?'

'Do you mean alive or antique?'

'An alive-thing first' replied our animal-lover.

'Well, darling, it was something I will never forget even if I live to be ninety. When we came to live here I bought a bicycle and sometimes if I wanted to go up to the grocers I would leave you in your pram at Mrs Clancy's and cycle off the three miles. One spring day I was spinning down the hill past the Park woods when I sensed a movement. And there over on my left racing parallel to me was a group of deer led by a milk-white hind. We kept silently alongside each other for hundreds of yards. I cannot tell you what a wonderful feeling it was. It just made my day!'

'Then I must have seen your white hind, Mummy. Helen and I were floating on the mill pool one day and it stepped out of the woods and stood in the rushes for perhaps one second and was gone. We were never really sure if we saw it or dreamt it! And now tell me about the loveliest antique you ever bought?'

'Well that is a puzzler! Can I tell you about the *lovliest* one I have ever *heard* about? And then its bed-time!'

'Well, it is perhaps the loveliest toy that has ever been made. A customer has been telling me about it. He has seen it in a London workshop where it is waiting to be repaired. It consists of a life-size swan in pure silver; she is mounted on twisted glass lustre rods on a pool as large as the top of a bath. When it works again the rods will revolve and look like the glittering surface of a lake and the swan will appear to glide over it. She will arch her neck, turn her head from side to side, preen her feathers and pick up tiny silver fish which she will swallow and all to the accompaniment of the sweetest music.' Then for a makeweight I told her yet once again how I had seen the great Pavlova dance 'The Swan.' Of her lovely dress of white feathers and the swansdown on her hair, how the spotlights turned the empty stage into a moonlit river, and how she floated and glided down it for the last time to the rippling music of Saint-Saëns.

When I went to tuck her up she was still thinking about the musical swan. As I drew the curtains the great white owls flew silently across the green, one can almost set the clock by them, they follow the same route night after night. We do not know where they nest now but one June evening last year Gordon came rushing into the kitchen and almost before I could get my apron off had me hurrying with him down the village to see 'You'll *never* guess what!' I had never seen him so excited. Several old elms, considered unsafe, near the Church, had been felled that day into an adjoining rick-yard. A dozen children

81

including Angela were springing up and down on the leafy branches and having the time of their lives and shrieking with delight, while several quiet ones were peering into a hollow trunk and there squatting like three feathery fawn footballs and quite unharmed were the offspring of the great white owls! A big boy took one home and tried to feed it but it languished and he had the sense to return it in time. The parent birds found their young and within a week they had flown.

One of the mild excitements of cleaning and polishing up antiques is the frequent discovery of secret drawers, sometimes as many as ten in a bureau or desk and they are almost invariably empty! So far I have discovered nothing more exciting than two ten shilling notes, out of date postal-orders and old stamps which have got behind drawers, although, like the Indian Rope Trick, one keeps hearing of people who have. Legally unless the bureau has been sold 'with contents' anything valuable should be returned to the vendor as the valuable found would come under the heading of 'stealing by finding.' So at an auction sale when a piece is offered that has its drawers full, it is just as well to pipe up and ask the Auctioneer 'With contents?' and to get those words on one's receipt too. This would protect one from any relatives or beneficiaries who might enquire later for any missing jewellery or valuables. Our grave-digger's wife told me how she once bought at the Church Jumble Sale a pair of Sir John's riding breeches for her husband. Weeks later he found three sovereigns folded in a piece of paper in a pocket. She took advice and was told she should return them. So next day she donned her best bib and tucker and walked up to the Big House. She sat in the kitchen enjoying a cup of tea while the master was informed. The Lady herself came to thank her, she rewarded her with a sovereign and told her that 'she was a good honest woman.'

❧ 30 ❧

THIS SPRING I had a letter from an elderly cousin. She wanted me to furnish an empty cottage for her. We had not met for thirty years but a mutual aunt had told her about me. She was retiring in June and her cottage was ready scrubbed with curtains hung but she wanted me to do the rest. She told me what I might spend and proposed paying half on account. She told me she wanted new divan beds and bedding and new rugs in plain colours, everything else antique, if possible, and for preference a dark oak gateleg table, wheelback chairs and a dresser with a rack.

A friend in the village rented me a garage and I had three months to find everything. For each bedroom I bought an antique chest-of-drawers and a pretty swing mirror and antique bedside cupboard. After all the essentials were found there was still a little money left over, so I included blue willow pattern china for the dresser, tiny pierced brass fenders for the bed-rooms, sprigged china chamber potties for the bedside cupboards and the sweetest little rocking chair for the guest-room.

Last Thursday I made the forty-mile journey with our local carrier and one of his henchmen. We got the key from next door and the men carried the beds and the chests-of-drawers upstairs for me. We unrolled the dining-room carpet and set the furniture in position. When they had gone I really set to and gave the furniture a good polish, made up the beds, put in the bottles, unrolled the rugs, laid the fire and put the matches handy, filled some jugs with flowers that I had brought from home and put a basket of home-grown vegetables in the kitchen. As a final touch to the dresser I filled one willow dish with brown eggs and concealed some farm butter inside another.

Fixing the stair-carpet was the worst job. By this time I was hot and tired with fluff in my hair. Half way down I had a 'breather' and thought of John working away for me. I felt I ought to have my head examined. Why, I could have been sitting under my little willow tree, mending or watching the kittens at play. When I got my second wind I did the lower half and got the kettle on and had a good wash. I left the key next door and cooled off waiting for the long distance bus home.

A week later I heard from my cousin and her letter made me feel it was all worth while as it began like this :—

Dear Anne,

When I turned the key and went into my cottage I shed fifteen years! How can I thank you enough . . .

I have now been married for twenty-three years and have put on twenty-three pounds! I could write a chapter on diets; several have reduced me ten pounds in two weeks, but as soon as I relax a bit I put it on again, plus an extra pound. Really I should give up all sugar, fat, milk and starch for the rest of my life! For energy there is nothing like a protein diet. On this I can work the clock round and feel not only that I could do it all again but enjoy it into the bargain.

In the Spring I had coffee with two women friends in the Pump Rooms at Leamington Spa. We waved aside the proffered cream cakes and discovered we were all taking Dexadrine on our doctors' advice. We asked each other how it affected her. Mrs A. said 'I am two jumps ahead of everyone else now and keep putting words into their mouths if they hesitate. They don't like it, especially my husband who says it wouldn't be so bad if I got the right word.' Mrs B. volunteered the information that she now got into conversation with anyone on the least pretext and had had an animated and witty conversation with the bus conductor all the way from Banbury, and between them they had had the passengers in tucks of laughter.

'Now what about you, Anne? Own up!' they demanded in unison, and I had to confess that on the way to meet them I had dived under the laurels as I crossed the little Park and pulled up a bucketful of weeds! We were all bursting with activity but not really quite ourselves.

Talking about energy, Mrs Avril, nearly an octogenarian, was chatting to me the other day at the shop-door when a regular hobo whom we have nicknamed 'Sprinter' trekked through the village at his usual six miles an hour.

'My word!' exclaimed Mrs Avril 'He means to get to the Workhouse on time.'

'Oh,' I said, 'he always goes at that pace. He is said to drink methylated spirits.!'

'Indeed' replied Mrs A. 'I must have a word with my Doctor, I feel that's just what I need' and moved away thoughtfully at her snail's pace.

⚜ 31 ⚜

SOMETIMES WHEN I AM TALKING to my children I think to myself 'My Mother said that to me' and when I am singing and hit a good note, I hear my Mother's voice, but when I am clowning and romping with the children I think 'This is Daddy coming out in me.'

My brothers and I used to try to keep awake if he were late, and he would come into the night nursery and do funny turns and recitations in the dark. Sometimes he would be an old Professor studying the stars. He would stroll around the nursery gazing at the ceiling and would keep falling over our beds nearly crushing us! Then he would use two voices for the next little turn, first a hollow macabre bass saying,

'Old man, old man for whom diggest thou this long and narrow grave?'

'It's all right, governor! We're only laying the gas pipes down!' would reply a chirpy Cockney one.

When he kissed us and tried to slip away we would plead 'Have the jumps! Have the jumps!' He would then hold the foot end of my little iron bed and kick his legs high up behind him. Yes, 'having the jumps' was our favourite. We stifled our laughter as best we could, but my Mother hearing various bumps and thuds would innocently call up softly 'Charles! Charles! You will wake the children.' The baby would sleep through it all but we older ones would lie there in paroxysms of laughter.

Two of us grew up on the serious side and two of us on the jolly side. A customer came in the other day. We had been at school together and had not met since we were eighteen. But she told me she had met my daughter at Art School and had asked Angela what I was like these days, and she said she had replied 'Well I suppose Mummy is too fat, but then you see she's very jolly!'

I have been looking back through my diary and seen Mrs Silver's name so often I think I will sort out some pages about her to-day. She was one of my first friends in Penny Priors at the beginning of the war. She died last week.

Dear Mrs Silver to tea to-day. How I love her to come! I should think she must be nearly seventy now. It's funny how some people look just the same for years and years, especially people whose hair goes white while they are still quite young. Hers matches her name, and her eyes are as blue as periwinkles. But it's laughter and Mrs Silver that you think of together. She owns the empty cottage near the wych elm. I must tell you about her and why it's empty and why she only comes to Penny Priors once a month. She and her husband once owned a lonely cottage along the Roman Road, and when she was not off on her bicycle visiting or nursing up the road then you could bet your bottom dollar she was doing the same thing down the road. So shortly before Mr Silver departed this life he bought her the cottage by the wych elm in the very centre of the village so that she would not be too lonely. As soon as she was safely installed and the curtains hung, he took his final farewell. Within a few months, Mrs Silver once more on mercy bent went to stay with an aunt and uncle who were both ill and both eighty-eight years old. Now I will tell you what she did, because it did not seem a rash thing *at the time*. She gave her faithful promise to the old dears that she would stay with the survivor till his or her death. When you think that they were both ancient, both ill — and you know what the Good Book says about man's allotted span — it did not seem a wild commitment! But nine swift summers and nine long winters have passed since that promise was given and with laughter and chuckles Mrs Silver tells how her cooking and care look like making the old gentleman a centenarian, by which time she prophesies *she* will be pushing up the daisies! A neighbour takes charge of the Uncle one day a month while she slips down to her cottage, opens the windows, tidies her garden, gathers a posy for her husband's grave and drinks innumerable cups of tea at various cottages. With semi-serious faces we enquire,

'How is the old gentleman?' and with a chuckle she answers shortly,

'Stronger than ever!' or 'planting potatoes.....'

You might well ask, 'Why doesn't she bring him to her cottage?' But no, he has to go into his Market Town every Tuesday and see his cronies. Or would they be the *descendants* of his cronies? — not knowing, I can't say.

Well, the old fellow did not quite make his century after all, and Mrs Silver had her last few years in her own home. She jokingly said that she had never had the chance to marry again. The old gentleman had chaperoned her too well; calling her in from the gate if she stayed to gossip, packing her off to bed, and turning out the lamps at nine o'clock. She always insisted that her ginger puddings were better than any tonic, and that each time he was a bit middlin' she would knock one up. In fact, she became so expert at it, that she declared she could make one with her eyes shut.

⛥ *32* ⛥

ANGELA OFTEN 'does' the shop window for me. She is slim enough to get right inside it, polishing the plate glass until it is invisible. The window has gone all 'Victoriana' at the moment. A French ormulu clock under a glass dome holds pride of place; a Parian figure, her arms full of grapes, poses on a carved ebony stand, looking down disinterestedly on a mother-of-pearl casket which is spilling out lockets, chatelaines and coral necklaces.

'How pretty your window looks these days!' remarked a faithful regular customer the other day. 'I often take a little walk round the village to see if you have changed it.'

'Yes, Angela does it these days. Quite an improvement on those two dead flies and a wasp in the old days.'

'Oh, it is,' she replied mildly, 'but it wasn't quite as bad as that, there were other things, if you remember.'

One day, I remember filling a silver resist teapot with a mixture of small herbaceous flowers, clarkias, columbines, nigella mimulus, godetia and phlox. Within an hour it was on its way to London, flowers and all!

For many years I have been collecting, and receiving as presents, pieces of lustre. This is a china, covered with a thin layer of copper or silver in its glaze. The prettier pieces have designs on them and are sometimes decorated in colour too. This china as tea services was originally made for people who could not afford real silver, but they are now becoming collector's pieces in their own right. I only keep any damaged pieces for myself, and have jugs, goblets, mugs and teapots, and a silver lustre hen without her nest. Whatever flowers I pick there seems to be a lustre piece to suit it. The velvety gillies go into a copper lustre tea pot, the tall blue cornflowers into a large copper lustre jug, its facets touched with blue. The sweet pansy faces into a copper lustre goblet, while the more elegant lilies-of-the-valley, sweet peas, jasmine and roses get popped into the dear old chipped silver resist pieces.

The metallic surfaces enhance the flowers, just as a silver or gold setting enhances a jewel, or an old gold leaf frame, a painting!

There is tremendous interest these days in the art of flower arrangement, another gift from the Orient. Some of the arrangements are so exquisite that they have to be seen to be believed. If someone could invent a spray to transfix them for ever, his fortune would be made. The first lovely ones I saw were studies in various shades of one colour, perhaps roses in every shade of pink from pearly pink to deep rose, or a number of different varieties of flowers all cream in colour — ivory carnations, white stocks, palest yellow penstemons and creamy roses, with dark green aspidistra leaves as a foil for their beauty. Then there seemed to be an Oriental period, when customers asked for oriental bowls and soup plates; in these they erected flowering twigs, surrounded by interesting wet pebbles. Next, if I remember correctly, we had to find the same ladies, two-handled bronze or Spelta goblets and urns; we called this the

Dutch Period, for in these vessels they created living flower pictures with peonies, old-fashioned roses, morning glory convolvulus, tiger lilies, passion flowers, guelder roses and what have you! They soon found out too that the beloved striped tulips of the Dutch Masters were never in bloom at midsummer and realised the painters had cheated a bit!

Many of my customers, who made this their hobby, have cupboards full of bowls, vases, sea-shells, dishes and stands, 'enough to stock a shop,' husbands have told me. When I have several inquiries during one week for 'a miniature something,' a glass dome, or something Victorian for flowers, I know there is a competition somewhere. Mrs Clancey's youngest grand-daughter now five, competed in our village flower-show this summer. Her grandmother began to offer advice and sugges-tions, but they were cut short by the little competitor saying,

'Excuse me, Granny, I know what to do. I have been in for competitions before, you know.' And sure enough she won a prize in the childrens' section for her 'saucer arrangement' of tiny heartsease faces! Angela once won a prize too for flower arrangement of wild flowers; she made a tight little Victorian posy, using a paper silver doyley for the frill. The centre of the posy was a single wild rose, surrounded by closely packed heads of wild blue scabius, then a circle of pink clover heads and finally white keck, pretty as lace!

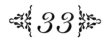

To-DAY, NEW YEAR'S DAY, January 1st 1955, I filled the posy ring with polyanthus, sprigs of pink stock, various pansies and three violets. I have had letters from my Cornish friend at Christmas sometimes naming all the flowers in her garden, but I have never had more than an occasional violet and the chaste helebore or Christmas rose. I wonder if this year is going to be topsy-turvey again, as it was three years ago in Coronation year. There is a Scottish prophecy that there would be no seasons in the year of the Three Queens. It certainly worked out like that when Princess Elizabeth became Queen, our Queen became the Queen Mother, and we had Queen Mary, the dead king's mother, still with us. I remember we picnicked in March, nearly froze in the summer and it poured with rain for the Coronation in June!

Everything seems to happen to me in 'threes.' I had three brothers. I have had three children, (there was a little daughter between Gordon and Angela who was only lent to us for one week), and I have three Godchildren. So far I have had two homes but if I could foretell the future I would say the next, and last, will be within sight or sound of the 'briny' to satisfy John. I even buy things in 'threes;' that is to say, if I get something rather unusual, I see or buy two similar pieces quite quickly. Sometimes I go for a year without buying a Chippendale corner chair, and then I buy three in ten days. I even did it with three antique staircases. It is a bit uncanny!

Talking about Chippendale corner chairs, I sold a very fine one to an impressive-looking Doctor last week; it was in my stable. He sat in it, leant back and relaxed. I had to smile and say, 'You only need to take out your snuff box to complete the picture.' Yes, you've guessed, he suited the action to the words and took a pinch. I have not seen anyone take snuff before, although I've seen it sold in tobacconists. I sold this same customer, on another occasion, a Breeches Bible, which he gave to his Church; in the third chapter of Genesis, verse seven, it says 'and the eyes of them both were opened, and they knew that they were naked; and they sewed fig leaves together, and made themselves aprons,' but in this edition the word 'breeches' was used instead of 'aprons,' hence the name 'Breeches Bible.' I bought it at a little cottage sale and then wrote up to the British Museum about it. They told me that a similar one had recently been auctioned for five pounds, and that is how I priced mine.

I have missed some wonderful books lately. I often chatted to the road-man who used to sweep our paths and trim the verges. He loved beautiful things, and no-one but a countryman would have left the heartsease, which had seeded against our garden wall. At one time he had been on the dustcarts, and had had permission to keep any book he particularly wanted. He told me of one that unfolded with maps of the roads of England, each road being about an inch wide; I have occasionally seen single sheets framed but never a book of them. Some months after his early and tragic death, I decided to call on his widow to see if she wished to sell anything. I was a week too late. She told me that the children had had a bonfire of his books and all his old junk on the previous Sunday! If anyone ever reads this and has something old they don't want, do, *do* give it to a Jumble Sale, a 'Bring and Buy,' or the Scouts, and let someone buy it who will treasure it. A chemist friend, a collector, bought a glorious Napoleonic drinking glass bearing the capital letter N in gold leaf. He found it at a Vicarage Sale of Work, in the South of England. A country woman standing in front of him bought it with five other glasses, and he asked if he might buy that one off her.

'Yes' she replied 'it doesn't match.' He had to press his half crown upon her! He feels sure that the glass had belonged to Napoleon III who, you remember, lived in exile in England.

Some people have the luckiest buys. A friend of Angela's bought a little Blue John vase in the Bermondsey market for a few shillings and a few weeks later bought the plinth belonging to it on another stall for a shilling. How about that for a bit of good luck?

Our dustmen call every fortnight and bring me all sorts of odds and ends. They have assured me that it is allowed, our Council do not even salvage paper, and anything I don't buy will go on the dump. Nevertheless we do all our transactions rather furtively in the shadow of the dustcart door and, if I settle with a treasury note, I fold it into a little square to add to the mystery! They once brought a pair of lovely carved wooden bird brackets; I spent an afternoon on each brushing it with a soft wire brush until it acquired a silvery beauty. Another time they brought some old carriage lamps and a pierced brass fender, and there seems to be an endless supply of old copper kettles and pot hooks. We simply love a pair of silver plated pheasants that they brought us. These were pepper pots for white and red pepper, I suppose, and they look beautiful on the polished oak table. I have told Angela that she shall have them when she marries. She is eighteen now and rarely mentions the subject. Ten years ago she decided she would like to marry a farmer and breed horses. She said she would have me to stay, and I should have breakfast in bed and strawberries and cream every day. She would lead me round the farm in a wicker chair fixed on the back of a shire horse. Quite the most suitable breed I should think after such a diet!

⚜ 34 ⚜

I HAVE NOT WRITTEN A WORD in my diary for months — in fact, I am in pretty low spirits. It is winter; John goes before it is light and comes home in the dark. Gordon is in Egypt and Angela at College and consequently away all the week. Her pony, Miranda, misses her too, and I often go to have a chat with her and get a bit of comfort myself. She is a lovely creature, a chestnut with blonde mane and tail and the most loving disposition. Angela says she has a sense of humour and is a bit of a clown, but personally I have never seen a beautiful clown myself. I tried singing to her this evening :—
    'Where is my quiet girl?
    Where is my gentle girl?
    Where is my quiet girl?
    Softer than snow . . .'
But she showed the whites of her eyes, so I spared her the next verse. After visiting a circus once, Angela and her bosom friend begged some old ostrich feathers from the shop and made up head-dresses of felt and nodding plumes for their ponies. When I came on the scene the ponies were trotting round an improvised 'ring' of hay, with boltins of straw for jumps. The girls, were riding bareback and *back to front* and being bounced off with perfect regularity. It would not have been so funny if they had not looked so deadly serious about it all.
    The other day a customer said to me,
    'I don't expect you remember selling me a wonderful oak table? We bought it at the beginning of the war: it was in your back garden.'

Yes, I did remember it, for it had puzzled me; it was like a short Elizabethan refectory table, but only carved along the one side. I discovered years later that it was an Elizabethan serving table or side table and I either paid three pounds ten shillings for it, or sold it for that figure, I cannot remember now. Another little discovery I made in the course of time was that draw-leaf tables originated in Elizabeth's reign, but I had thought they were a twentieth century invention.

This started a train of thought and I began to think of some of my best pieces. I have only had one credence table, this also was a sixteenth century piece and came out of a cellar in Chipping Norton where it may have been used by a Catholic family after the Reformation. This little table would have held the bread and the wine before it was consecrated. It was a collector's piece, but in those days I had few customers who knew what was what. People seem to forget that all our old Churches were Roman Catholic until the Reformation and someone has lately written in the Visitor's Book in Brailes Church, 'Beautiful but stolen.'

Another of my early buys was a very lovely solid walnut refectory table, and its home now is a fine old one-time Rectory in Warwickshire. I saw it at a Saleroom Sale and, little thinking that I would be able to buy it, began to sketch it in my catalogue; but a few minutes later it was knocked down to me for eight pounds! The people who bought it sold me an Elizabethan bed which I sold to a very important oak buyer in the trade. Somewhere in my diary I have written about an Elizabethan staircase which was one of three antique staircases that I had in a matter of months.

The finest piece I have had up till now was an eighteenth century domed pine cupboard with shaped doors, standing on a chest of drawers base, still with its original pierced brass handles. A favourite doctor customer bought this, but was not able to take delivery for some months as he had planned to have it built into the recess of a house he was building. Lots of customers saw the cupboard in my stable, with its little red SOLD ticket, and it made their mouths water. I could have sold a score of them! I have been to tea with this cupboard in its new home, the doors stand open and the shelves are filled with a fine green-bordered Coalport service. I found this doctor another lovely pine piece, a Jacobean moulded dresser base for seven pounds ten in a junk shop!

Shortly after the war, at a local sale, I bought my finest piece of walnut furniture. The sixty pounds was the highest price I had ever paid for anything up till that time. It was a superb Queen Anne walnut chest of drawers, having six drawers, and on a base with bun feet which also had a drawer in it. It was cross-banded and had herring-bone inlays. Both the colour and the patina were wonderful. The drawer linings were of the finest feathered oak and the beautiful drop handles were original. John took it to an old cabinet-maker for me and he rsstored it perfectly for another twelve pounds. We kept it and enjoyed it in the cottage for a year, and then sold it for a hundred and twelve pounds which included delivering it by taxi to Reading.

Like other dealers, I always sell my best pieces very quickly, often before I have had time to gaze my fill. One of the things which does cheer me up is to think of the hundreds of antiques that I have found and had beautifully restored by craftsmen. One of my customers literally rescued a chair like this on November 5th, when he rushed out on to the Green with one of his old kitchen chairs and persuaded the boys to reseat Guy Fawkes Esquire in it, while he returned home triumphant with a Chippendale 'arm!'

As I am so strong and good at lifting, I do not hesitate to buy large pieces, providing they are early ones, but I do now draw the line at monstrous Victorian sideboards and spinets. The last one nearly pulled my arms out of their sockets. I used to wonder how Stonehenge was built but not any longer! If you saw this 'frail woman' move a large Jacobean chest-of-drawers from her store to her shop, you might get a clue. Modus operandi :- First remove all the drawers, and carry each separately; then procure two old rugs and turn the chest-of-drawers on to its side on to rug one, then turn the top of the chest-of-drawers on to rug two, then other side on to rug one and proceed until destination is reached. To return to Stonehenge, I believe I have read that some of those immense stones came (or rather were rolled) from South Wales. During the War there was a notice pinned up somewhere saying, 'If it is difficult, it takes time; if it is impossible it takes a little longer.' This may have been a motto of the Druids.

I HAD HOPED TO BUY a little load in Cheltenham to-day. I received a statement from the Bank this morning and, for the second time only in my life, my account was healthier than I thought.

My Cheltenham Uncle met me at the Bus Station. The dear fellow had been to the Public Library and written out a list of all the Cheltenham dealers and furniture brokers. We had an early lunch and a good talk over our coffee.

To-day has not been a lucky day for buying. The first dealer had some lovely little papier maché chairs, inlaid with mother-of-pearl and painted with passion flowers, but alas, their price tallies of 75/- each all bore SOLD tickets. At the next dealers, I liked half a dozen pieces but they all needed restoration and I already had a shedful in a similar plight.

Taking a short cut down a side street, I recognised a cheery fellow I had often talked to at Auction Sales. He had a second-hand, bicycle-cum-antique shop. The thing that caught my eye was a beautiful bronze real seal skin coat, suspended from a beam on a coat-hanger.

'How much is the fur coat?'

'It's fifty shillings. But *you* will never get into it!'

'You are very rude. I think I shall, I've reduced twenty pounds!'

I donned it, certainly the front edges only just touched, but the shoulders, sleeves and length were perfect.

'Now,' said my friend, 'shall I fetch the tin-opener to get you out?'

It's rather stiff but I shall be advised by a good furriers at Oxford and, if it isn't wearable, I shall make sealskin moccasins for all the family. If it is a success as a coat and anyone asks where I bought it, I shall say,

'At one of those little shops, just off the Parade in Cheltenham' and when you come to think of it, all fur coats are second-hand. I remember once examining a little feather toque in a second-hand shop in Banbury, and I was surprised to find that the chicken skin was cured and still adhering to the feathers. I mentioned this to a farmer's wife, and she said that she always skinned her boiling fowls, it was done in a trice and none of them liked the fat skin anyway.

As I made my way to the bus station, I passed a really grand emporium where antiques were being unloaded at a side door and, there on the footpath, waiting to be carried in, was a simple Spanish refectory table. The top and the pierced ends are of solid walnut and the ends are braced by wrought iron rods which run up to the centre of the underneath of the top. I was amazed to find the price was only eight pounds and they are delivering it to me next time they send a van near Penny Priors. So my journey was not in vain!

This evening one of the inn chimneys caught on fire. It was really frightening! The flames shot six feet into the air and myriads of glowing sparks came showering down on to the neighbouring thatched roofs. Balls of red hot soot, as large as cricket balls, came bowling along the main road driven by the wind. We were all thankful to hear the fire engine dashing up the hill. Ten minutes can seem a very long time when one is waiting for it.

I have two customers who collect fire signs. These signs or plaques, of iron, lead or copper, were fixed to the front of a house. If one belonged to that particular society, it would send its horse-drawn or man-handled apparatus, if summoned. If one did not 'belong,' I suppose one relied on the buckets and strong arms of one's neighbours. This was before the days of a Public Fire Service of course. In a church near here, there are poles with iron hooks attached for tearing down lumps of burning thatch. Near here too, I have seen two rows of gutted thatched cottages, both fired, I believe by frying pans catching on fire. In one case, the flaming pan was carried out through the front door and it ignited the edge of the low thatched roof. In the other case if only the person, who phoned the Fire Station Officer, had said the chimney was in a thatched cottage, the row might have been saved, for the hoses would then have been despatched. N.B. Here is a safety tip for housewives . . . a flaming frying pan should be covered with a folded wet cloth.

❧{ *36* }❧

MY SHOP is not a good one for gifts. Desperate shoppers come in at times, on Saturdays usually, saying they have to buy a present for a Christening next day.

'Is it a boy or a girl? Oh! a boy. Now let me see.' One thinks of rattles, of everlasting silver spoons, silver serviette rings, pewter mugs, silver egg cups. Not one in stock! One can hardly suggest a silver cigar case or a silver patch-box for pills!

'I have a rather fine magnifying glass? If he collects foreign stamps or butterflies later.'

'Just the job Mrs Summers! Can you find me a little box?'

'Do you think young people are as romantic as we used to be?' asks a stalwart bearded customer.

'Of course not!' I reply. 'But why do you ask?'

'Well, here I have a list of suggested wedding presents, written out by the bride herself — a beautiful creature! Just cast your eye down that.'

What do I read?

Washing Machine
Spin Dryer
Vacuum Cleaner
Carpet Sweeper
Shower Bath Fitting
Turkish Towels
Frypan
Mincer
Doormats.

'Yes, it is rather ominous,' I agree. 'She's certainly going to keep him clinically clean.'

'The mincer and the doormats sound more ominous still, don't you think? What would you do, if she were your niece, and as lovely as a dryad?'

'Well,' I said after a thoughtful pause, 'I would ignore the list I think, and give her a Dresden mirror to reflect her beauty, or a silver candelabra to suggest dining by candlelight, or possibly a magnolia tree for their lawn. This might inspire your dryad to a moonlight pas seul!'

'We are looking for a silver wedding present' inquire a very young couple. Now that is not too difficult as there is a mirrored table covered with plated articles, cake-baskets, entree dishes, toast racks. They choose an oval silver Victorian photograph frame, which now contains a little mirror, in place of its original moustached gentleman with his riding crop.

'We are in search of a golden wedding present,' inquire a middle-aged couple. 'Can you help us?'

I put on my thinking-cap again, 'I'm afraid I haven't the goods to back up my ideas,' I reply.

'It's very difficult, they have everything they need for the house, and Mother does not care for jewellery. Can you suggest *anything*?'

'Well, in modern Worcester porcelain, I have seen gold lustre cups and saucers, and I believe they make little porcelain trays to match. Rather lovely as a modern déjeuner set for them, perhaps? If I sell you anything in brass, it would only make more work. Had you considered giving them anything for the garden? A collection of golden roses in different varieties perhaps?'

Jane Tudor can usually make up her own mind, but this time she almost pleads,

'What *can* I give him? Something he cannot lose? He's ploughed his last two pipes into Sixpenny Field, and Heaven only knows where his last wallet's gone. Probably in the middle of a rick!' She finally decided on some early farming books, from our village jumble sale and strangely enough, within one, was a description of a farm (in the eighteenth century), that they know well and visit.

I don't often tout my wares but I did on this one occasion At a furniture dealer's, I had espied a lady's exquisite black cloth cloak, quite eighty years old, but in mint condition. The material, similar to felt is called face-cloth, I believe, and the whole of it was adorned with black silk braiding and fastened with two black mantle clips. I slipped it on. Most becoming, très chic! But certainly not me, nor Penny Priors! I wrote to a favourite young customer with a beautiful wife, a brunette with creamy complexion, saying I had something to show him, which I thought he might give her as a Christmas present. He agreed wholeheartedly when he saw it, and we wrapped it up.

Next time he brought her, she exclaimed,

'It's fabulous! But what made you think of me?'

'I just saw you inside it!' I answered truthfully.

Wedding presents are easier to find than personal presents. Most decanters seem to be sold for wedding presents and antique swing mirrors are favourites too. Chairs are a fairly safe 'buy.' Everyone needs quite an assortment and these are really my speciality. I usually have several antique chairs for children in stock, and these are more often bought by God-parents and grand-parents than parents. The earliest cradles I buy are English oak ones and always panelled. The eighteenth century ones are of mahogany, sometimes panelled, but the easiest to buy these days are Welsh pine ones, with little rockers, and knobs at the corners. The simple little hoods to these cradles sometimes have a small opening, like the hole in a dove-cote, which was to hold an old-fashioned feeding bottle. The long black rubber tube from it would serpent down to the babe below, and terminate in a bone ring with a teat attached to it. Most hygenic — in fact, deadly!

At the moment I have two identical folding bassinettes, except that one is made of iron and the other of brass. They have netted sides and will look adorable when they are draped; one is stamped on its canvas base with the words 'As supplied to her late Majesty Queen Victoria.' Other Victorian cradles I have had, have been of mahogany, and have had canework panelled sides and hoods and been suspended from mahogany stands. These are practical for modern needs as when the cradle is unhooked, it will slide on to the back seat of a car, and travel 'with baby and all,' just like a Karri-cot. Some customers, with large rooms, have bought them to hold magazines and I have seen them looking quite lovely filled with potted azaleas and ferns. I believe it was Barrie who said 'A cradle's such a homey thing to have about the house.'

To return to my favourite chairs for the last paragraph, I once saw an exquisite little miniature wheel-back chair about eight inches high. This was at an Antique Dealers' Fair and it sold immediately at fifty pounds! This would almost certainly have been made as a pattern, as it was too large for a doll's house; or it could have been a fine 'prentice's piece. Through the years, all dealers get miniature pieces of furniture, bureaux bookcases, pedestal tables, little four posters and so on, but they get rarer and rarer. Somewhere in my diary I mention a little pine wardrobe I kept for years, which I bought in the back room of a little milliner's shop! The lively 'dolls' tea and dinner services,' often found in antique shops were really travellers' samples and, in the old days the salesman would arrive on horseback, he would call at manors, rectories and farm houses, unpack his basket paniers and display a whole service in miniature, and take orders for dozens of everything in those days of large families. This was of course before the printing of illustrated catalogues. Other travellers, not so respectable, were known to call on antique owners and persuade them to let them replace their beautiful brass handles, with turned wooden ones which 'did not need cleaning.' The bright fellows would then jog up to London and get a good price for the discarded handles from the fine cabinet-makers there.

❦ 37 ❦

I was really glad to wake up this morning. Like other dealers, I have many customers who are actors and actresses, and this particular nightmare was that I had to be an understudy for an actress who was ill. 'But, I don't know the *words*!' I kept protesting.

'That doesn't matter,' my actress customer kept replying, 'You have only to be yourself!'

'But I don't know what myself is — am,' I pleaded.

'You've just got stage-fright,' she replied firmly. 'Everyone has it. You wouldn't be any good if you were confident and sure of yourself.' She compelled me to close the shop, but as I turned the key I awoke!

As I am so ignorant about the theatre and everything pertaining to it, I keep quiet usually and listen, but one day I forgot this golden rule and it caused some merriment. John and I had attended Matins at Holy Trinity Church at Stratford-upon-Avon the previous April. It had been Shakespeare Sunday, and all the ambassadors and V.I.Ps. proceeded through the West door, the sun shone, the organ rolled, the choirs sang and of course the Church was packed, but what impressed us most, was the reading of the lessons. John and I looked at each other. We had never heard the Bible read like that before. In my shop a few days later, I told an actress-cum-friend-cum-customer about this, and she remarked,

'Well, Anne darling, that's not so suprising! Ralph Richardson read the first lesson, and John Gielgud the second!'

Several times I have delivered goods to the wardrobe department of the Shakespeare Memorial Theatre, and seen the dozens of young people there working away at the clothes and armour for the next production. All the chief characters are drawn individually with their costumes shown in detail and the colours suggested in wash. These sketches by the designers are called cartoons. Needless to say, these drawings are very much sought after and can become quite valuable. They lie about among the sewing-machines on the work-benches and cutting-out tables with scraps of velvet, brocade and felt pinned to them, for reference or approval. One of the real problems, I was told, was to keep the costumes down to a wearable weight, as the padding required (and the footlights) were exhausting enough!

The last time I called I was taken across the road to the theatre and shown the fine new dressing-rooms, and I stood on the deserted stage by the ship-wreck and other stage props, all ready for the evening performance of The Tempest. It was strange to get the actors' view of the auditorium, completely empty, except for one still silent man sitting right at the back. I wondered if he was trying to conjure up Shakespeare's ghost, struggling with a thesis, or just dreaming dreams.

I had a real working day yesterday, so to-day I am taking it easy, catching-up with letter-writing, and rattling off a few pages of my diary.

What started me off working yesterday, was a snow warning on the seven o'clock news and, as I had a large shabby Persian carpet spread out on a lawn, there was no excuse. Years ago, I missed a real bargain of a Persian carpet for £5! It was certainly more holey than righteous but, as the auctioneer's hammer fell, I realised that I could have scrapped the central worn part and made runners of the still magnificent borders. This time however I was ready and I bought this one for £9. I am going to use the worn part to carpet the shop and the upholsterer shall join the two long borders into a fine fifteen foot runner, and the ends into a rug. Yesterday, using a very sharp blade, I cut it up very carefully and rolled and folded the pieces and packed them away into one of the sheds. By this time, I had really got the working-bug and set to on the shed. This was swept and restacked by 3.15 p.m., seven hours non-stop, no tea-breaks, just enthusiasm! And I had kept a bonfire going too, as a side-line. I then decided to have a hot bath and to take a cold lunch upstairs with me. So I lay there and steamed, with a leg of cold chicken, a huge cup of coffee and the packet of salt. I didn't wash my hair though, and when John kissed me at his home-coming, he enquired if I had enjoyed my bonfire?

The first fall of snow arrived as promised, and the birds are returning to their table; often three or four blue tits at once, and also great tits and cole-tits. There is one little fellow with two white stripes on his head, I must look him up in the Observers Book of Birds. John says it sounds like a Lesser Corporal!

Angela will be home for the week-end. She hopes to get the National Diploma of Design next year and is working very hard. The students are divided up into little groups this last year according to the subjects they are taking. She is with three boys or, I should say, young men. Angela says all of them earn money in the holidays when they can get jobs. One helps a stonemason and cycles off to village churchyards and adds names and dates to old gravestones, and another worked for one day only as a window-cleaner at a huge mental institution. When he was several floors up, a group of patients who were quietly walking in the grounds decided to remove his ladder. He clung to a window-sill until rescued by a male attendant. Angela said he added point to his story with spirited little 'pin' drawings of the assault and the rescue. Another fellow will sit on some convenient town bench and sketch an adjoining Hotel or shop, and human curiosity being what it is, the proprietor invariably comes to look and a guinea or two may change hands. I believe it is this enterprising young man, who has the Grandfather in the North, who pays surprise visits. His wire causes a crisis every time, as the student's parents have secretly put all the old gentleman's antiques into store and refurnished their home with 'G-Plan.' I gather from Angela 'though that the family gallantly rally round each time, and 'Operation Furniture Swop' is quickly completed. The family form a sort of human chain down the street, doing a 'General Post' with the 'G-Plan' into the store, and the antiques back into the ancestral home.

Whenever I read a bit of my diary, I always seem to be in such good spirits, but this is far from the truth. I must just feel like writing when I am jolly. So I will write about one of those other days now. Early last week a farmer's wife had told me, on the bus, that she had some old things to sell and gave me minute directions of where to leave the bus, and how to take the short-cut to her farmhouse. So on Friday, I set forth and followed her directions, skirting the sides of two ploughed fields. Great thunderheads of cloud rose against a purplish blue sky, a dozen gulls followed a plough. Somehow I felt I was on a wild goosechase. The advance barking of farm dogs, quickly changed to friendly yelps and the kitchen was welcomingly warm, but it was characterless and too clean. I had had visions of old settles for sale, bacon cupboards and polished brass meat jacks, but it was not to be. In the back hall I stopped to look at a snow-white black-bird in a little glass case.

'How beautiful!' I exclaimed, 'We have one in our garden with a white head, but I have never seen a pure albino!'

'Oh yes,' she replied, 'and it was so tame too, it used to come right on to the kitchen mat.'

'You were very clever to find it,' I answered, 'they usually hide away when they are going to die.'

'Oh it didn't die,' she said, 'we killed it and had it stuffed.'

I lost all interest in antiques and got away as soon as I could. I was in low spirits all day, and it's made me sad again writing about it, so I will close my journal and put it to roost, where it usually lives, on top of the dresser.

❧ 38 ❧

ANY DAY, ANY DEALER may make his fortune. Is it this fact I wonder, that keeps so many of them youthful and full of fun? Our lives are one long search for the old, the rare and the beautiful. A perpetual adventure! Perhaps the shortest cut to fame and fortune would be to find an old Holinshed's History or a Hall Chronicles annotated by Shakespeare! Scholars say that he drew freely from these two old Histories. What an extraordinary thing it is, that only four signatures are known to exist in his own hand! Just think of all the notes, rough jottings, corrections and fair copies that made up a single play, let alone twenty years of continuous writings. What could have happened to them all? Are they still waiting to be found? Did his favourite daughter Susannah have them? She inherited nearly everything. No one knows.

Many dealers far from making their fortunes give up the trade and change over to modern furniture or to the scrap metal business. This seems to be prospering but it needs a hefty fellow for the actual work and a shrewd one to know when to sell, as prices fluctuate so.

In the meantime the second-hand dealer goes on being a second-hand dealer. His criterion is the newness and shininess of his goods, and he must often be puzzled or amused at the price offered by an antique dealer for some moth-eaten old tapestry, or battered picture lying in his back-yard.

Antique dealers who start in a small way keep replacing their stock with better class goods, and if they are reasonably priced they are easier to sell than to find. Some antique dealers are also first-class cabinet-makers and they get opportunities to purchase from their customers treasures which are stored in old attics and cellars and, but for them, might never have seen the light of day again.

The two greatest assets to an antique dealer are good taste

and capital. Some bankruptcy figures were analysed in the press recently and by far the largest cause of failure was lack of capital, not lack of industry or knowledge as one might have suspected. One dealer, now dead, told me how he had a shop in one town where sometimes in a week no one crossed his door-mat. It was a town that people passed through. He moved only twenty miles and did all the trade he wanted. Another friend opened an adorable shop and showroom on a village green, plenty of room for parking, shady cedars to picnic under, streams of traffic passing through — everything you would say. But no, it was fifteen miles from the sea, and drivers passing south wanted to complete their journey to the coast, and cars travelling north, had a long day ahead of them, and were fully loaded anyway with luggage, prams — the lot!

There seem to be live shops and dead shops. I have passed one antique shop for forty years and have yet to see the door open or anyone inside, yet it is a corner shop and in a wonderful position. Perhaps the most alive business I know is Miss Hughes' place at Towyn in Merionethshire. She rents the old Town Hall as her father did before her. The centre of it is filled with trestle tables set out with farm produce, salty Welsh butter, dressed chickens and great baskets of eggs, while on others are fruit and vegetables, golden and green, stacks of oranges and apples and from above hang drapes of imported grapes. Set around are chips of early peas and gooseberries, while standing in silvery buckets are flowering azaleas, peonies red and white, tall iris and a great bowl in a corner holds tall branches of white magnolias. The walls of the hall are lined with fine old dressers, their hooks hung with antique lustre jugs; old tridarns stand there, softly lustrous with the polishing of generations. There are sets of country Chippendale chairs, old oak bureaux from the reign of Queen Anne, narrow little pine cradles and spoon racks. High about in the gallery, are old Welsh spinning wheels, comb back chairs, and ladderbacks waiting to be re-rushed.

The people, streaming in and out, are local farmers and their wives with sheep dogs at their heels, holiday-maker fathers with children riding shoulder high and mothers filling their baskets for beach picnics. Landladies hold musical conversations in Welsh, and buy carefully for their guests. It is a hive of industry and life. John lets me off the lead and says there is room in the back of the car for something. He will move the bathing togs, and the picnic basket into the boot of the car.

'Good morning, Miss Hughes, do you remember me?'

'Of course I do! It's Mrs Penny Priors, now just give me a minute, I'll remember. Yes! Its Mrs Summers, how are you?'

We compliment each other on our rude health.

I choose three of my favourite wooden-seated country Chippendale chairs and a little iron table with a base of sportive dolphins. I write my cheque at her beautiful knee-hole desk. She gives me a bouquet of golden azaleas and we say goodbye for another year.

❧ 39 ❧

THE VICTORIANS loved to put their treasures under glass shades, their clocks, stuffed birds, wax fruits, china figures and their own arrangements of dried flowers and grasses. Sometimes one finds artificial flower arrangements under them, wonderfully made with wire, silk and wool, and occasionally real masterpieces in seashells. I have only ever had one like this and that was rather badly damaged. The middle of it was stuffed solid with newspapers. I carefully removed this and the silly coloured crepe paper packed between the exquisite flower sprays. Dozens of different kinds of shells had been used and wired to resemble real flowers around artificial stamens. The loveliest to me were twigs of syringa of soft pearl-like shells. An Oxford gentleman bought this arrangement of shells and shewed me photographs of his collection of these treasures. They were nearly all flower arrangements, but one was of a hen with her chickens around her; all made from sea-shells. He had paid over a hundred pounds for some of them and was now very 'choosey,' sometimes trading in one of his less valuable ones in part payment for a gem of a one. He bought mine for the shells to repair one of his imperfect pieces. Of course I had to read the old newspaper I had pulled out; it was a Birmingham daily, either 1870 or 1874, I forget which. There was the report of the previous day's Titchbourne Case. I had read the book of this trial when I was a girl. It tells of an imposter returning from abroad and laying claim to a great inheritance. It is fascinating reading. The questioning of the scores of witnesses and the fellow himself went on for weeks. He knew a tremendous amount about the family and his 'mother' in inverted commas, claimed that he was her long lost son, which complicated matters! In the advertisement columns of the paper were advertised mangles, clogs, goffering irons etc. and lock-up shops for as little as 1/6 a week including the 'use of fire;' which I suppose meant that the tenant could boil a kettle, fry a sausage, or warm his toes in the owner's sitting room behind the shop.

At the moment I have a magnificent flower arrangement standing two feet high under its glass dome. The flowers are wonderfully realistic, the petals are of wool-work and the centres and stamens are of silk. There are moss roses, fuchsias, lilies, passion flowers, clematis, parrot tulips, morning glories, geraniums and trails of smylax. The rose alone would take me a week to make and the whole creation years; but perhaps it was made a hundred years ago by a family of career-less daughters awaiting their Prince Charmings.

If I saw stuffed birds at Sales twenty years ago, I used to say to myself—

'Now steady on Mrs S. don't bid for those!' although I often disobeyed myself. During the war I went to an old Post Office-cum-farm sale at another village where I had once lived. One friend said,

'How much do you think the dresser will make Mrs Summers? I want to give it to our Billy as he is getting married in the Spring.' Another,

'Would you bid for me for the grandfather clock, Anne? My Joe wants it and I'm nervous of bidding!' Another asked,

'Do you think I will get the coffer for a "fiver", Anne? It once belonged to my Uncle Bob.' Yet another,

'You won't bid for the chairs will you? Our Milly has set her heart on them.' In the end there was nothing left for me *to* bid for except some old oak panelling and the stuffed birds. There was a case of them about five feet long on a mahogany bench made to fit the case. They were all game birds, pheasant, quail, snipe, blackcock, and so on. One day when I was gardening, Angela who was nearly five came to me excitedly and said,

'Mummy! Mummy! Mr Prosser's in the shop!' and tugged my hand. I didn't see what there was to be excited about but followed her in. She led me to the great case of stuffed birds and pointed to the French partridge — yes, it was Mr Prosser all right, full eyes and white 'cuffy' if you know what I mean. Mr Prosser to a T! I had this case of birds for months and it eventually went to a sportsman and now adorns his gun room.

With a mixed lot, I once bought a stuffed barn owl in a glass case, on the back was a label saying,

'Found in Longdown Woods, Christmas 1844.' The glass was shattered, so I took the owl out of its case and for fun stuck it in a corner of the thatch. A day or two later Mrs Horton who lives by the weir spotted it as she passed. She quietly crept away, fetched her camera and stealthily photographed it. She then realised it was not alive and thought it very funny.

Now, when I see stuffed birds, I try to buy them as they are fashionable. They usually go to London customers. Some have said that their rooms are so severely furnished with modern furniture that they must have a bit of nonsense. Other customers have remounted two or three brightly coloured birds on the perches of little gilt birdcages and fixed their electric lights inside and very gay and unusual they must look.

Talking about birds makes me think of ostrich feathers. For years I have tried to have little things to give to customers' children. Sometimes cut glass lustre studs which make rainbows round everything they look at through them, and at other times little mother-of-pearl counters. These may be oblong or round and engraved with doves and bamboos, or shaped like tiny fish. Just lately I have had three odd lots of ostrich feathers, dozens of them, and if you were to pass my shop any day now, you might see two or three very small children following their parents across the green to a parked car, each child proudly holding aloft a curly ostrich feather.

⊰ 40 ⊱

As I have mentioned, Angela is taking her National Diploma in Design and she has decided to write her thesis on 'The 'Sporting Print of the Eighteenth Century.' Needless to say it had to be something to do with animals, preferably horses! She has had lots of books from the College Library and spent her 'present' money on others. I have enjoyed swotting up the subject with her and I doubt if there are two better informed females on the subject within fifty miles.

I thought last week that I had found a Stubbs! I was at a farm sale and the canvas of a group of mares and foals lay face downwards across the rafters in a stable but, when I had blown off the chaff and given it a good dusting down, I found it was only an oilegraph of a Stubbs painting. Perhaps the best horse picture I ever bought was a small oil of a white horse that I bought at the Redesdale Arms at Moreton-in-Marsh. It was unframed, I paid 6/- for it and after extolling its beauties for a year managed to get 26/- for it. It turned up beautifully framed at the Grosvenor House Antique Dealers Fair in June. Three separate customers recognised it there but the price had risen slightly — to 120 guineas to be exact!

A horse-dealer calls sometimes to sell me a warming-pan. He says he has bought and sold hundreds and gets the best price for those with a peacock on the lid. He once sold me one with the words 'Who scorched the sheets? Not I,' round the lid. He said he had one that he would never sell as it had saved his mare's life. She was very ill with colic and he had stayed up all night, filling and refilling the pan with red embers, and sliding it along back and forth below her belly.

I often used one on the children's beds when they were little, and because of this they used to undress in double-quick time. Of course the pan had to be kept on the move and the usual cold corners were the hottest bits. This encouraged the children to stretch out, and lie straight.

This horse-dealer called recently to say he had a Romany caravan for sale, and for only £50. I had visions of painting it in glorious technicolour, and keeping it in the orchard as a studio-cum-den. I hired Mr Bede to take me to see it. It stood in the middle of a little field occupied by a Hereford bull. Mr Bede seemed to imagine we would leave the taxi outside the field and enter the field. He could not have been more mistaken! So he patiently drove into the field and slowly circled the caravan. I soon decided against it, as personally I would have described it as a roadman's hut on wheels. I once saw a most pathetic sight involving one of these. It was the home of a hop-picker, his young wife and two babies. They were mercifully in the lorry which was towing their caravan when it broke loose, zig-zagged down a hill, turned on its side and disintegrated. Out fell old tin trunks, their clothes, a big bed, push chairs and little broken toys — it was pitiful. The poor girl kept brushing away her tears and the babies lifted up their voices and wailed.

This horse-dealer told me that he was always hard up until the war started, and then his luck turned, and everything he touched turned to gold. It started with a just completed house which he had built for £600 and sold very profitably. With the proceeds of this he bought a derelict farm very cheaply. The lead on its roof (which no-one else seemed to have noticed) and the timber on the land showed him a handsome profit and he still had the farm. He picnicked out in this old farm for a year or two, spruced up the stone walls, rehung the gates, reglazed the windows, cultivated the garden, and let the grazing. By this time, to continue in his own words, 'my two neighbours were outbidding each other for the place. When it was high enough I decided to play and, believe it or not, when I was on the way to the solicitors with the deeds, I had to pull up sharpish in a line of traffic, and the driver behind me crashed into my 'posterior' and I got a new car out of it too.'

When I am at sales I try not to get into conversation with my neighbours but it is difficult if they keep borrowing my catalogue and making remarks. I had a dear old countrywoman sitting next to me on Friday. I didn't let on that I was a dealer, and she kept remarking 'By Guy! Forty shillings for that!' or

'By Guy! I wouldn't give it house-room! Not worth tuppence!' Then for good measure she added 'If you take my advice you'll put your money in livestock not deadstock. That's what my folks used to say, and we listened to our parents in those days.'

The auctioneer leaned over and said,

'Now ladies, I know you enjoy your day out, but if you want a gossip, there's a tea-shop next door.'

'Listen to him!' continued my cheery friend, 'Isn't he a one? Yes, that's what my Dad used to say, put your money, my gal, in livestock not deadstock. Pigs was what he put his money in, and he once fed a hog that scaled thirty-six score and not a word of a lie. The butcher reckoned the beam in the dairy could not be trusted, so the carcase was strung up in the great oak by the back gate. My dear, the head alone weighed ninety pounds. People came from far and wide to see that great hog, and not a word of a lie, or may God strike me dead!'

'Ladies! Ladies!' pleaded the harassed auctioneer and wagged his finger at *me*.

I managed to buy a few lots in between, and was glad Angela was not with me, as we would have given each other the giggles. A second-hand dealer bought the contents of a vast bookcase for 10/-. I asked the pig-keeper's daughter to keep my chair for me, and went to have a look at the books. 'Can I buy a few for 10/-?' I whispered to him. 'Help yourself, Mam,' he replied. I looked out seven old ones and slipped him the note. One was an illustrated account of the Trial of Charles the First. I wept over it on Sunday afternoon. It was the most moving account I have ever read in my life — no wonder he was called Charles the Martyr!

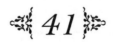

41

CAROLINE, my dear Goddaughter left the village to-day with her family, and things will never be quite the same again. Of course, we gave them a happy 'send off' and they have only gone to

London. The wife came visiting at the beginning of the war, and only meant to stay for six weeks. She laughingly said to-day,

'I came with two suitcases for a holiday and I am leaving after seventeen years with five children, two furniture vans, one dog, two cats and a canary!'

The whole family are real characters, and the oldest boy has kept up the good old custom of calling on new people, as well as all his old favourites.

I sold a lovely walnut chest-of-drawers to a retired Doctor and his wife, who arrived in the village, and came to live opposite to this family. I was asked round one morning to coffee and to get my cheque.

'Tell us about the family opposite, the Doctor and I are so delighted to be able to see all their comings and goings — and what beautiful children they are!'

She memorised all their names and I prepared her for the official 'call' which she would almost certainly receive from eight year-old Michael.

'A quiet little knock will come one day, shortly after 4 p.m. and more likely than not he will be flanked by two small sisters. So be ready and ask them in for you will have callers!'

'Oh I will! I will!' she replied joyfully.

As I walked up the village I thought to myself 'well *she's* going to be happy in Penny Priors! She's a giving person, and as I passed the Church I remembered the words, 'we love Him, because He first loved us.'

Two Sundays later as we were coming out through the Churchyard gate, she caught up with us and whispered happily, 'He's called! He's called!'

I once saw, on the cover of a humorous magazine, a picture of a lighthouse, and on the rocks at the foot of it was an open sports car. Below were the words, 'that salesman must have been some salesman.' Well! To-day I sold an eighteenth century mahogany cradle to a middle-aged spinster. I expect she wanted it for potted plants — I hope it was not for dogs, nice as they are.

A very charming old lovey-dovey theatrical couple call in very occasionally. The first time I thought I was going to sell out, but not any longer! He is the would-be buyer and she is the brake. The conversations run like this :—

Husband. 'Here! Look what I've found, darling! A perfect little table for the coffee, don't you think?'

Wife.   'Yes, it certainly is sweet, but where should we put it?'

Husband. 'Look darling, let's buy this little pine rack for displaying your Worcester mugs!'

Wife.   'I love it too, darling, but there is one just like it in our cellar. Remember? You were going to strip it for me?'

Husband. (still not discouraged) 'Would you like this bureau, my sweet? I haven't given you your birthday present yet?'

Wife.   '*Dear* James, how kind you are! But you must have forgotten that I am having Aunt Margaret's one day. She has willed it to me.'

An hour later they will go off happily arm in arm. They should be happy, for they've enjoyed exploring and they are not a penny the poorer! I'm the misery! It's past my lunch-time and I've lost my appetite!

An engaged couple from the States were in the other day, also at lunchtime, and I have my doubts about their future. I don't think that they will be as happy as the 'darlings' in fifty years' time.

He picked up a pewter tankard and regarded it seriously.

She   'What do you think of it?'

He   grunts

She   'Were you thinking of it for Uncle Hiram?'

He   grunts

She   'Do you mean "yes" you were thinking of it for Uncle Hiram?'

He   'No.'

She   'Come on and say something, Theo! You leave everything to me!'

He   'I don't know.'

She   (standing firm) 'He's *your* Uncle.'

He   'Yes. Shall we think about it?'

She   'I have thought. You *say*.'

He   'Let's have a meal first.'

I felt like saying, 'Them's my sentiments' but didn't. The discussion continued, while Theo changed the tankard from his left hand to his right hand, put it down, picked it up, handed it to his betrothed, took it off her and set it down again. After forty minutes they left, saying they would think it over. My chop, left under the grill, was now pale golden and wafer thin. It snapped in two when I touched it.

I told Gordon about them when he came home. He put his hand on my shoulder and said,

'Dear old Mum, you have done something to improve international relations. They must have thought you were very kind and patient.'

I suddenly felt better and said brightly,

'Yes, that's exactly what they did say!'

42

THE CHILDREN have gone together to a Young Farmers' Dance and I am sitting with my diary. Gordon is twenty-three now and Angela is eighteen. We have some lovely girls in our village, including our own. Nearly all are slim and tall with long necks and fashions are so becoming too, with tiny waists, crisp petticoats and shortish skirts. The girls look like flowers in their summer dresses. Angela is wearing a full-skirted diaphanous white cotton dress with a silver thread and her crystal necklace. She has piled her hair up high and has little curls in the nape of her neck, just like my Mother.

When she came downstairs, her brother told her that she looked like a snowflake! What a nice husband he will make one day!

I should really be sewing, not writing. Some generous soul has given the material for eighteen surplices for the choir and we females on the Parochial Church Council have received instruction from the Rector's wife on how to make them. She unpicked an ancient one in the Vestry to obtain the pattern, and has successfully made up one, with its tricky little square gusset, within four flat seams under the arms. The President of the W.I. has also managed one, but confessed to doing the gusset by hand. Anyway, if anyone shews signs of examining our handiwork during the services they will be discouraged. So will any outsize (o.s.) man in the congregation, who carols too loudly to attract attention. The six men we have are obliging stock size, bless their hearts.

A Doctor customer who is a clock addict came in on Saturday evening. On the way here he had given a lift to a young hitch-hiker, a young German, a Prussian. He asked the Doctor the English for a certain German phrase and the Doctor said,

'The nearest would be, "one man's meat is another man's poison."'

'Meat? What is meat?' asked the H.H.

'Flesh,' replied the Doctor.

'And the meaning of poison?' asked the H.H. again.

'If you eat it you die.'

'I understand not.'

'If your cat is very ill, you give it poison to make it die,' explained the Doctor.

'I understand not.'

'Goering ate poison, he died.'

'Goering? Goering? *GOERING! Oh!*'

Silence all the rest of the way to Penny Priors!

I do not seem to have written down one of my favourite stories, though I have told it to customers. This woman friend is a terrific character, older than me I think, and fatter, but a ball of energy. She does not drive either but scours the country for lovely things for her business, which is in the lower storey of a Georgian residence. The showrooms are always interesting but her home above is a treasure house — an Aladdin's Cave. But only favoured customers are invited upstairs.

On this particular day, when she was walking in London, an open lorry overtook her, moving slowly in the heavy traffic. On its deck she espied a really fine antique Queen Anne walnut armchair with some shreds of its upholstering still clinging to it. She gathered her strength and began to trot after it. Sure enough, it soon stopped, but before she reached it the red light turned to green and they were off again. This pantomime had happened several times before she saw it turn and disappear down a side street. When she turned the corner, there was the lorry and the chair, but no driver. He returned after a while and she bought the chair at her own price. But her troubles were not over! The first few taxi-drivers pretended that she and her ruin were invisible, but finally one took pity on her and whisked her off to London W.1. Here she carried the chair into a top-notcher's showroom, and had her reward.

A dear old fellow, a Mr Dance, looks in occasionally. Sir George has given him permission to fish in his grounds. This man is an unusual craftsman. He has a one-man business, making glass eyes for taxidermists to use for their stuffed birds and beasts. He dispatches these eyes all over the world and has his workshop in Leamington Spa. When Gordon was small, he gave him a golden glass eye for a crocodile which lived in his pocket. Mr Dance told me how he made a glass merry-go-round for his daughter when she was a little girl, adding to it when he had time, but alas before it was finished it was shattered. One day the child raced into his workshop into his arms, and his masterpiece was no more.

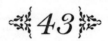

WE HAD A TWIG of the family tree to mid-day dinner on Sunday. We expected three little nieces, their parents plus a mutual great-aunt, so with the four of us it was to be a houseful! One evening I went through into the shop to select a few extra chairs to polish up and bring through into the cottage. In the back of the shop was a nine foot refectory table, looking rather beautiful. It gave me an idea. Why not have the meal in the shop? So after I had closed on Saturday night, I stacked some of the other furniture out of the way and polished and arranged all the hooped Windsor chairs I had around the table. Then I gave the table top the polishing of its life, (there is nothing better than beeswax and real turpentine), and from the beams above I hung some witch balls, a couple of galleons and all the lanterns and 'chandeliery' things I had. Down the full length of the table I laid a narrow strip of puce brocade. For a centrepiece I used an old wooden mixing bowl piled high with fruit, flanked on either side by lumpy old wooden candelabra. The silver had an extra polish too, and when the table was all laid and ready, it looked quite exciting.

I decided on the Sunday to draw the curtains and light the candles. I do so hope the little girls will remember it. They certainly thought that it was very funny to have a meal in a shop.

When I was a small child, about five or six years old, I was taken to Worcester for the day by our 'domestic;' it was her 'day off.' Her parents kept a grocer's shop. I cannot remember the journey or how we got there, but I do remember the shop. I was given a paper bag and the glass-topped biscuit tins which fronted the counter were opened for me and I was encouraged to make a selection.

It must have been their closing-day, for it was decided that we should go for a picnic. We piled into a little padded trap and drove between high green hedges until we stopped on a hill-top and unharnessed the pony.

Here I was allowed to chase about with the family dog which was a collie. I was told not to touch him as he had 'the mange.' This was a new word to me. I thought it meant 'bite.' (perhaps I have a French ancestor) so I was obedient.

Being a little girl, the man of our party, our maid's father, was the chief object of my interest. I thought he was very funny and very nice. He said the things were cold and kept putting food into his pocket to 'get it warm first,' before he would eat anything. He made me hold his apple with both my hands to 'get it warm first.' He kept exclaiming 'How I love to hear that child laugh!' He kept looking over his shoulder when he said this. It was rather queer. I looked too, but there wasn't a child anywhere.

This morning, I bought one of the largest dressers I have ever seen, 8' 4" to be exact. It had four drawers and three banister legs along the front and a pot-board below. It is in magnificent condition with beautiful patina. It has its original brass handles and across the back a long row of little spice drawers with wooden knobs. It is of fruitwood. I only found it just in time for a cabinet-maker had bought it privately, and was going to make it into a pair of two-drawer dressers. Nearly everything this dealer friend buys he makes into something else; that is unless I get there in time. I say 'But how much is it as it is?' Probably the thought of all the work he is going to be saved, has a softening effect on his already reasonable prices! Little does he know how much of my stock goes into farm-houses, manor houses and even churches.

This cabinet-maker changes little circular marble topped commodes into wee book-cases, spinets into sideboards and dressing tables, knee-hole washstands into writing tables, shattered bureaux into chests-of-drawers, broken backed carved oak chairs into stools and mirrors, old-fashioned fire-screens with swept legs into little occasional tables, grand-father clock cases into gun cupboards, circular Victorian table-tops into bed-heads, and bedposts into standard lamps! In fact, a half-remembered song I've heard should have been dedicated to him! It runs something like this:—

'Take the legs from some old table,
And the arms from some old chair,
The neck from some old bottle
And from some old horse the hair . . .'

44

WHEN CUSTOMERS ask me for an old Welsh dresser, they almost always mean a dresser with a plate rack. Certainly many Welsh dressers do have racks, but just as many do not have them. In fact, there is almost a different design of dresser for each county in England and Wales. Take, for example, a Pembrokeshire dresser: this is usually made of pine, with two drawers, two cupboards, and an arched space between the cupboards where the farm dog can curl up on his sack to keep from under folk's feet. I can still buy these dressers for five or six pounds, but there is the carriage home, and then another fiver to have them stripped. This is quite a job, as there are frequently layers and layers of paint, often with a top crust of grained oak and varnish. Then I replace the poor wooden handles with good brass ones and have to do the final waxing myself. I once had a number of these pine dressers and settles shot-blasted very cheaply, but the double lot of carriage added up and then they had to be sandpapered by hand.

In a Barmouth Sale-room in Merionethshire I once found a couple of painted dressers for which they had been unable to get a bid. I paid ten pounds for the two, for the proportions were good and the racks were prettily pierced. To my delight, when I got them home (by rail), I found they were of pine. They were beautiful when they were stripped and waxed. All dealers have their own methods of waxing pine. I used to use liquid wax which looks like top milk and is bought at dry salters' shops. I used to apply it, or rather scrub it in, with a soft scrubbing brush and next day scrub it hard with a dry scrubbing brush and then finish with a soft duster. Lately I have been giving the pine pieces a thin application of Ronseal with a soft paint brush and, when dry, a good waxing with a natural coloured polish. I use Waxol, the polish used in the Royal Households. I always used to fix very simple brass handles (as approved by men dealers) to these pine pieces, but, since acquiring an odd lot of magnificent French Chippendale handles, I try to use something so lovely that the first woman customer will fall for it!

One of these two dressers from Barmouth had never had any handles to its drawers. They were flicked open by inserting one's middle finger into a little recess cut under the drawer. I soon remedied this however and used some old brass handles I had been hoarding. Several customers who saw these dressers marked 'SOLD' kept popping in to see if some more had arrived, but alas they do not grow on trees!

Before the war it was a different story. One dealer friend told me he bought scores of Welsh dressers at £2 a time. His look-out man was a porter on Aberystwyth station who would send a postcard when he had gathered up a dozen or so. My dealer friend would then register him the money and along they would come, by rail, at 6/- a cwt.

A Lancashire dresser is usually a very important piece and

119

made entirely of oak. This dresser usually has a rack with a filled in back and the lower part is enclosed, consisting of a number of drawers and cupboards, frequently with wooden handles. I have twice seen them with a brass faced clock incorporated in the rack, but these are rare.

I find a very quick sale for any Cardiganshire dressers I manage to buy. In fact, they are so pretty that they sell like hot cakes and are what people mean when they ask for 'a Welsh dresser.' They usually have an open rack, that is to say, backless. The four front legs are banister type and there are frequently arched aprons between these legs. There are usually three shallow drawers and sometimes two little extra ones in the arches. Below is a pot-board where the copper kitchen pots and pans once stood when the dresser was in its original home in the kitchen.

I am on the look-out for a first class illustrated book on dressers. What a fascinating subject for research!

The first dresser my daughter bought was sold to her as a Dutch pewter dresser. It cost ten pounds. I have never seen another like it, and only wish that I had made a careful sketch of it. The rack was unique in that the top shelves were deep ones and over hung those below, which graduated down to shallow ones, only deep enough for wee pewter measures.

While on the subject of dressers let me write about my favourite, a Queen Anne one. This was a simple oak seven footer English one, on the pale side, with the most glorious patina, the three drawers were cross-banded with walnut, the front legs were cabriole and the magnificent pierced brass handles and escutcheons were original — simple, beautiful, right. Alas, it went to Italy.

I have lately palmed one off on to John, one that is *not* right. It is a golden two-drawer elm one with simple Chippendale swan handles. It is much admired in his Welsh cottage. I bought it legless for three pounds ten shillings. I decided to have the top board cut across and the halves applied at each end and nicked at the bottom like the ends of an early coffer. Then a new elm coffin board with fine figuring was bought for the new top. It is already beginning to respond to its weekly polish. We have it in the lilac bed-room and use it as a dressing table. I notice that American customers call dressing tables, dressers, and they call dressers, sideboards. Incidentally, they call jugs pitchers! I thought a pitcher was the bowler in a game of baseball. They might be surprised to know that a bowler is a hat! Life gets tricky doesn't it?

45

My first caller this morning was a grubby old tramp. He stood outside the high iron gate, eyeing the Cairn doubtfully. She, for her part, had no qualms about him. Her whole anatomy wagged its welcome.

'Scampi is like us, Mummy, she likes tramps and gypsies.' said Angela one day, 'I expect its the smell of hedges, ditches, bracken and hayricks — everything a Cairn loves!'

This fellow held out not the usual smoky tin for his tea, but a yellow plastic beaker. Really even the men-of-the-road are getting demoralised. He rubbed Scampi's ears and settled himself into a broken-kneed Welsh chair behind the willow-tree. He tucked into some heavy fruit cake while I pierced a large empty coffee tin and threaded it with a stout wire handle in the traditional way. Each time I approached him he took rude loud sniffs and muttered 'Lovely, lovely woman!' I accepted this as an unsolicited testimonial for Johnson's Baby Talc.

My next caller was my cabinet-maker. He brought back a beautiful little Chippendale commode, whose false drawers he had made into real ones. This was an eighteenth century piece with its original handles and little bracket feet and in fine condition. He also returned a collection of six country Hepple-white chairs with wooden seats, two had needed stretchers, three of them had to be stripped of white paint, and all had had to be reglued, repegged and recramped. The last thing he had restored was a Victorian papier-mâché box, smothered with inlaid mother-of-pearl roses and painted with misty blue forget-me-nots, the prettiest casket I've had. He had replaced the strained hinges and conjured up a missing foot for it. We had coffee together. I settled up and we reloaded his truck with another collection of temporarily disabled antiques. The man is a magician. He helps me and another dealer. We would both like him full-time. He doesn't like private customers. He told me that once on returning a Queen Anne walnut bureau with his bill, the lady gasped and exclaimed in horror,

'What! Twelve pounds ten! I can't see what you've done!'

Little did she know that she was paying him the greatest compliment. She would have been surprised if he had answered,

'I've made and replaced seventeen pieces of cock beading and matched, cut and replaced fourteen pieces of veneer. I've cut and replaced five inches of herringbone inlay. I've reglued and cramped the bracket feet, copied, cut and replaced one missing back plate, and replaced the grub-eaten back, replaced four worn drawer runners, cleaned and oiled all the locks, injected the carcase with Rentokil and cleaned and rewaxed the whole piece including the fitment.'

I am catching up with my diary this afternoon. I am sitting in a saleroom waiting for some antique lots to come up. At the moment, the porters with their aprons still 'whiter than white,' are struggling with beds, carpets and park benches of all things!

Yesterday, a customer called who was feeling on top of the world! He was a gigantic American, a man of forty or so and as happy as a boy by a river! In one huge fist he held two magnificent walking sticks which I admired. He asked me what I thought they contained. I guessed they were sword sticks, but when he said 'No,' I guessed they were yard rules, but was wrong again. He gleefully unscrewed the first. It was a gun-stick, wonderfully made and deadly; the second when assembled was a four piece fishing rod. He had paid £15 and £12 for them.

'Well you are lucky!' I exclaimed, 'I have never seen such fine ones!'

'I'm off to Cheltenham now to see a sword stick,' he said.

'Just a minute,' I said, 'I have a walking stick here that you might like, not as fine as yours but interesting and only fifty shillings.' His face was a study as he unscrewed its knob, and fished out four inches of amber and screwing it into the knob, found he had a smoker's pipe in his hand. He had found them all on one day. He went on his way rejoicing.

Most Americans are very hard work and spend very little. They fly here, and their purchases are restricted to a few pounds in weight. A happy exception to this rule are the American service people who are stationed here for three years at a time. They come in with their wives and children and love this part of the world. They have a passion for grandfather clocks and American wall-clocks and really love the things for what they are, not for the possessing of them. After a few visits they begin to trust me and we get to like each other. Their children speak English of course, as they attend our schools. It sounds rather quaint, coming out of a pale little Yankee face, under a base-baller's peaked cotton cap.

When I refer to them being hard work, let me give as an example last Monday. By 11.30 a.m. I was flagging over a late cup of coffee. The morning started with two charmers from South Carolina who stayed an hour. They thoroughly enjoyed themselves, remarked on my reasonable prices, but spent nary a dollar. They went off happily with a gratis 6d 'I Spy Book' on antiques. They were 'thrilled' with it!

The next couple, equally unprofitable, stayed an hour and a half, but they were rather dears. They looked at every price ticket and remarked that my things were 'less than in the book,' in a whisper to each other! What is this book? I must find out. Is it something they swot up on the liner coming over? 'What to pay for Antiques in England or some such title, perhaps? I might advertise under a new slogan 'Less than in the Book!' As they were leaving they admired my hedge of Albertine roses, now in its full beauty. I heard my silly voice say,

'Let me cut you a bunch!' Really I need my head examining. They loved them, they loved my shop, they loved the village and even me.

I returned to the kitchen, literally licking my wounds, from the rose thorns. I put on the coffee pot but, before it was hot, I had to photograph another pair, male and female this time, against the shop window. The lady remarked that,

'You surely have the cutest little shop in all England!' Incidentally, she didn't spend anything either.

I am beginning to think I might do quite well as a museum curator since I send them off so happy. And I can always let off steam in my diary!

In the 1920s, as a schoolgirl, I would see loads of antiques being packed off to America from Warwick, but they were not bought by holiday-makers. The American customer, apart from trade-buyers, is a myth. The holiday-makers from the Continent, especially from Sweden and from Italy, do buy.

An elderly Southport dealer told me how he used to go off on buying expeditions for these Americans trade buyers long ago; he always went with an old Warwick dealer, now dead. He said they were always up to fun and would be away several days and nights at a stretch, lodging where they could and often having to share a room. On one of these jaunts, he, the Southport dealer, bought what he considered was a very fine pair of large oil paintings — portraits. His Warwickshire friend ragged him about them and said they were no good. The Southport dealer, being still convinced that they were valuable, insisted on getting them out of the van each night and lugging them up to their shared bedroom. Each morning when he woke up, he found that his friend had nipped out of his bed and placed the pictures so that the subjects were gazing down upon him when he opened his eyes.

However my Southport friend had the last laugh for when the pictures were being unloaded in Lord Street, a gentleman followed them into the shop and bought them at a very handsome profit.

⚜ 46 ⚜

LAST WEEK I was sitting next to a new woman dealer in a saleroom. She asked me if I still made blunders. I sensed she must have made one and asked her what she had done.

'Well,' she replied, 'any coins I happen to find in old boxes or vases, I put on a plate and sell at 1/- each. The other day a school-boy asked me, 'is this *really* only a 1/-?' and after he had settled up he told me it was a sovereign!'

'You will find you have got a regular customer anyway,' I

chuckled, 'and he won't be able to resist telling all his young friends.'

I assured her I still made blunders too and it started a line of thought. Here are some of my prize ones, though I must have made scores more unknown to me.

Just after the war, when petrol was still rationed, we hired a cabin-cruiser for a week from Messrs. Salters at Folly Bridge at Oxford. It was the month of April and the weather, the river and the whole week was out of this world. We borrowed two more youngsters, making up our family to what I think is the ideal number, two boys close in age, a breather, and then two girls close in age. I know I am going off at a tangent, but I must write something about the river. I've said already, it was April. This means that the trailing weeping willows were just coming into leaf and caressing the flowing Thames. The swans were beginning to nest and selecting sites on sudden little islands. The banks were starred with celandine and the gardens were softly green and newly mown and the sun shone and shone. The children decided amicably where we should tie up each tea-time for the night, but even when somewhere lovely was found they would agree to 'let's see what's round the next bend.' One evening, to John's amusement, they voted unanimously to tie up within sight and sound of a great iron railway bridge and the illuminated trains tearing across through the night gave our country children a new experience!

One of the places where we stopped for bread was Henley-on-Thames. We tied up by the bridge and the children called after me 'Don't be long Mummy.' Something made me look in a china shop however, and there, sitting on a shelf at the back of the shop, were three little blue and white pierced porcelain bowls.

'Yes, you can have them if you want,' said the shopkeeper 'but they aren't new you know and this one has a chip. Shall we say a pound for the lot?' They were beautiful, like little baskets without handles, and where the tressis crossed over the entices were decorated with little rosettes or little flowers. I priced them at 45/- the three and let the trade have them for two pounds. Years later I discovered they were Dr. Wall Worcester baskets.

I sold a pill-roll last year; anyway, that is what this dealer told me was the name for the square little Delft plate, with decoration in blue, that I had hung on a hook in my shop. I let him beat me down from 30/- to 25/- and doubtless, feeling he owed me a bit of information, he added that there was another one he coveted in Oxford, one decorated with little rhinoceros, but alas it was £100! As the name implies, these little plates were used for the making and rolling of pills.

On another occasion I had viewed a sale upon the hills, and I had dismissed my taxi, thinking I would phone the carrier to collect any furniture I bought and travel home with it myself. But after further consideration I felt it would be a waste of time to stay. So, the day being glorious, I started for home on Shanks Pony, with a spanking four miles walk ahead of me all down hill! I was shortly overtaken by a dealer friend who buys beautiful things for museums, and he insisted on giving me a lift home though Penny Priors was rather out of his way. He asked to have a peep in the shop and said, 'Now, I am expecting you to find me something good!'

'Just look at this little drawing,' I said, putting it in his hands. 'I know a bit about drawing, and personally I think it is exquisite. I bought it at the Manor House, here in the village, and I cannot think why no one buys it.'

My friend studied the little picture, examining it with his glass. The drawing was of a young shepherd boy sitting under a tree playing his flute, with his flock around him.

'Yes' he commented 'I like it. It's a Boucher, and it's signed and dated. What is the price to me?'

'Twenty-five shillings,' I replied. I had never heard of Boucher and knew nothing of him. Five minutes later, however, I had looked him up and did! I should add that this customer, shortly afterwards had a 'turn-out' of furniture and oddments and nearly gave the load to me. One of the pieces he jobbed off was an immense high-backed bowed settle which I quickly sold for twelve pounds.

A delightful young Army officer calls occasionally. He calls himself my 'Fourpenny Customer,' as he once bought from me an old Geographical Gazetteer for that sum, and resold it for two pounds. On another occasion he noticed two curious objects, which I had used for years as door-stops to keep open the stable doors. The easiest way to describe them, perhaps, would be to say that they were the shape of swing boats at a Fair, with high curling prows. He asked me what I thought they were, and I said I thought they might be a kind of iron stirrup and giving one a rub, I pointed out they were beautifully damasceened with some metal, possibly silver. Anyway, he bought them for a few shillings and told me later that he had had them looked at at the British Museum. Sure enough they were Chinese stirrups of I forget what Dynasty, but certainly very antique. They are now polished up and adorn his flat topped desk I believe.

Before I forget, I had better write about a pair of elegant dove grey gaiters which I had for sale during the war. In those days anything which was free of clothing coupons sold itself; but these gaiters were too narrow for all of us. One day however, a really thin customer, armed with one of my silver button hooks, made a really determined effort to get the little buttons through the tight little buttonholes. She looked uncommonly like one of the Ugly Sisters wrestling with Cinderella's slipper! Suddenly she gave a guffaw and exclaimed,

'They aren't for humans. They are for horses.' She was right.

I had a quiet chuckle on another occasion just after the war. I was at a country sale and noticed that two village women had 'got the giggles' as they came out of a stable where the auctioneer was selling the riding tack. I edged my way in and saw the reason for their mirth. The Honourable — — had had a coupon-free overcoat made for himself, out of a yellow horse-blanket. He had perched himself in a hay crib, so was as visible as a mannequin at a dress show. The top half of his fluffy coat was conspicuous enough, but the hemline was pure haute couture, for round it ran stripes of scarlet and black!

❦ 47 ❦

OTHER DISEASES beside the plague have run like wildfire through these islands. For years now, hundreds of our women customers have suffered recurring bouts of a disease, which we in the trade have nicknamed 'lampitis;' not to be confused with 'mastitis' which only affects mothers. Patients suffering from the former complaint search untiringly for any object, be it of glass, stone, wood, china or metal that can be transformed into a domestic table lamp! The frenzied pursuit of vases, bottles, candlesticks, jugs, jars, urns and 'what-have-yous' sometimes abates towards sunset and the tired patient may be soothed in some strange way by watching resurrected Victorian lamps which shipped themselves to Hollywood and now flaunt themselves in ancient movies on Television. Two similarly affected patients may find relief in talking together of their symptoms and discussing fonts, shades, galleries, chimneys, wicks and 'Hinks,' whatever they may be!

There are now signs of another craze and in all honesty I must admit to an early attack of it myself. This complaint may be referred to in years to come as 'screenitis.' Our Victorian grand-mothers started it with their folding draught screens which they adorned with early Christmas cards, 'Valentines' and 'scraps' which could be bought in packets at toy shops and Penny Bazaars. A picture restorer whom I know has made himself a truly beautiful screen. On one side he has pasted and varnished coloured prints and on the reverse side he has used prints in sepia. The whole effect is subdued and chaste.

On the way home from seeing it, I remembered that I had scores of old 'Collectors' Guides' and 'Connoisseurs' stacked in piles on the workshop floor. Their superb covers and illustrations would be wonderful for a tired four-fold screen of mine which nobody wanted to buy. What glorious evenings I had sniping round these illustrations of priceless treasures. That was last week. Now I have a screen, or rather half a screen (only one side is done) of real beauty. Where the corners of the pictures meet, I have softened the square effect by adding cut-outs of bejewelled watches, milliflora glass paper weights, gilded snuff boxes and Pratt pot-lids. I found that if I included the shadow of an object in the cut-out the effect was almost three dimensional. I sit and gloat over it at night when I am listening to music. Soon I shall get up steam to do the reverse side.

I SEEM TO GET ON with writing my diary at a great pace when I am in a train or bus, and being under the hair-dryer seems to have the same effect. John says it's the vibrations. I am writing this on the bus, the windows are steamed up, but the world outside is white and beautiful except for the great banks of defiled snow tossed back by the snow ploughs.

I had a letter from the Inland Revenue people last month. They wanted to know why my profits had risen last year although my turnover had not. Really I did not know, but I got out my stock-book to try to solve the mystery and was surprised to find that I had sold over four hundred pictures last year. These had been mostly around the twenty-five shilling mark and none more than ten guineas. These pictures were mostly bought at county sales in two or three pound lots. I reckoned I had doubled or trebled my money on these. Private buyers are very chary of buying, say, a dozen pictures in an attic when they only want one, but dealers expect to work, and all that hareing up and down those flights of stairs is all in the day's work, apart from its slimming properties.

The profit margin on the antique furniture is nearer 30% gross, though some pieces show much more and others much less. One dear old dealer calls every fortnight like clockwork. He invariably spends eighteen to twenty pounds each time and has very special trade prices. One day however I sold him an early oak spice cupboard. This was rather like a small hanging chest-of-drawers. I bought it at a Cattle Market Sale for three shillings but had been prepared to pay three pounds for it. I sold it to my old friend for three pounds fifteen and the next time he called I asked him if he had sold it all right.

'Yes' he chuckled, 'sold it to the trade on the way home for seven fifteen. What *should* we all do if we didn't take in each other's washing?'

I remember well the loveliest of those four hundred pictures. I bought it at a house sale at Warwick, a house in the shadow of St. Mary's Church. The picture hung over the drawing-room mantelpiece. It was a beautiful needlework picture in a fine eighteenth century gilded frame. The subject, a lovely young woman, was in profile, and waist length. She wore a fitting bejewelled gown, a little crown and in her long slim hands she held a single rose. The background showed a distant castle against a cloudless sky. The children also loved the picture and we hung it for a while in our sitting-toom. I often wondered who she was and felt I must enjoy her for a while. One winter's night when I was alone and the children asleep, I unhooked it and carefully removing the picture began to gently clean the frame with weak ammonia and soft rags. The radio was on, and I was half listening to a quiz programme. Question followed question and then I heard the question-master ask,

'To which Queen of England was a cross erected at each place where her funeral cortege rested on its way to London?' There was a pause — I did not know the answer myself, but the picture seemed to say quite clearly,

'It was I, Eleanor.' The answer on the radio came a few seconds later,

'Eleanor of Castile, Queen of Edward I.' This is perfectly true. At the time I was not so much surprised, as delighted to know who she was at last. She now resides in a Cotswold Manor House.

The beamed ceiling in our downstairs rooms are very low, but the modern kitchen which has been added is long and lofty; in fact it is the only place where I can stand the grandfather clocks. Sometimes I have as many as seven at once. I don't like to sell them until they are working perfectly. Of course I am used to setting them up by now, and soon have them ticking away if they were in working order when I bought them. But they take time to regulate, and John teases me about them and says when the end one strikes three, and the little one strikes seven and the brass-faced one begins to growl it is ten to five. I love to hear their voices if I wake at night, but it is our church clock that we rely on — it is infallible. I can see its face, as I sit in my wing chair.

The other day a Welsh parson called in, and he told me this little story about a grandfather clock. A colleague of his was visiting one of his old parishioners in the Black Mountains. She asked him if he would kindly have a look at her grandfather clock which had stopped. He studied it intently for a few minutes, peered inside and then putting his arm down into the bottom of the case he lifted out a dead mouse and holding it up by its tail said to the old dear,

'How can you expect it to go, Mrs Williams, when the little engine-driver is dead?'

My own funny story about a grandfather clock fell rather flat. I had a brass-faced one in recently, bearing the maker's name, Hughes of Pembroke, on its face. I was in correspondence with a Pembrokeshire dealer at the time, and sent a letter to him worded like this:—

Dear Mr Oliver,

Please find enclosed my cheque for the pine dresser and the two cradles. I am always interested in the latter.

I had an old gentleman from your way come in on Friday, a Mr Hughes of Pembroke. He looked rather unusual as he wore a hood and had a case with him; his face was shiny, his voice mellow and I particularly noticed his beautiful hands. I wonder if you know him?

Yours faithfully,
Anne Summers.

I have not heard from this dealer since. Gordon says he probably thinks I have gone 'bonkers,' and added that too many clocks affect some people like that.

⫷ 49 ⫸

FOR YEARS I have been buying antique pieces from a huge old store in town. It is close to three town dealers. They would not be amused to know that several of the pieces they have bought from me have only come a stone's throw from their own premises. There have been antique coffers, chests-of-drawers, two refectory tables, (one was walnut,) a set of nine period mahogany chairs, leather screens, some gilt pieces, bureaux and a Queen Anne settle. I have just about scraped the barrel clean and my last piece was delivered on Friday. It is an immense bath chair with shafts. It is lined and button-padded with navy cloth of the finest quality. I am going to offer it to a customer who breeds Shetland ponies. She has a herd of them, but the latest pet is a house-trained baby donkey who follows her into the house, and lies on the rug at her feet as she has tea.

My Godson and one of his sisters have been earning some pocket money polishing it, and as it stands on the front lawn I am getting teased about it.

'Afraid you are feeling your age, Anne!' or 'Can I sell you a horse?'

Another unsual chair I have at the moment is a skater's chair. On Christmas cards you may have seen a knicker-bockered gallant skating across a frozen pool pushing before him a bemuffled lady in an iron chair on skids. Well, that is what I have. The vendor and I both thought it was a rocking-chair at first which had been immobilised, but the bolt holes in the base gave us the clue that it had been mounted on runners or skids.

A woman dealer sold me a few things last week. She saw my chairs and said she had recently bought something unusual too. She was returning from a very disappointing day, when she overtook a cavalcade of tinkers, and noticed a highly decorative knife-grinding cart being towed behind one of the vans. She pulled up ahead where the road widened and succeeded in buying it as it was never used. She sold it next day and rather wished she hadn't; she said it looked marvellous in her forecourt, all red and blue with shining brass knobs. She said it would have stopped the customers.

Many years ago three chairs were made from the wood of a mulberry tree felled in Shakespeare's garden at Stratford-upon-Avon. They were sold separately each with printed particulars about its history. Well, some years before the war a London gentleman, who owned one of them, was driving very early to a conference in Birmingham and, on the way as he passed through Stratford-upon-Avon, he saw a chair exactly like his own. It was in a shop window, and as the shop had not opened, he decided to call on his way home. Shortly after it did open however a Birmingham dealer saw and purchased the chair for £7. 10. 0. The old dealer (now dead) tried in vain to get £8. 10. 0. for it. Within three hours it was on sale in the Birmingham dealer's shop window and, as the fates would have it, the London gentleman saw it there. He could hardly believe his good fortune and felt sure he would be the proud owner of the three chairs before the day was out. The price, £135, was more than he bargained for but he settled for £130 and the chair was soon in the back of his car.

He left for London in good time and pulled up at the country shop, but the chair was not in the window. He entered and enquired about it.

'No, I'm afraid it's sold. I sold it before ten o'clock this morning,' said the old dealer.

'Well I *am* disappointed,' replied the gentleman. There were three made you know. I have one at home, I bought a second one this morning in Birmingham and yours must have been the third.'

'In Birmingham, did you say? I sold mine to a Birmingham dealer. Was it in Mr . . . . . .'s shop?'

'Yes,' replied the gentleman, 'it was.'

The old dealer hesitated, and throwing in a 'Sir' for good measure enquired,

'Er . . . could I enquire, Sir, what you gave for it?'

The gentleman told him. The poor old fellow (who under stress always knocked off his own hat) sent it flying, and began running round the car in circles. The customer was astonished at this performance, but when he was informed of its country price, he was quite affected himself.

⁂ 50 ⁂

AFTER ALL THESE YEARS I still get asked for something I've never been asked for before. This morning two brown-eyed youngsters inquired if I sold 'pigeon's milk.'

'Pigeon's milk?'

'Yes, the Marlow Boys told us you sold it at 3d a pint.'

'Pigeon's milk?'

'I think someone has been having you on,' I replied. I told them how the parent birds feed their young squabs with regurgitated food, and that the name for it is pigeon's milk.

'Well, thank you for putting us wise' replied the elder, a young man of perhaps eight summers. 'We must think of some trick to play on *them*.'

I then suggested they should get the Marlow Boys to hare off to the High Cross to see Farmer Turville's field of macaroni. 'Tell them to be quick, he is just going to cut it,' I said. To be on the safe side, I told them the facts of life about macaroni, and that Farmer Turville's field was just a field of wheat.

I feel I have made two friends this morning, but knowing the Marlow Boys of old, I feel they will win the last round. I have quite a few boy customers. They usually ask for one of six things, swords, guns, rods, coins, foreign stamps or stuffed birds. I like the direct approach.

'What have you got for a shilling? or sixpence? or three-pence?'

Last school holidays when I was clearing out the front shed, I found three young customers for three sets of stags' antlers. They cost them a shilling a head plus their threepenny return fares. When I saw them vanishing into the distance with their long walk ahead of them, they were still clasping their purchases to their foreheads, like the stag dancers of Abbots Bromley.

Children seem so much more confident these days and thus must be spared agonies of shyness. A teacher was telling me the other day how the scholar pianist had failed to turn up at 'prayers' and the Head asked for a volunteer. Within two seconds the gangway to the platform was a threshing mass of arms and legs as the volunteers collided and fought for the honour.

Another teacher, a colleague of the lady in the following little story told me, that at her school, a little child in the Infants Department, had been found to have T.B., and it was thought advisable that all the children in that class should be x-rayed. When, however, the x-ray apparatus was trundled into the room, several children, *not* so confident, began to cry and all looked alarmed. The teacher put on her happiest and most reassuring smile and asked if '*she* could be done first.' This worked like a charm and the children calmed down. A week later the results came through and all was well but the Headmistress sent for the teacher and said that the Doctor would like to x-ray her again. She feared the worst. Her colleagues tried to cheer her up and she told them, and herself, that she felt as fit as a flea. After a second examination, the Headmistress informed her that an eminent heart specialist would like to see her in London, and that all her expenses would be paid.

To cut a long story short, the specialist told her that her heart was on the wrong side, that it was lying down and that she had not got the usual number of ribs. He made quite a fuss of her and she had a wonderful shopping spree in town. The interview also solved a mystery for her — she now knew why her 'bras' never fitted properly. Not enough ribs!

This has not been my day. The boys and the pigeon's milk were the one bright spot. I phoned three people who were out or on holiday. Some promised carpet has not arrived. Mr Bede took me in his taxi to a sale that was no good, so we came back before it started, and this afternoon, when I was turning out the shop, it rained on all the furniture on the footpath.

❧ *51* ❧

I HAVE ONLY BOUGHT ONE THING that really frightened me and that was an innocent looking cotton patchwork bedspread edged with scarlet. I bought it from an old gent in Devon. It was in immaculate condition and I thought it was just the thing for Gordon's bedroom as he had a plain red fitted carpet. But each time I made his bed, a feeling of terror seemed to come upon me. This terror passed up my left arm, across my chest and down my right arm. Ruth made the bed some days, but passed no remark, and neither did Gordon report any nightmares, but each time this dreadful sensation passed through me if I touched it with both hands. One day I folded it up and put it in the shop, it is sold now. It has not been returned.

I did once have a little figure in the shop, an odd little figure in porcelain, that made me feel queer. Ordinarily I would have bought it from the lady who brought it in, for the price was reasonable, but it did not appeal to me. A few weeks later this customer called again and I asked her if she would take it back as 'it made me feel queer.' She looked rather surprised and said it made her 'feel queer' too, and that was why she had decided to sell it.

What tales old things could tell. I have a little doll whose tale would greatly interest me personally. She is a little bride doll of my great grandmother Sarah. My mother told me that before the days of photographers, a dress-maker might make and dress a pair of little bride dolls (one for each side of the family) exactly as the bride was dressed, making the clothes from little left-over snippets of the real bridal garments. I must look up the exact date of the wedding on the Family Tree, but from memory I believe it was 1825 — late Regency. The watered silk gown is long and stiff, it is full enough to have covered a crinoline; the bodice is low cut and it, and the half sleeves, have appliqués of lace and two long panels of the lace continue the line down the front of the gown to the hem; here and there are stitched little clusters of white lily-of-the-valley flowers. The doll's head is of porcelain and probably French I should think; the hair is dressed with a centre parting, with a low shining knot of plaited hair in the nape of the neck. The underclothes are of white cambric, except for a white flannel petticoat; the pantaloons are ankle length and the petticoats much betucked, with white embroidery insertions. The stockings, handknitted in a lace design are of white silk; the little white satin shoes have flat bows. For three generations this lovely little object has lain wrapped in white tissue, but now that she is mine she is standing under a glass dome and delighting her twentieth century descendants.

I wonder what this little bride-doll could tell? Did she see my great grand-mother dressed for her wedding? Did she have the vapours and need smelling salts? Did she carry a prayer-book or a posy? Was the young doctor-bridegroom her own choice or her parents? Was she happy?

⊰{ 52 }⊱

THERE ARE ALL SORTS of short cuts in housekeeping and cooking. I think a leaflet should be published for the small woman shopkeeper, or rather the small shopkeeping woman. Such a lot can be done before the first customer appears on the horizon in the morning. It saves time to dry up the breakfast things and put them straight on to the tray for the next meal, adding anything else needed. The drying up itself is done in half the time if one uses a Turkish towel and, if the silver is dried twice a week with a silver cloth, there is no need for silver cleaning sessions.

Having two jobs makes some people just feel tired, while others just feel it is a challenge. A lot is done these days about Time & Motion Study in factories and farms, but of course it can be applied to housework and gardening too. Take shelling peas for instance, or rather let's gather them first. There are two

137

ways that I know about. Method One :— you hold the basket with the left hand, you gather one pea pod at a time or possibly two or three, straighten your back and drop them into your basket. Method Two :— you place the basket on the ground, gather with both hands and fill the basket without straightening your back. Then comes the shelling of the peas, one at a time perhaps, or you can fill your left hand with full pods, shell with the right hand which quickly fills with empty pods. I like to sit down in the garden to top and tail my gooseberries with a pair of sharp scissors, but the speedy way is to whirl them round and round in one of those coarse net carrot sacks. This has to be done outside, of course, just as one dries wet lettuce leaves in a linen cloth. New potatoes should be dug daily, an old garden fork can be left in the row but instead of scraping the potatoes with a knife, they can be rubbed clean in a trice with a nylon scrubber. Poultry also feathers very quickly if done while the bird is still warm.

Making pastry is one of my patents. I do this in a steep-sided pottery bowl and use a flexible knife, working the lard into the flour until it looks like breadcrumbs, then mixing in the water with the blade too, and out it comes on to the floury board untouched by human hand. Then if the shop bell does ring in the middle of the operation, one can appear unflurried and 'unfloured.' Slicing onions without tears would go into that leaflet too.

Gordon at the growing stage had a passion for suet puddings. I have timed myself making one and my record time was less than two minutes, I believe, but I am writing this from memory. The *modus operandi* was as follows — S.R. flour into the mixing-bowl, a pinch of salt, a shower of shredded suet, mix under cold water tap into a stiffish lump with the same kitchen knife; a dollop of raspberry jam into the greased pudding basin, in with the out-size 'tennis ball,' on with the patent clipping lid, into the boiling water and on with the saucepan lid. Not very exact ounces and measurements perhaps but foolproof!

Vegetables and sauces can be prepared early in the day, and simple sweets such as apple charlotte and fruit crumbles; fresh fruit sliced into a bowl of tinned peaches will improve with standing a few hours. Casseroles of meat and vegetables which can be left for hours in the oven are a boon to those of us who dash off to auction sales, and three cheers for mixed grills, say I, which seem to please everyone.

A favourite sweet course in the autumn was always 'Plum Cream.' Just halved ripe uncooked desert plums set in a good red jelly. Our favourite combination was Monarch plums set in a strawberry jelly and served with cream it became 'party food.'

Last autumn there was a glut of plums in this area. One wished they would store like apples. Everyone was trying to give them away or borrow a boy to pick them. Even the Speaker at the Women's Institute closed her talk with, 'by the way, if any of you could do with some plums, do bring a basket and help yourselves.' A great sigh went up from all of us, for we had been bottling, jamming, picking or eating plums all morning. We began to feel like plums.

I will round up this cookery section with THE most delectable receipe for Plum Conserve, for it is much too superior to be called jam. It not only tastes simply scrumptious but looks so beautifully home-made too.

PLUM CONSERVE

3 lbs. desert plums
1 large orange
1 lb. seeded raisins
Juice of one lemon
1½ lbs. sugar
½ lb. pecan nuts

Wash and stone the ripe plums and cut them into pieces. Choose an orange with a thin skin, slice it very thinly and cut it into small pieces. Chop the raisins roughly or put them through a mincer with a coarse cutter.

Put these three ingredients into a preserving pan with the lemon juice and cook until soft and pulpy; than add the sugar, and cook again until the mixture will jelly. Add the nuts a few minutes before the conserve is ready, or some of the plum kernels may be used instead.

Now I will finish off my gardening section, in this unwritten Know-it-all-do-it-yourself leaflet, with a receipe for growing potatoes (untested I must admit), but I shall certainly try it next spring, if I can buy an old barrel cheaply at a sale.

Ingredients

1 old barrel

1 large healthy looking potato (a King Edward
   for preference)
Earth

Modus Operandi

Place barrel in garden, open end up. Put 6 inches of good
garden soil in bottom of tub. Place the potato on earth, cover
with 6 inches of soil. Await appearance of shoot above surface
of soil. Cover with earth, and keep on covering it as it keeps
appearing, until the barrel is full. Leave it until the greenery
of the potato plant fades in the autumn. Spill out contents
carefully. It is possible to grow fifty to a hundred pounds of
potatoes from one tuber in this way.

A farmer-customer-friend gave me this gardening information, and it really works. I think it might also work with a
Jerusalem artichoke.

⚜ *53* ⚜

ONE DAY IN THE SUMMER, I took a train into Birmingham and
spent a wonderful morning at the Art Gallery, where there was
a visiting Exhibition of Van Gogh's paintings. I had never seen
an original of his work before, only countless reproductions
which seem wonderful until one sees the real thing. The
orchard scenes in Arles appealed to me most of all. I shuffled
slowly past them, one of a hundred thousand in an endless
stream of townsfolk, mostly young people.

I once read an article about visiting museums and galleries
and the writer stressed the importance of studying one man's
work and then coming away. Wandering round aimlessly seems
to blunt both perception and memory, like nibbling something
from each course of a banquet perhaps. All Galleries have
catalogues and it is a first-class investment to buy and study
them. One can leave one's shopping, possibly one's cares too,
and compulsorily one's umbrella at the entrance and ascend the
stairs into a world of beauty and inspiration. I love to sit in front

of a favourite picture for a while, close my eyes and try to recall it, and then gaze again.

Lately several of us in the village have been having lessons in oil-painting. We have tried to paint the old pollarded willows by the river, a bit of the village, a corner of the Churchyard and various cottages. On wet days we work in the artist's studio, and try our hand at still life and flower painting. So far none of us has produced a masterpiece, but oh, how wonderfully our eyes have been opened to see — to see 'lilacy' shadows, reflected lights, different textures of petals and leaves, the softly blending colours in an old stone wall, the glistening beauty of dead grasses. It could fill a book!

I feel the same thing applies to reading too. If one enjoys a superbly written book, it is enriched by reading the author's biography, or better still his autobiography, and then perhaps all his other works. It seems such a pity, after leaving school, to stop studying. When I was in my twenties I read all J. M. Barrie's books, and after a summer in Spain, I got every available book on the subject from the library. Most dealers have at least one trade magazine each month and how we gloat over it. I find it helps to study the illustrated advertisements too and say to myself, 'that I think is a Florentine Coffer probably in walnut,' or 'that is a Georgian Baby-Walker in mahogany,' *before* I read the description below. Occasionally I get three photographs of pictures right in a row, say a Rowlandson, a Shayer and a Bonnington, and then I feel quite elated and say to myself, 'you're learning, you're learning.'

Many older dealers are most kind and love to help and to tutor a beginner. I remember once an established middle-aged dealer coming in with his son, just demobbed, and the father was literally pumping information into the young man. I wondered if he knew how fortunate he was.

Cabinet-makers and antique restorers always appear unhurried and are wells of information, so too are collectors, who revel in displaying their treasures and so often let one get 'the feel' of the piece, which is an invaluable help.

A Welsh lady, a collector of Swansea porcelain, has lately left this district. More than once she had invited me to see it, but now I have missed my chance and could kick myself. Whatever I do, I must not beat my breast, as I have had a hen's egg down my neck all day, for the hen forsook it when nine chicks had hatched, but I fear this one is addled as it is getting steadily colder.

Yesterday evening a dealer friend arrived with some goods for me. Believe it or not he has a genuine old Queen Anne chair in his hen-house. An American lady saw it there and said that when she got back to the States, she would be able to tell her friends that we even furnished our poultry-houses with antiques! He has promised to let me have it sometime after he has cleaned and polished it up. He says he, 'will get it out one day when the hens are not looking.'

Across the road lives a large and very fierce Alsatian dog who loudly objects to strange men carrying things away from my shop, but yesterday evening he fiercely objected to this dealer *delivering* goods. My friend, thoughtfully rubbed his chin with one finger and remarked,

'What shall we do? Will you carry the urn table while I beat him off with the euphonium or shall I carry the table, while you beat him off with the euphonium?'

The Alsatian (like Queen Victoria) was not amused by our mirth.

Through the years I have bought hundreds of pieces from this friend and never been stuck with a single one, although there was a sequel to one purchase. This heavy wooden object, quite two feet square and six inches through, consisted of many complicated moving parts, obviously antique and interesting too, if you knew what it was. He affirmed it to be an antique rat-trap, and certainly there was a square little aperture leading into it, or could it be out of it? Anyway, I sold it as such (unseen) to the County Pest Control Officer of Warwickshire. He brought it back before long and laughingly told me that it was an early water ram. It is now in an agricultural museum, rubbing shoulders doubtless with old flails, breast-ploughs, linen smocks and Vicky scarecrows!

I must pop in a bit here about my Cheltenham Uncle who at eighty is still just as full of fun as ever. As a young man he went with a friend to view an Exhibition of Modern Amateur Inventions. The friend became involved in a lengthy conversation with the curator, and my Uncle, who was several stands ahead, became bored. With his walking-stick he mischievously pushed on some exhibit cards by one place, thus 'a speedy potato-masher' became 'a latest tyre inflator' while 'a de luxe fish fryer became 'an improved moustache-trimmer,' and so on.

⋙{ 54 }⋘

As soon as John had gone this morning, Angela and I drained the coffee pot and settled down to two catalogues. I tossed her the promising one and slit open the other for myself.

'Listen, Mummy, Lot 17 Pair of angel candelabra.'

'*You* listen, pet, Lot 14 Pink lustre tea-service.'

'Mummy, Mummy, Lot 32 Silver gilt model of the Golden Hind.'

'Lot 46' from me again 'Six silver baby-rattles.'

'Mummy, listen! Lot 55. Ship's figure-head of a mermaid.'

'*You* listen, Angel! Lot 60. Parcel of gems including emeralds, rubies and sapphires.'

'Mummy — you are making it up, you and your gems.'

Yes, I was making it up. The things in my catalogue sounded as if they were suitable for Bonfire Night. Angel's catalogue was wonderful. The collection of a lifetime was to be dispersed. The Sale is widely advertised in the Dealer's Journals and in the London dailies so I expect all the world and his wife will be there. Still we would go if possible and gaze our fill. One antique dealer's motto is, 'Never miss an opportunity of seeing anything beautiful.' The gardens at this house are famous, and they kept an army of gardeners before the war. It would be lovely to take a picnic and slack off for a day and who knows we might find some pods, berries or explosive seeds to jump in our handbags. After breakfast, at Angela's suggestion I decided to retreat to the attic with my diary and pretend I was out.

'Don't forget to tell about Jemima, Mummy.'

'Of course I won't, but not to-day.'

'What *are* you going to write about?'

'Bad buys.' I called back.

'Oh!' she replied, 'I tried to read that bit, I thought it was "bed bugs" Your *writing* Mummy!'

'It's as good as your spelling.' I called back and quickly closed the door.

But to return to bad buys,

'Do you still make bad buys?' I asked an experienced dealer the other day.

'I'll say I do, my dear. Still buy chairs with a leg missing. You know what it is, you arrive late at a sale, the stairs are solid with people and you can't see, or you are talking and bid for the wrong lot, or you get something really good and the heaviest lady there sits on it, and it's a "gonner" The thing to do with a "bad buy" is to job it off yourself or to stick it in a sale. The bit of money you get for it will soon start earning again.'

Some dealers in the trade belittle anything they want to buy until the vendor may feel he will be lucky to see his purchase price back. Farmer customers too are most awful rascals like this. If there is a price ticket on an article it rather cramps one's style, but if it is not priced one can add a bit, to have it knocked off and everyone is happy. I once tore off a ticket as I saw a customer like this approaching. He had previously beaten me down on an oak settle, and said he would call again soon as he wanted a pair of brass candlesticks. When we were arguing about the settle he said,

'You let me have it at my price and I will send all my friends to see you,' and I replied,

'If they are like you, I would be obliged if they would stay away.' He didn't seem to be the least offended and here he was again after the candlesticks. These were in the window and priced at 30/- the pair. Clutching the price ticket in my hand, I said,

'I am only going to ask you 50/- for the candlesticks as you are a farmer!' I let him beat me down to 45/-.

I felt a bit guilty another day when I asked £24 for a lovely little bombe Dutch chest-of-drawers. This customer had always haggled before, but this time he pulled out his cheque book and wrote his cheque without a murmur. It was rather awful as his wife is a special friend of mine but as the chest was still good value, I decided not to lose any sleep over it.

The other day I bought a fine wheelback armchair in yew wood. It had cabriole legs and a crinoline stretcher but it had been restored. I priced it at twelve guineas and stood it outside my shop-door saying to it,

'You will soon stop someone, my friend.' Sure enough within an hour a dealer acquaintance bounded in. He shed crocodile tears over it, and kept saying,

'Oh, if *only* it hadn't been restored! Oh, if *only* it hadn't been restored' and I replied,

'Don't buy it, I wouldn't like you to lose money over it,' and I showed him something else. But no, he kept bringing the conversation back to the chair and I really enjoyed myself heading him off. He departed a sadder but perhaps not a wiser man. I'm sure he didn't know if I was trying to be kind, or having fun at his expense. I sold it later in the day to a farmer's wife who was thrilled with it. She has an enormous gateleg table and is slowly building up a set of twelve wheelback arm chairs. I promised to remember her when I had another. My dining-room is furnished like this, but our wheelbacks are all cut down ones. This means that the legs have been shortened at some time. Stone floors were often damp and if one toe rotted a bit I suppose the easiest thing was to shorten all the legs. These cut-down chairs cost much less than the perfect ones which we describe as being 'up on their toes.' Although these chairs were originally kitchen chairs, they are now much sought after. The design in the back splat may be a pierced wheel, or a solid wheel which is called a draught back, or a fleur-de-lys, or a tulip or a shield, contained within the wheel.

Along one wall of our dining room is a rather lovely narrow elm settle. It is seven feet long and bowed, and made to stand against a wall. It has a very high back and open arms and only the polishing of generations has given it its lovely patina. When I was newly married I received a cheque for a guinea and a half for a pen and ink sketch. I went into town to spend it on a hat and a scarf, but somehow — don't ask me how — I found myself in an auction room and within minutes had bought this settle for 30/-. When I was paying the clerk, the auctioneer leant over from his rostrum and in a fatherly way said,

'Never mind, Missy, we all make mistakes sometimes.' He would be surprised to know that years later I refused £30 for it. When the children were little they both loved to race up and down it, it swayed slightly which added to the excitement and Angel often had to be rescued when she threaded her little legs through the arms and couldn't get back. This was very galling to her independent nature.

Our only picture is a framed sampler worked by my mother in 1879 when she was ten. This is in brightly coloured wools, a typical Victorian one. It has several lines of letters and numbers then her name, age and the date, an embroidered rose and lastly this little verse,

> Not mighty deeds make up the sum
>   Of happiness below,
> But little deeds of kindness
>   Which any child may show.
> Our Heavenly Father loves to see
>   These precious fruits of love,
> And if we truly serve Him here
>   We'll dwell with Him above.

❧ 55 ❧

If I had three wishes, I know what one of mine would be. I would love to have an immense picture book of the village and be able to turn the pages and see how it looked fifty years ago, one hundred years ago, two hundred years ago and right back a thousand years to show the stone-masons at work on our first church here.

I know what our cottage looked like twenty years ago because we lived here then. It had a green wooden gate but this has been changed for a rather lovely old wrought iron one. It took me six years to find it and it came from the Borders of Herefordshire. The little porch roof is new and is supported by two carved oak brackets. The thatchers have been twice in that time and we have planted a golden weeping willow in the middle of our lawn, which makes a play-house for children and a secret sewing place for me. The dove cote now fifteen years old has been re-thatched too, and the flight of the fantails keeps any borrowed baby happy in its pram for hours.

To return to Penny Priors : when old Miss Cunningham died, I had to pack her belongings in boxes and cases for her octogenarian relatives. It was then I discovered some old post-cards of Penny Priors, which I wished I could have kept. The inn looked just the same but adjoining it was a high brick wall, a garden wall doubtless, but this has now vanished to give way to a car park and a bus shelter. The little girls posing in the foreground wore sun bonnets and long white aprons with frilly shoulderpieces—about the year 1906 I should think. Also among those post-cards was a view of three little cottages. Forty years ago these were purchased by a London gentleman who made them into one dream house, a wing was thrown northward and linked to an old barn which was given a sprung floor and made into a ball-room or banqueting hall. Italian gardeners were employed and they devised a lovely garden alongside the river. What a transformation.

The picture of the church looks the same, but the great elms have gone. I wrote about them in another part of my diary and the three young owls we found inside one. The Church gate has been repaired, and there is a new wooden notice board with no capital letter for our dear Saint's name. The bells have been recast and rehung but of course they do not show. The spire, our lovely landmark, looks just the same, but we have had it repointed. We hardly dared look as the masons hung suspended from the top, kicking their way round in little swing seats. I used to drink my 'elevenses' in my garden, looking up at them, with the cup rattling in its saucer. 'Why look, Mummy, if you are frightened ?' 'Because it *is* so frightening, darling.'

There is a fresh line of graves by the newly planted beech hedge. All the old people, who were old when we came, have gone of course — old shepherds, farmers, agricultural workers, old grannies who lived their allotted span, retired merchants, a rector's wife, young lives cut short by the war and a poisoned child and a drowned child.

Let's turn another page.

A little watercolour of our cottage forty years ago shews it with an ivy-covered porch and a little cobbled path in front. We have had to replace the front door but we have had it copied exactly in English oak by the village carpenter, and he has reinserted its little window and remounted the old knocker and the old iron handle and lock. The key which I call my little latch key is five inches long and weighs a quarter of a pound. Writing of the little window reminds me that of all our cats, only one, dear Jet, a glorious black Persian (one of Mrs Muffit's many) used to spring up at the door, peep through the window and bang the knocker as she dropped back. She was quite a star turn at it. This door also reminds me of another picture which would make an illustration for my diary. I would call it 'a picture of a surprised customer.' On this particular day I must have shut three pigeons in the cottage and when the customer knocked and I opened the door, they departed in formation and at great speed, one over her head and one over each shoulder.

My Cheltenham Uncle, who had been reading in some old book about Penny Priors, asked me where the starch factory was. Why, it's the huge barn near the south wall but it houses tractors now and shelters young stock in bad weather. There are no longer four great shire horses in the Big Ground. It used to be yellow with cowslips every Spring, but they gave gone too. Could there be any connection?

The little mud hut down the road is still there. My children were told that Queen Victoria stopped there for a drink of milk, but my little mud hut and brick stable has been demolished and the road altered. Little children now in their thirties used to stand there and solemnly watch me milk the goat, and some-times I would fan a giant rhubarb leaf and the baby swallows, thinking the draught was from their parents' wings, would crane their little necks out from the nest above us.

Yes, I was sorry to lose my old stable. My enormous bargains went in there and sometimes there would be three gentlemen's Chippendale wardrobes at once, often bought for a maiden bid. Into it went my old four-posters, panelled settles, old staircases, and huge mirrors beloved of little gown shops.

A hundred years ago, according to Mrs Clements, there was an annual fair on the village green, at which there would be donkey rides and everything. The wheelwright would have a busy week putting on new rims and mending shafts. In the book that I have not got, would be pictures of the bowmen practising on the green by order of the King. That would be four hundred years ago. One of the arrows is supposed to be still embedded high up in the great wych elm. The green is a model of neatness now and is mown and velvety. The wheels have gone and the seasoning timber, the old ladders and the shafts that once were propped against the great elm. Some children knocked the other day and asked if they might play with Spot on Mr Bryan's lawn.

'Of course you can, Mr Bryan mows it but it belongs to all of us,' and I still think he would be a bit surprised if we carried out trestle tables, and had a good old-fashioned wedding feast and dance there, but we would only have to turn back those pages fifty years or so.

❧ 56 ☙

MR CLANCY and my dear John are not the only patient husbands in Penny Priors. On Monday, Mr Smedley-Corbett called and asked if I would be interested in buying his old Sheraton four-poster bed. The conversation went like this:—

'I can explain to you, dear Mrs Summers, you are married yourself, and you know how devoted I am to my dear wife, but I have ordered twin beds. It is like this — we are both confirmed tea-drinkers and now we are getting on, we seem to disturb each other. Annabella gets up at 2 a.m. to make tea and again at 4 a.m., and then I get up at 6 a.m. to make a brew for myself and she says that she has 'just got off nicely,' and I disturb her I fear.' The bed was a beautiful one, but my customer will have to modernise it. The straw palliasse is supported on wooden splats and the top mattress is a feather bed. Most of the eighteenth century mahogany beds had visible posts at the foot only, the head being a framework of stout wood on which brocade was stretched. Early American four-posters were literally four-posted ones. I once sold a set of posts (two very similar pairs) to the Birmingham Repertory Theatre. These were made up into a bed for the play 'Mourning becomes Electra.'

Some other furniture of mine also went on the stage. This time it was to the Royal Shakespeare Theatre at Stratford-upon-Avon. A scout arrived first with a sheaf of delightful sketches of Victorian furniture required for Chekhov's play 'The Cherry Orchard.' I had three chairs just like one of the sketches and some tables seemed suitable too. A week or so later the scout turned up again, but this time with a car-load of men-folk. He introduced the producer M. Michel St. Dennis & Abd' Farrar and others. They filled the shop so we stood outside on the footpath and left them on their own. They chose the chairs, two tables and some rush-seated country chairs for another production on the Continent, then off they went to another dealer who had some likely lamps and sofas.

Just recently Angela had had the thrill of seeing one of her little customers on Television with an old doll that she had dressed and sold in her shop. The little girl, seven year old Karen Dotrice is the child in Walt Disney's film Tomasina, one of Paul Gallico's beautiful stories. During the making of the film Karen became very attached to the doll and the little basket work perambulator she used in the film, but alas they were not buyable as they were lent by the Victoria & Albert Museum. By happy chance Mrs Dotrice came into Angela's shop and there was almost the beloved doll's twin sister.

Going back to the subject of husbands, there is another in Penny Priors who I had better not mention by name, so let's call him Mr Green. He has a cross to bear in the form of a worse half, but when he gets teased about her in the pub, he remarks that his shoulders are broad and that he wouldn't swop his little pepper-pot! When however she cannot incite him to strike her, she will depart to her mother's in a pet for a few days. Then he gets quite a few invitations to come in for a bite and various wives will pop on to his kitchen table a basin of tripe and onions, faggots or something else tasty. My speciality is an apple-pie properly made with cloves. When he returns the pie dish he remarks that 'it was a bit of alright.' I didn't tell him that John had courted me on the strength of my mother's apple-pies and my brothers had said that if ever John left me, I would only have to place one of my Mother's pies and a lighted candle in the window and he would come back. When the chastened Mrs Green returns she finds her spouse sleek and fit — and a few extra basins on the larder shelf I should imagine!

People quite often call and ask me if I will value something for them. It does take a bit of explaining, that nothing is really valuable as an antique unless it is rare, well-made and in fine condition; damaged porcelain is only worth shillings instead of pounds. Also people seem to think that if anything belonged to their Granny who died aged 93 ten years ago then the object must be 103 years old, when quite probably she bought it when she was sixty-five or shot it down at a Country Fair! I have even heard them say 'This was my mother's, she lived to seventy-seven and it was her mother's before that and she lived to 87.' They add both the ages together .

I had rather a strange experience about a valuation two years ago. This is a bit spookey but absolutely true. A roadman brought in what looked liked a silver half-crown only very light in weight. He said one of his mates had dug it up and could I tell him anything about it. I asked him to leave it and call back. I scrubbed it with a nail-brush and it shewed quite clearly a portrait of Sandow, the strong man, on one side, and an advertisement for cocoa on the other, while round the edge were the words 'Keep this and you may win £1000. I wrote out the particulars and told him the tokens were given in ¼lb. packets of cocoa at the beginning of the century. I also gave him a few particulars about Sandow and his almost super-human strength. He was convinced he would live to a hundred but died tragically after lifting his car out of a ditch singlehanded. I began to read my writing to the roadman and when I got to the part 'you may win £1000' he stepped back suddenly and exclaimed,

'But he has, Mam — on the Pools!'

'Good heavens!' I exclaimed and paused, 'Well, tell him I am going to keep his token for a few more days till after the Premium Bonds Draw on September 30th.'

Ernie did not turn up for me and I returned the token a week later. A few weeks later Angela said to me,

'Do you realise, Mummy, that Auntie died and left you her money when you had that token in your handbag?'

It was perfectly true. She died on October 5th at the mellow age of ninety.

⊰{ 57 }⊱

A FEW DAYS AFTER I knew I was to be a grandmother, I bought the most lovely miniature pine wardrobe standing about twenty inches high. It has moulded doors, little shaped shelves inside and stands on bracket feet. I am keeping it for the grandchildren — note the plural — to play with when they come visiting. Quite often I find some wee piece to pop inside — a tiny fan, miniature cups, saucers and jugs, little candlesticks, a pair of bellows carved in bone and an inch deep little hamper with Mrs Tittlemouse inside has been given me from Beatrice Potter's home in Cumberland. Last week in a drawer I found a red morocco leather book tooled in gold. It is the size of a postage stamp and inside are the words 'given to Dorothy Brown by Mary Brown, July 19th 1831.' It is entitled 'a Token for Children — being the account of the conversion and holy life of several young children' and it begins like this :— 'You have heard my dear lambs what other good children have done.' I shall have to read it one day with a magnifying glass. I have a feeling it will make me cry! Someone once said that modern children's books tell children how to live and old-fashioned ones tell children how to die.

I am also keeping a cow cream jug — I expect you have seen them? The cow's tail is looped to make a handle, the cow's open mouth is the spout and the milk is poured in on the centre of the back, the hole being covered by a little lid. I hope this will enchant the grandchildren as they come along but of course all the little folk, who come to tea, see or play with these old things. The cow still stands on my dresser but I have rather gone off her. A six year old who came to tea last Sunday remarked in a polite little voice,

152

'Don't you think, Mrs Summers, it rather looks as if the cow is being sick?'

Another piece I am hoarding is a lace-maker's chair. You might well think that this was a child's high chair. It is tall and straight and lightly but strongly made. The seat which is surprisingly high is an oval filled in with cane work. The lace-maker would perch on this and have a sloping lap to support her pillow, which was like an oblong horse-hair pin-cushion and on to it she pinned her lace, and from it hung her bunches of coloured bobbins. These bobbins, the size of pencils, might be of bone, ivory or wood and wired on to them were coloured glass beads to simplify the pattern. I once sold one of these chairs as a lace-maker's chair when it was really a Regency music chair. This had a square seat and a lyre back, which should have given me the clue but otherwise it was identical to my lace-maker's chair, and both had been used by children, as the turning on the top front stretchers had been worn flat by little feet.

We still find these chairs in Warwickshire, though alas scores have been exported. I said to one young dealer who asked me for one, 'You let *me* buy them from *you* for English parents, they simply love them.' The chairs are now much rarer than spinning-wheels and spinning-chairs. I have had numbers of wheels through the years, the loveliest have been made of yew tree, fruit wood and walnut. All these three woods attain a satinlike texture with the years. The yew wood ones are particularly beautiful as the figure in them resembles a bird's eye and the wood may become rosy in colour. One day a lady called and enquired for one to use. As my shop was very overcrowded, she lifted one I had off the top of a chest-of-drawers, and carried it outside on to the footpath, while I followed behind with a three-legged stool. I wished that I had had a film in my camera and a tape-recorder. The lady was plump, middle-aged and very pretty with curling white hair. In fact, she was a picture. She settled down at the wheel and talked and crooned to it until she had it running sweetly, and then softly under her breath she sang the old spinning song.

Another picture, which I would like to have had, included myself and was also on the footpath in front of the shop. A local couple riding by on horseback, pulled up and enquired if I had any wall tapestries for sale. I was lucky enough to have one about seven feet square. I carried it outside, and tried to hold it up. The gentleman gallantly dismounted to assist me after giving his reins to the lady. When we had it fully extended a great puff of wind billowed it out like a sail and the great hunters took fright and reared above our heads. It was frightening and funny too!

Another scene I remember perfectly although I saw it quite fifteen years ago included a little girl, who is now married, but the memory is as clear as yesterday. I was the guest of a collector of rare and beautiful things, many of which he had arranged like a museum in his great timbered attics. As we descended the stairs, he tapped on a bedroom door, saying,

'I have a little friend staying with me.' The door opened and there in a great draped four-poster bed, a little girl with long flaxen hair was sitting up, with a folded shawl over her shouders. Her mother, a young war widow, sat close against the bed reading the beloved bedtime story, the soft light of a candle illuminated their gentle faces — they might have been a painting by Gherardo delle Notti!

All dealers have memories like these, of something choice, something complete, or a word we use in a different way from other people — the word 'right.'

❧ 58 ❧

There is a funny story going around about a Mr Brown and a Mr Blenkinsopp, partners in an antique business.

One day a customer entered their shop, saying,

'Good morning, Mr Brown. To-day I have something to sell you. Something rare and wonderful. From his pocket he produced a little twig, and went on to say 'This is a little bit of the Tree of Life. Would you be interested in buying it?'

'That is certainly very unusual,' replied Mr Brown, 'but I

don't know what to say. Let me call my partner.' He shouts upstairs 'Mr Blenkinsopp! Mr Blenkinsopp!'

Mr Blenkinsopp appears and the customer tells his tale again.

'Yes, it is a genuine bit all right,' says Mr Blenkinsopp, 'but we already have several twigs of it, rather larger than yours, in the warehouse, so I am afraid we are not in the market for any more at the moment.'

A day later the customer appeared again, with a bit of the Ark this time. Again Mr Brown could not make up his mind, so whistled up Partner Blenkinsopp.

'Yes,' said Mr Blenkinsopp, 'and a very nice fragment of it too, a good specimen. We do not want it, as we have numerous pieces of the Ark, but keep it safely, it will appreciate.'

The following day, the customer reappeared and glancing quickly around the shop, to make sure that Mr Brown was alone, he slapped on the counter a little circle of old leather.

'That' he said emphatically, 'is one of Julius Caesar's shoes, and before you call that fool Blenkinsopp, there is the pair to it!'

☙ 59 ❧

LAST SUNDAY John and I gazed upon our first grandchild. Gordon brought all his girl friends home from when he was eighteen and ten years later married the dearest one of all — Joan. We could not be more pleased, and her family think the world of him. This babe is the first grandchild on both sides of the family, so there are great rejoicings.

No wonder they did not hear us turn down their lane or park the car beneath the tall beeches for the wind tore through the great branches and the sodden leaves swirled about us. We had to pass their sitting-room window to reach their door, but of course we couldn't pass. We gazed in. All was warmth and light, Gordon dark and protective in the background, Joan slimly curled in a corner of the settee, the little white 'sausage' in the crook of her arm. They must have felt us there for they turned with lovely welcoming smiles, and we saw the dear little face with its pointed chin, eyes shut and little pink mouth tightly closed.

Lots of people say that swallows bring happiness with them. They came to us the year that Gordon and Joan became engaged and Angela met her future husband. When John and I came back from a long week-end we found that Gordon had left us a little note on the dresser shelves. It read,

'Look out! Swallows building in the outside lav!' The cup-like mud nest was complete and there was one egg already. Soon there were four and the birds began to sit. All were safely hatched and the parents began their tireless job of feeding. They sped in above the closed door, clung for a few seconds to the edge of their nest, stuffed the hungry beaks and were away. If anyone was 'in residence' they were away like lightning, but we found that if we half opened the door and stood in its shadow, we had the most wonderful view of the flying buffet, as the nest was only six feet away from the floor and an arm's length from us.

On our way back from Gordon's, I pointed out to John William Shakespeare's antique shop in Tewkesbury, I have bought from him several times and he has promised to take me round to his store next time, if I 'phone him first. I laughingly said to him that I was going to stick a label on everything I had from him saying,

'This once belonged to William Shakespeare.' But since everything I have bought from him was made of mahogany I doubt if anyone would have swallowed it. In Shakespeare's time all the furniture was made from English woods, mostly oak, elm and the fruit woods — cherry, apple and pear. Then followed what is known as the walnut period, in Queen Anne's reign at the beginning of the 18th Century, much of the walnut coming from France; then, half-way through the 18th century, mahogany and other foreign woods began to be imported in great quantities. This was the great century of the famous cabinet-makers and designers — Chippendale, father and son, Hepplewhite, Sheraton, Adam and many others.

A few days after Joan had written to us to say a babe was on the way, I overheard this conversation on the bus; the mother and child were sitting immediately behind me, so I could not see them. The child began,

'Mummy, Mummy, do leave me with Granny.'

'We'll see. Perhaps she won't want you.'

'She *always* wants me, Mummy.'

'She wouldn't be able to take you walks, you know.'

'I know, Mummy, it doesn't matter.'

'And you wouldn't have the boys to play with.'

'I know, you are going to leave me, aren't you?'

'And Granny can't play games with you, remember?'

'I know, that doesn't matter. *We just like to talk.*'

I could just see that grandmother and little girl together, for it was a little girl about five years old. I had a good look when they got off at Penny Marston. Now that is the sort of Grandmother I want to be. Only I *do* hope I am not going to be housebound. I should love to take my grandchildren to the woods to look for primroses and to drop twigs in the river above the waterfall and to gather basketsful of fir cones and walnuts, just as I did with their parents. I will tell them how we used to sing the Teddy Bear's Picnic there and sometimes sit absolutely still and quiet, to watch the squirrels play.

Lots of children seem to have an almost passionate desire to know about 'grownups' antics.

Years ago when I was bathing my two, I just happened to mention in passing, that Uncle Joe once had an Uncle who was so heavy that he had to be got out of his bath with a rope from a pulley in the ceiling. That did it! They wanted me to make a serial of it. As soon as prayers were over and they were safely tucked up and last kisses given one or other would shout out as I tried to slip away.,

'*Now* tell us about Uncle Joe's Uncle.' I then had to mime the little Aunt's frantic struggles with the rope and the pulley, the slipping mat, the more slippery soap and the constant failures, the loud splashes and the despairing cries from the overweight gentleman. To tell you the truth we never did get him out, but I'm game to have another go at it, if this little granddaughter is interested in the subject in a few years' time and providing of course I've got enough puff left!

⫷ 60 ⫸

SOME DEALERS are investing in rather wonderful cameras, which cost about sixty pounds each. A finished glossy print can be taken from the camera a minute or so after making the exposure. They can be invaluable, they say. A gentleman calls who wishes to buy a bureau for his wife, or a director who is looking for a board-room table. Five minutes later, he can be on his way with a photograph in his wallet to show to the interested party. Or a dealer, who has promised to let a client know when he has a certain piece, can enclose a photograph with his letter. So far I have only run to doing little sketches, but even these can save a multitude of words. During the war when films were unobtainable I remember a dealer asking me to do a sketch of a chandelier for him to post to a woman client, who did not want to use up her petrol ration just to come to see it. I did a rough sketch in his showroom, (the chandelier was like a glorious inverted cascade) and when I got home I did a better one in pen and ink and put in the 'sparkles'! Next time I saw him he said he had made the sale, but he added that his customer said the sketch flattered it. I had a feeling that he said this to keep me sweet for another day.

I almost invariably put in little sketches with my letters. It helps, if they cannot read my writing, and it is a fact that lots of people have no notion what one means by an apron, a stretcher, a pot-board, a dentil cornice or a blind fret. It sounds like swearing perhaps.

My whole pattern of buying has changed since Angela has had her shop, and we now share a little van. I used to spend a whole day at a country sale, or a whole day in some town, calling on the dealers, the second-hand shops (furniture brokers to give them their name in the classified directory), demolition contractors, and sometimes builders' yards too for good measure! Now we more often than not view a sale and decide not to stay, perhaps just leaving a price on a couple of pieces, and then do a run of sixty or a hundred miles, calling on dealers from whom we know we can buy. We load up the little van and its roof rack and I get my local carrier to collect the larger pieces the following Saturday, or leave it a couple of weeks if there is not enough for a load.

More often than not we do not stop for a proper meal but picnic on a hillside on fruit and crispbread and salady things. The Cairn chases around, agog with joy at all the fresh scents and smells. By three-thirty we are usually on our way home and beginning to flag. We pull in somewhere for a cup of tea *with* sugar and a cup of coffee *without*.

Yesterday, Angela and I drove through the Vale of Evesham calling on various dealers. The plum and pear blossom is starry white and the apple buds softy pink. In every orchard the ewes and lambs complete the picture. Gillies and forget-me-nots gaily fill the cottage gardens and the grassy churchyards are bejewelled with primroses and wood anemones.

When we reached home, a round ball of cowslips awaited us on the doorstep — from my Godson, I expect. Bless his heart!

Our arrival home is timed like a small military operation, for the meal is to be ready at seven!

Angela backs the van down the Green.

Mrs S. runs down the Green with Cairn and unlocks front door.

Into kitchen, switches on kettle, hot-plates and grill.

A match to the laid fire in the sitting-room.

The switch down on floor-heater in the dining-room.

Removes coat, washes hands.

Season lamb chops and under grill.

Prepared potatoes on to a hot-plate.

Water boiled ready for cauliflower.

In with the salt and the mint.

Angela has unpacked the interior of the van.

Together we lift the Georgian commode, Bentwood rocker and Delft rack off the roof of the van.

The Cairn circles us at speed.

Mrs S. turns the chops.

Angela garages the van.

Mrs S. upstairs to wash again and mend her face.

Lovely smells from kitchen.
Angela's turn upstairs. She is expecting her Love.
Sounds of men's footsteps.
'Have you had a happy day, dears?'
Dears have!

⋘ 61 ⋙

How LUCKY I AM! As I lie in my bath I can see the top of the
great pear tree, which is in full bloom now against the blue sky.
The fruit is good for neither man nor beast, although Angela
would nibble it at a very tender age, but she would sample
anything — mustard, green gooseberries and even morella
cherries!

We have few pictures on our walls. For one reason the
beamed ceilings are very low and, for a better reason, the view
from each window is a picture in itself. We have lately made
another window, a modest one through a thick stone wall at a
cost of £30, but the view is worth £100 to us. It looks across
Mrs Clancey's damson orchard, bridal white before all the
other fruit trees, and royally purple with fruit after all the
others.

'I love your climate!' exclaimed an overseas visitor the other
day.

'And so do I' I seconded her, 'ever changing, ever beautiful.'
Only yesterday I was coming down the orchard and saw the
whole village in a new light, the reflection of a dramatic sunset
gave it a backcloth of lilac and rose. One early morning I shall
never forget. The children and I had been mushrooming below
the Fox Cover and, as we turned for home, a silvery mist began
to rise from the Great Meadow and above it, as if suspended in
the sky, floated our lovely Church, the spire catching the first
rays of sunshine.

Even weather forecasts are as vague as racing tips. A
promised sunny day may be enlivened with a thunderstorm, a

160

cloud burst, or a hail-storm. This lady and I like variety and we get it in full measure, and the suddenness of the spring with all its freshness and beauty still surprises this ol' body.

I keep my ex-pair of reading specs permanently wedged between the edge of the bath and the wall, and dash off a bit of my journal when I feel like it. I have to give them a polish on the curtains when they get steamy, the sponge rack makes a book support and I suppose that if I had one of those tropical fish heater filter arrangements, I could keep at just the right temperature for hours.

It is my closing day to-day. I have sold very little for ten days although lots of people have been in to enquire for things I have not got. I have looked down the 'Wanted' column in the local paper. There are inquiries for feather beds, broody hens, homes for unwanted kittens and a lonely farmer is looking for a lady-love. Sorry I have none of these in stock at the moment. I must get off a few bills, and liven up a few slow-payers. My customers are wonderfully good on the whole, but a surprising number of people go looking for furniture without their cheque books or any cash! I have been warned about several 'beauties' in the neighbourhood and every single one of them have tried it on.

At a sale last week a little group of us were discussing debt-collecting about which everyone had his own ideas. A healthy-looking fellow in a flat cloth cap remarked,

'I don't beat about the bush. I bangs on the knocker and when the door opens, I sez "Morning, I've cum for me money!"'

'I always send the wife,' said another dealer, 'I pay her 15% and she enjoys it. Last time she had a sherry at most of the houses. I deal with the nobs, you know!'

My method of enclosing a stamped addressed envelope seems rather mild I know, but I work on the assumption that my client is too lazy to open her bureau. When goaded, on rare occasions I have sent a letter saying, 'On Friday at eight a.m. my carrier will collect the gateleg table I lent you nearly a year ago. I trust this is convenient. Yours faithfully, etc.' The cheque always arrives before zero hour!

Years ago an important and successful dealer gave me three pieces of advice, 'Never' he said, 'say that trade is quiet — it snowballs. Everyone is quiet sometimes and it is a chance to do some of the hundred-and-one jobs that need doing, to increase the value of one's stock.

'Never' he said 'stop buying; just get "choosey" when money is in short supply;' and thirdly he said, 'Go after trade, we do, don't wait for it to come to you.'

Pondering over this last bit I wrote one January when trade was dead, to an important dealer who specialises in the finest oak pieces, saying I had an Elizabethan four-poster, part of another one and an early oak pew. As I posted the letter, I thought, 'Well, I have only wasted a 3d stamp.' But next day I had a telegram, followed by a letter next day, followed by two dealers, complete with spouses the following day. They bought the oak pieces and all my best mahogany pieces and a very fine credence table costing £100 from the dealer friend who had given me such good advice.

On Saturday, an American Air Force Colonel who is stationed near, asked me if I would be on the look out for any Christmas plates, as his mother collected them. I admitted I had never heard of Christmas plates. He explained that in Holland, each year a prize was offered for the finest design for a blue and white plate, and that only a limited quantity were made. They were sold for charity and the pattern destroyed. Each plate bore the Dutch word JULIE, for Christmas, followed by the date; as for example, JULIE 1910. His mother, he said, had bought one from a little half-pint woman dealer in the States. When she had inquired the price, the little lady first exclaimed, 'It has hung there for seven years and you are the first to ask the price!' Incidentally, it was seven dollars.

We say in the trade that we learn something every day. I was very surprised years ago to learn that 'antimacassar' meant 'to protect from macassar oil.' Well this bit about Julie plates was the first thing I learnt on Saturday. When I picked up the Daily Telegraph, I saw the words 'Osprey Suite makes £9,500 in London Saleroom.' On reading further I found that it was a gilded French Suite, called that, because the cushions were stuffed with osprey feathers.

⊰⊱ 62 ⊰⊱

It's may again! The sun is shining. The hawthorn hedges are crested with bridal wreaths, while child attendants of pink campion, bluebells and buttercups follow in their train.

We have been on a buying spree. Angela has pulled the van on to the wide grass verge beside the Roman Road and we have just finished our picnic luncheon. Through a break in the hedge, I can see three mares with their new-born foals. The Cairn is lying near me, her dark muzzle resting on my shoe, but she is not asleep, one brown eye is watching a bee among the flowers. She is happy and I am content. I hope Angela is having sweet dreams, for she has nodded off. Next month is her bridal month. Her home is ready and her gown and veil, chosen in January, await her adornment in June.

How quickly the years slip by — the babe a child, the child a girl, the girl a woman, all in so short a space, yet old age lasts so long a time. Three of my Aunts have lately died; they were all in their nineties and were old when she was given to us.

We are both closing our shops for a fortnight before the wedding, and I sometimes mind hers for a day, when I can. She gets more collectors than I do, as she buys jewellery and countless small things rather than furniture. I suppose there must be collectors for everything under the sun, from fans to furbelows!

American holiday-makers invariably ask for cranberry glass, Mary Gregory pieces and Wedgwood. Some ladies collect tea-pots, little boxes, miniature furniture, needlework samplers, wee shoes of glass or porcelain, chatelaines and little china cottages and castles. Others ask for old card cases, which can be works of art in silver, tortoiseshell, or mother-of-pearl. Boys always ask for coins, stamps, or anything warlike, like swords, Zulu shields and spears. She occasionally has had archers' bows and arrows that she has found in some old attic. Young girls ask for Victorian jet earrings, and how beautiful they look against a youthful neck. Long silver chains are also favourites with the younger set, especially if complete with a little watch or fob. Old bead bags and old lace may hang fire for weeks, then a collector comes along and joyfully buys the lot.

Angela's trade customers quickly snap up all her more beautiful table lamps and the hanging ones, while the occasional student's lamp sells itself. Dealers' hands go out to bits of Spode and Rockingham and Old Chinese porcelain as if drawn by magnets.

Just as in my own shop, the best pieces sell most readily, miniatures on ivory for instance, the occasional silver vinaigrette, sets of enamelled waistcoat buttons and old piqué and cameo brooches.

63

SOME FAVOURITE Bristol customers called yesterday. They always call each June on the way to the Chelsea Flower Show, and always give me a little list of things they want to find.

'Good morning! How lovely to see you again,' I greeted them. 'And how is your Aunt? I hardly dare ask; is she still alive?'

'Yes, very much alive thank you, and she sent her kind regards, but I'm afraid we are all sadly out of favour at the moment.'

'Oh dear, I am sorry, what is the trouble?'

'Well, since her hundredth birthday, we have insisted that she should not go out alone and she strongly objects, as you can imagine! But with all the rebuilding and broken paths it really is not safe in Bristol.'

'Does she still play the piano?'

'Oh yes, every day. We call it her hymn of praise!'

'Well be sure to give her my warmest regards.'

'Indeed we will. We hope to bring her next year, but she

has a friend visiting for a few days, so could not come this time.'

They had hardly gone when old Mr Thorn propped his bike gainst the front wall and called 'Good morning!' He disappeared into Mrs Clements, cottage with a posy of columbines. He often cycles over with flowers and Mrs Clements is his last call. He leaves posies with two other widows on the way and reads them his latest poem. He jokingly says,

'I don't know if I does it to stop the gossip, or to keep them guessing! But anyway there's safety in numbers they say!'

When I had finished dusting the shop, I joined them for a cuppa. I knew the cosy would be on the tea-pot. Whereas my Bristol customers had been having 'Aunt trouble,' old Mr. Thorn had been having 'Niece trouble'.

'Yes, I've gone and done it proper this time,' he explained, 'I've told her I sha'n't be able to cycle over another Christmas, the eight miles there is alright, it's the eight miles back that gets me down, in the dark you know, when I'm full of roast goose, plum puddin' and dandelion wine and all. It's too much!'

'Surely she *must* understand Mr Thorn!'

'But that's just what I'm a-telling you ma'm—her *don't*! Her says if I can follow the hounds across county, then I can get myself along a good metalled road.'

'You love to follow the hounds, don't you Mr Thorn?' I said trying to get him off on another scent.

'That I do,' he replied with feeling, 'but I'm failing! I'm failing! Its the running over the ploughed fields carrying me bike that knocks the wind out of me, and I haven't been in at the death since I was eighty-three!'

While on the subject of old biddies, we seem to have a fair assortment in our own family and some of their remarks have become family classics, as for instance, 'How is your Father? I never liked him,' and another by a great aunt who, discovering some loathed coconut in a home-made biscuit, remarked 'Little did I know what I had let myself in for!' This same lady out-shone all her previous efforts when I took her the photographic album of Angela's wedding. I felt it would give us something to talk about.

'That's cousin Bessie, you remember her don't you?' I asked.

'Is it? How little she looks. She must have shrunk! Who's that?'

'That's Jonathan.'

'It doesn't look like Jonathan, and who is that?'

'That's Mary Gregory.'

'Wouldn't have known her, how fat she's got! That can't be Philip? or is it?'

'Yes, that's Philip.'

'Good heavens! He looks quite middle-aged.'

'Well Aunt, he is, we are all in our fifties now.'

'And who are those two? Their skirts are very short.'

'Those are cousins of David's.'

'Do I know *her*?'

'No, that's David's sister.'

'What a lot of strangers! What did you want to ask them for?'

'Is that you?'

'Yes,' I confessed.

'I never liked big hats. They shade the face; and is that your Uncle Ralph?'

'Yes, he's eighty-five now. Wasn't he a sport to come?'

'Pity he has lost his hair. He was quite handsome when I was a gel.'

'You haven't said anything about the bridegroom Aunt?'

'Well, I must admit he looks strong and healthy and Angela was clever to find someone taller than herself!' Should I say she was only five feet six? No, I decided to save my puff and say,

'We were sorry you did not come Aunt.'

'Well,' she said with a sigh, 'to tell you the truth Anne, I prefer funerals to weddings.'

I gently wrapped the white album in its tissue and packed it into its white box. It *had* given us something to talk about.

I have been reading the last few pages of my diary and I cannot think why I sound so cheerful. I have been feeling thoroughly frustrated as I have got an overdraft. I dare not go out buying until a cheque for £280 comes in. It has been owing for six weeks. Yesterday I discovered the Bank manager in my shop and nearly swooned. He said he wanted me to find him a mahogany bureau. I wonder what he thinks I can use for money — cowrie shells perhaps.

My next customer was a local farmer. He had come to collect a fire-basket. I told him of my encounter and he said,

'You don't want to worry yourself about him. He's new. That's his only trouble. Old Jake Hirons caught him peeping over his hedge counting his cows last week.'

After he had gone, I felt better. I felt heaps better. I took some pennies and hied off to the telephone-box. I rang up the offender and asked, politely, if my cheque would soon be along as I was only in a small way of business.

'Oh my dear Mrs Summers, haven't you had it? How naughty of William. It shall be in the post to-day without fail! Do forgive us.'

I could see by the smiling face looking back at me from the mirror that they were forgiven, and sure enough, there it was in the shop letter-box this morning. It was keeping company with a catalogue of a lovely sale where I expect, and hope, to spend the lot!

⊰{ 64 }⊱

JOHN HAS ACCEPTED an offer from a builder for the little field adjoining the orchard. I hope the children who live there in years to come will love to watch the sunset as much as our two did. There is nothing man-made to spoil the distant view of gentle hills and pollarded willows in the foreground fringe a stream that reflects the glories of the evening sky.

John says he is not going to put this money into the family business, but buy a cottage with it within sight or sound of the sea. I thought this was coming one day, as for years we have been renting little places for holidays, cottages on quays and old coast guard houses in Cornwall. Now that the children are married we can get away quite often and it will be for cottage-hunting! It will have to be big enough for all the family and we shall have to add bunks or hammocks as the grandchildren come along.

One of the best ghost stories I ever heard, and a true one, was about a lady who was house-hunting. The story was told to me by a young friend, who is the friend and contemporary of the lady's daughters. When their mother was widowed, she announced that she was going to sell up and buy a house in the north of England. She promptly got her name on several house agents' lists, and almost every post brought particulars of some desirable residence. She was unable to drive herself and was always getting her daughters to drive her up north on some wild goose chase. Quite often she wouldn't even look over the house. 'No' she would say firmly 'it's not my house, I shall know it when I see it.' The daughters would try to reason with her, but no, she was adamant. She *knew*.

Well, one day after many fruitless trips north, they set out yet once again. They slept a night on the journey and at noon the next day they turned into the leafy drive of the advertised property. The daughters could hardly believe it when they heard their mother exclaim,

'This is it. It's been waiting for me!'

They drew up at the welcoming porch and a young maid answered the door, but had nothing to say and left them standing there. A few minutes later an elderly gentleman appeared, looked at them closely and invited them in. He asked them to be seated and the maid reappeared with glasses of sherry. A few minutes later he offered to show them round the house. The mother kept taking the words out of his mouth and exclaiming,

'Yes, I know! This will be the music room and here is the little window I love. Here's the funny little back staircase. Isn't it all delightful!'

They made their way upstairs, their mother leading now and exclaiming happily as she opened each door. 'This is *my* bed-room' she said finally and walking across the sunlit room she went over to the stone mullioned windows and looked down into the rose garden.

'Yes,' she said again 'it's all just like I knew it would be. Oh, I am so happy!'

The quiet little party made its way downstairs and they resumed their seats.

The gentleman said,

'Well Madam, I will put all my cards on the table. I like this house and would like to stay here, but I cannot keep any domestics as the place is haunted. But I do not feel that you need worry. The ghost is *you*! We have seen you many many times about the house and gardens.'

Well, the house is now hers. She has been there for four years and that serenely happy woman you can see below in the rose-garden is not a ghost any longer, but my friend's friend's Mother.

When I told Angela the story she said,

'I wonder, Mummy, if you are haunting your old Priory?'

This is a glorious old place which has stood empty for seven years. John and I discovered it too soon. We saw it first when we were travelling down to the coast, when it stood bathed in the early morning sunshine and looked like a miniature Mandalay. The fourteenth century windows came down to garden level and the upper windows each had a little iron balcony of the Romeo and Juliet variety. John pulled in the car and we crossed the little trout stream and peeped in each window. The old glass-house had collapsed and the vines had died; as we stood at the back entrance we were overshadowed by an ivy-covered ruin and from beneath our feet came the sound of a rushing underground stream. John thought it all rather spooky, but woman-like I saw it as it had been and could be.

When we got home again we wrote for particulars. If we had sold up we could have scraped up the money I guess, but what about John's business, the children's lives and family ties? We had found it years too soon!

Three years later it still stood empty and one day when John went off on a sea trip, Angela and I got up at six o'clock and caught an early bus to the Annual Goose Fair. The driver set us down in the village adjoining the old Priory. We had a tray of coffee at the Inn and found out all we could about it, and then got the keys and spent two wonderful hours exploring it. There were eighteen rooms and one of them was a small private chapel approached by a circular staircase up a little tower. Angela kept exclaiming 'Oh Mummy, Oh Mummy!' and loved it as much as I did.

Ever since that day, when I have bought an early piece or anything particularly beautiful, like a Spanish screen, or a credence table, or a great refectory table with benches, I have thought how lovely it would look there and Angel has read my thoughts and said,

'Just perfect for your old Priory Mummy.'

In my dressing-table drawer lies a sketch of it that I did from memory and occasionally when I have had a wakeful night, the place has been my 'escape-hatch.' I have effortlessly hung my lovely curtains, spread the Persian rugs, filled the great inglenooks with sawn logs, set the furniture in place and carried in armsful of flowers from the old garden.

Since the children have married and Angela settled near I have not wanted to go so far, but when this money from my Aunt came along I thought I would *just* write and see if it was still on the market. The reply came back by return of post 'we regret to say that the old Priory was sold only last month.' I can't pretend I did not suffer a pang or two, but all of me is here again now and John and I are looking for a cottage on the coast.

❦ *65* ❦

IT WAS STARTING TO SNOW when we got the little van out on Friday and set off to a sale on the hills. The furniture, pictures and everything, had been carried out of the house and arranged in a great marquee in the garden. Fifty or so chairs were set out in rows in the centre. We were early, so put our baskets on two chairs in the front row, then each with our own catalogue began to view. Angela marks the lots she wants and puts a dot by those she thinks I will want and I vice versa. We then compare notes and discuss prices. We always try to view systematically starting at Lot 1, but it is easier said than done and it's so easy to miss a lot, especially if one starts talking to friends. Although the first lots are often only old garden tools and salting leads in the stables and sheds, among them *may* be something delightful, perhaps a box of wooden decoys, duck and drakes, or pigeons painted most realistically, or a collection of three legged milking stools. a gun-rack perhaps, a stove trough, and occasionally garden figures.

Very few people turned up at this sale, which was rather surprising. The worse the weather is, the more bargains are expected and the world and his wife usually turn up. We sat down and compared catalogues. Almost instantly the cold seemed to seize us and I wondered how long we could bear it. Angela fetched an old velvet curtain and some packing rugs from the van; we wound ourselves into a sort of Siamese cocoon and topped it with a prehistoric plaid round our shoulders. We wriggled our toes in our sheepskin boots, we turned our cuffs over our hands and threaded our fingers up the opposite sleeves. Waves of intense cold descended from the tent roof and through a slit in the awnings, we could see that it was snowing steadily.

We forgot our troubles when the bidding started and bought lots of small pictures, a quantity of Sheffield plate, some beautiful table cutlery, several lots of china and glass, two gilt overmantels, a dumb waiter and a Bible box, and all quite reasonably. After two hours the thought of home was sweet. We were almost too stiff to move but managed to stagger across to the nearby refreshment van and thaw out our fingers on the mugs of boiling coffee. We settled up and were soon away with thoughts of the fire left ready laid and the welcoming cottage. The van heater soon had us properly thawed out, but we really felt we had earned our bargains. A pair of Angel's little oval 'prints' turned out to be signed pastels dated 1775 and she sold them right away.

This is late November, so for a change of temperature I have turned back only sixteen weeks, to a hot July day, and found the page where we called on a Lowbridge dealer. He had sent word that we might find some saleable things among the stock of an old ironmonger cum storekeeper, whom he had bought up. Everything pre Great War! We took our poultry coats and put them on over our summer dresses prepared for a good rummage. Everything had been put into an old-fashioned caravan and we were left on our own. The first thing we did was to put outside an old galvanised bath and into it went all our little finds, — wooden butter moulds, butter hands, three legged iron pots, brass door knobs and handles, gold powder, candle sconces and lots of little pairs of silk openwork gloves marked 2¾d a pair. We left behind boxes of 'plated' stockings; Angel had never seen any before. We could hardly move at all for the old boxes. When Angel breathed out, I breathed in! The heat from the corrugated roof was almost unbearable and before long we looked like a pair of red-faced Gretchen dolls. When the bath was full we decided to call it a day and come again.

Another place we have to visit for a third time is a large storeroom behind a big modern furnishing store only ten miles away. The proprietress's father, long since dead, must have used it as a warehouse, for across the vast room run long racks once holding oil lamps, glass chimneys, china tureens, great meat dishes and so on. We bought up what was left and now only have to hunt through shelves and shelves of dusty old books. There are collectors for everything or nearly everything — certainly for old-fashioned children's books and early novels. I did not know until recently that novels have only been written during the last hundred years or so. Books especially in demand are those with coloured plates of birds, flowers and fashions. They just sell themselves.

The most profitable books I ever had were from an old gentleman's sale nearby. The 'Lot' consisted of five magnificent atlases. I was short of cash at the time and decided I must not pay more than £5 for them. The auctioneer, however, started the bidding at 2/- and they were knocked down to me at 4/-, which is what we call a maiden bid. I wrote up to the Bodleian Library at Oxford about them and they offered me £3 for one and said the Provost of Oriel College would like another for £5 and the remaining three I sold for £3 to a holiday-maker.

All these old prints and maps are coloured in by hand and usually most beautifully done. It is hard to tell without a magnifying glass whether they are printed or hand coloured, but if done by printing press the colours show up as myriads of dots.

When I go out on a buying spree, or to a sale, there are other things I have to take besides the magnifying glass, but first a word about my handbag. I always have one with a handle or rather two handles. After a sale one needs both hands for packing and loading and if there is only one handle the bag may hang open when the clip gets tired. I take of course, all the cash

I have in hand, my cheque book and pen, chalk to mark any lots I may have to leave for the carrier to collect, a tape measure and small flashlight, some trade cards, a stamped addressed envelope to myself to give to anyone who says they may be selling some things. Also into my bag, of course, go my comb and make-up, silver for tips, and a penny for myself.

⚜ 66 ⚜

THIS MORNING it began to snow, or rather, sleet. By eleven thirty I was sinking with hunger and to be honest, greed. So thinking no customers would forsake their warm cars for my chilly emporium, I switched on the grill and got out the frying-pan. All was ready, when the first customer arrived! By the time he and two others had left, an hour and a half later I returned to the oven. Yes, I had switched it to 'low' and removed my plate. The three sausages had been transformed into little dead fingers, the rashers into brown sticky tape, and the little black 'full-stops' dotted here and there had been mushrooms. However, my hunger has passed, so I have settled for coffee and two digestive biscuits; and here I am by a glorious fire, with my diary in front of me.

I am getting more and more interested in books, and so is Angela. An old dealer said to her, 'Never sell a book Missy, till you have given it a good shake. All sorts of things fall out of them!' He certainly could be right for it is a fact that seventy-one one thousand pound notes are unaccounted for. I have heard of Victorian Valentines falling out of them, as well as interesting letters and embroidered book-markers. Librarians report finding more curious things, strips of bacon rind, and even back-bones of kippers, also book-markers one assumes! Only this week, I found in one book a Christmas Card printed in Jerusalem, with a shiny photograph of a local scene on the front, but inside a beautiful little dried flower-arrangement of 'The Flowers of Palestine;' I can recognise the greenery as tiny

173

sprigs of mimosa foliage (wattle to our Australian cousins), and a little blue flower that looks like monkshood.

I have been lent P. H. Muir's little book on 'Book Collecting as a Hobby'; a book suggested by a Jew, written by a Scot and published by an Irishman. It is packed with information. I find there is a name for each part of a book, just as there is for a chair. What I called 'the back', is really 'the spine'; the two blank pages at the front and back of a book are called 'end papers.' I have often been puzzled by fine old books I have bought, with plain thick cardboard covers. I now know that these were made for well-to-do customers who wished to have the books bound themselves to match the others in their private libraries.

I feel I can recognise a First Edition now. In simple language it is the first impression of the first edition. In his book Mr Muir writes that in ninety per cent of books, there is proof that they are NOT first editions when they are printed later. I thought I had a number of first editions of Beatrix Potter's little books. Now I know that I have. I bought a batch of them at a country house sale in Gloucestershire. Five of them are first editions, but alas four of these five are in 'nursery condition,' and the others are just early editions. The title page of a first edition is like this :—

The Tale of

Mr. Jeremy Fisher

By

Beatrix Potter

Author of

'The Tale of Peter Rabbit' etc

London

Frederick Warne and Co.

and New York

1906

(all rights reserved)

Later editions do not bear the date. Miss Potter wrote and illustrated one of her lovely little books each year. You will remember that the end papers in these books are illustrated with little water-colour paintings of animals who appear in these stories? Well, this copy of Mr J-F has a picture of him with his name in the end papers, whereas my copy of 'The Tale of Peter

Rabbit' has not. Although not a first edition, it was therefore a reprint before 1906 — simple deduction and detection, but fascinating.

In Mr Muir's book he writes of the first edition of 'Alice's Adventures in Wonderland,' and how it was stopped and almost all the copies withdrawn. A second printer then printed it in the following year, so in this unusual case, there are two first editions, both rare and valuable, but the first one more so. They appeared in the years 1865 and 1866.

Another wonderful find would be a copy of Izaac Walton's famous book for fishermen; the original title page bears these words :—

The
Compleat Angler
or the
Contemplative Man's
Recreation.
Being a discourse of
Fish & Fishing
Not unworthy of the perusal of most Anglers
Simon Peter said, 'I go a-fishing : and they said, we
will go with thee.' John 21.3.
London, printed by T. Maxey for Rich. Marriot,
in S. Dunstans Churchyard. Fleet Street, 1653.

One of these books, originally sold at about one and eightpence, recently made £5,000 at an auction. There were writers on the same subject before him. One of the earliest books was written in 1486 by a Dame Juliana Berners, and in it she dealt with hunting, hawking and heraldry. She too philosophised happily like Mr Walton two centuries later. Nobody seems to know who this lady was, but it has been suggested that she was an Abbess. When I read that Izaac Walton was by trade an ironmonger, I wondered if there was any connection with the joke about the fisherman complete with rods and reel, who when questioned as to where he was going, replied 'To the iron-monger's to get my photograph taken.' Could this be a corruption of 'to the ironmongers for my gaff & line?' Certainly no more of a corruption than the name of the Inn which changed from 'God encompasseth Us' to 'The Goat & Compasses!'

I have customers for children's books, sporting books, gardening books, military books, topographical books, geographical books and another for very early books on any subject. This customer has a wife who is an expert book-binder and restorer.

On my buying expedition last Wednesday, I bought, among other things, an enormous late eighteenth century Geographical tome, 'incorporating the journeys of famous explorers up to the time of Captain Cook, with the latest accounts of the convict settlement at Botany Bay.' I spent all the late evening, slowly turning its six hundred odd pages, looking at old maps, engravings and reading snippets. Certainly women's queer fashions are not peculiar to this land or age, neither can we claim to be the inventors of crinolines or bee-hive hair 'does.' Some of the ceremonies in these far lands are so brutish and appalling, one could swoon in horror, but they were perpetrated against adults and animals — not children, as has happened in our lifetime.

Last summer I asked a Welsh farmer, who deals a bit, if he had any books to sell. He led me to an enormous Victorian bureau-bookcase, packed solid with books, standing in a dark corner of a calf-pen. He left me to my search. Until that hour, I had not known that so many boring books had been published. When he reappeared to see how I was progressing, he found me still hard at it and decidedly dusty. I asked him if any other dealers had looked through them, and he replied that a Cardiff dealer had bought thirty the previous week. I think he must have been a very thorough man. He had however left some old ration books and 'The Disection of the Dog-Fish,' and I too gener-ously left them for the next enthusiastic book-lover!

❧ 67 ❧

JUST AS STAMP COLLECTORS swap stamps, so dealers swap addresses; addresses where furniture and other treasures may be bought at down to earth prices. Two ladies who were in my shop last spring told me that they had found a man in Wales with sheds of furniture behind a little beach.

'Come along,' I said, 'you tell me where and I will give you the address of a local man like that.'

'Well,' one replied, 'this chappie — whatever is his name? — and his sister often take a lorry up to London of all places, and scout around buying things, all sorts of things from builders yards, demolition contractors, furniture brokers and sale yards. A friend of ours bought from him one of the toilet fitments from No. 10, Downing Street, which is being renovated you know. It is blue and white, *most* decorative, pure Victoriana!'

'My!' I said, 'one could charge *twopence* a time for one like that!'

'Yes, easily!' she replied laughing, 'it's gorgeous, and I've remembered the dealer's name now, it is Danny Davis. He lives in a little place you will never have heard of, called Cwm Tydu, pronounced Come Tiddy, it's off the Fishguard to Aberystwyth Road.'

'Cwm Tydu' I exclaimed, 'we once had a holiday there, years ago. We took the two children, Ruth and the 'daily.' We rented a large old-fashioned three storey-house so like the one from which I was married. It rained for the whole week, every day. A seal haunted the quiet beach. His head was always popping up to see what we were doing. It must have been monotonous for him because we were only walking in the rain, paddling in the rain, standing in the rain, or looking at him in the rain looking at us in the rain. The house itself, however, was full of surprises; although in a woody valley, the wind assaulted it from all points of the compass. We wedged the windows to stop the rattles, but the doors were more difficult and constantly crashed or banged shut; the catches did not catch and the knobs sometimes flew off leaving one imprisoned, with only the loose knob.

We joked about the house and said it was haunted by a gang of children; during mealtimes we would hear them on the top floor romping, banging doors and racing about. Then down the stairs they would come, like an avalanche of shoe-trees and repeat the performance on the first floor. They seemed to be happy, whatever they were up to, and it was infectious.

At night we had 'watchers.' These were of flesh and blood, and we heard them arrive on distant motor bikes. When I went upstairs to draw the curtains, it was a bit spooky to see one or two figures standing in the shadows of the dripping trees, silently watching the lonely house. They regarded some curfew however and departed just as quietly at ten o'clock!

Well, to return to the little beach and Mr Danny Davis and the furniture — that's exactly what we did last June, and it was still raining! John gave me half an hour 'off the lead,' and I spent a bit, but the larger pieces would have cost a lot to transport, so I regretfully left them. It was just the place to buy furniture for a country inn, a youth club or a holiday cottage. I had to be satisfied with a little walnut davenport, a Regency liqueur cabinet in rosewood and ormolu, some antique boxes and a brass standard lamp embellished with exotic birds.

❦68❦

LAST NIGHT I went to sleep repeating the name David Harropp, David Harropp — hoping I would dream about him, but I didn't. All afternoon and evening I had been examining his journal which began in 1697. I bought it in the autumn with a quantity of other books at a house sale in Oxford. I promised myself the pleasure of reading it when business went quiet after Christmas, and it couldn't be much quieter. The snow began to

178

fall on Boxing Day and it has been getting progressively more arctic ever since. There has been a blizzard in the West Country and thousands of miles of roads are closed, farms cut off and animals starving. Helicopters have dropped supplies to the great prison on Dartmoor, but hundreds of ponies are believed to have perished there. Little groups of sheep have been seen from the air, standing together and apparently encased in ice, and even the sea in the harbours is frozen.

Now to return to the journal, it is a little leather-bound book about six inches by four, with a little brass clasp stitched on to a soft leather flap. The pages are rather yellow of course, but the black ink is still bold and clear. On the fly leaf is written,

'David Harropp's Booke 1697' and underneath the words 'If I thee lous do as you would be done by.' Then there are two amusing little drawings done with a continuous line — one of a bewigged gentleman, the other of a dog or a sprightly sheep, I cannot tell which.

The book itself is unbelievably hard to read. Some letters are quite unfamiliar, the letter C is like an S with a line across its waist and a pointed accent above it, while any E at the end of a word is shown as an O. Also the words are spelt differently even on the same page. He spells the word 'uncle' as we spell it and four other ways — a jumble of Ks and Os and Us and Cs! Also as ONKLE which is how Shakespeare spelt it, I believe. Also there are scores of words unknown to me — What is 'A barril of Manchester?' or 'A pogging of rung?' There are references to another book he kept, but this one records monies paid away and family events. One of the first pages runs as follows :—

'I bought household goods when I began which cost me as followeth of a Gorgs Goodbone at Caddow' Then I can only puzzle out four items

'putor spoons	2d	
2 pots	4d	
2 blankets	10/-	
22 yds. of cloth	2. 13. 0.'	

There are pages and pages of accounts of money paid out for ploughing, harrowing, shearing, etc. Such as

'Daniel Knott 2 days ploughing	8d
You and your son 1 day	7d
You and your sons 1 day	8d

Harrowing marsh 12/-

You owe me a fortnight and 3 days when you was sick March 4th, 1717.'

There were also Birth dates :—

'Dun mare foled of horse coult May 27 1712.

Bay mare foled June 4th 1712'

Three of the earliest entries are as follows :—

'My Uncle John Smith died on Michaelmas Day 1697 Received of my Uncle Jonathan Smith Nov. 24 1699 one pound that my Uncle had left me.'

'Sarah (John's child) born March 18th 1700 paid you at her crissining April 20 3/-'

March 1700 The year of greate snow on 21st day of March.'

With a double page all to itself is a list headed 'the time when my children were born.'

'Sarah 22nd day of June 1703' The hour of birth is recorded each time. Mary followed in 1705. Ann 1708 David 1709 John 1712 James 1714 Jonathan 1716 Jonah 1719 Elizabeth 1721. Thus the oldest child was almost eighteen when little Elizabeth arrived. Strangely enough all the Christian names are popular now, with the exception of Jonah.

On other pages are recorded loans of money which are signed for by the borrower, and records of the renting of fields and the hiring of looms. School fees are referred to as wages. The girls went to school too and the last is recorded as,

'Elizabeth wint to ssoule Jan 23 1726 (she was not quite five years old)

The first grandchild arrived in 1722, another Elizabeth, her little Aunt Elizabeth was just one year old. The father was Lawrence Wright, and he must have married Sarah. Mary, David Harop's second daughter, died when she was 20 and little Jonathan died aged 8.

No address is given, but there are frequent mentions of Manchester and they worshipped at Oldham spelt OULDHAM. For a time he recorded the text of each Sunday's sermon giving the Chapter and verse like this :—

'Monseigneur Sogden upon Psalm 112 v. 7. He shall not be afraid of eveil tidings. His heart is fixed, trusting in the Lord. Sep. 25. 1709.

He used this little book for a quarter of a century. Inside the back cover he had drawn a skeleton with a book in one bony hand and an arrow in the other. I must close it now, and my own diary too.

❧ 69 ❧

DIFFERENT THINGS make different women feel rich, happy or content; mink coats for instance, new hair 'do's,' music, and motherhood of course. A wave of content always flows over me as I wait outside the Ashmolean Museum after a buying day in Oxford. It's not so much the purchases, the sunshine, or my imposing backcloth, it's the little notice screwed to the post above my head — it reads COUNTRY BUSES. Lucky, happy, fortunate, me!

I like to sit on the wide seat, at the very back of the bus and here, with much rustlings, I undo my purchases, put on my specs, and have a really thorough look at what I have bought so quickly in my slap-dash way. Really I must get into the way of putting on my specs when I buy small things now. To-day at the Oxfam Shop in Broad Street I bought a rather beautiful two handled pewter goblet, lovely for flower arrangements I thought. On closer examination, (in the bus) I found that it was engraved; I had an award for cycling the mile in record time in 1891! Another purchase, from a woman dealer, sold as a 'lovely little gilded frame with a "cut-out" picture in it, proved to be a charming little water-colour of an Oxford street. This vendor needed her specs too. Angela will smile gently when I tell her and say, 'You really *are* a silly old thing!'

She is on holiday at the moment. When she was married I did not shed a tear, but now there is talk of them possibly leaving the district, tears fly out unexpectedly when I am dusting and make little smudges on the furniture.

It was the same when Gordon was married. I was so happy for them both, but just seeing the name Hereford on a bus blinds

181

me with sudden tears. They are not for myself, but for the end of our life as a family, under one roof; each part had seemed the best as it came along — till then.

⚜ *70* ⚜

THE GREAT FREEZE UP goes on and John had taken to going to bed in my green angora cap. It suits him. I have borrowed a pair of his long woolly pants to wear under my diaphanous nightie. I hope I don't die in my sleep, I should hate to be found like that. The milk bottles are feeling the cold too. The frozen top-milk pushes up the little metal caps about two inches above the bottle necks and my young Godson and I have cut off the protrusions with a knife, sprinkled them with castor sugar and eaten them with tea-spoons. Scrumptious!

Last week we ran out of coal for one day and burnt a pile of grub-eaten bannisters and a complete set of Walter Scott — a miserable edition. I have made several bus journeys to view furniture, and have borrowed the car rug. No wonder they are called travelling rugs, as passengers long ago in coaches and unheated trains always used them. One of my travelling companions was a country-woman, and I said to her that I had dreadful visions of antique furniture being burnt in homes and farms that were isolated. She confessed to doing that very thing herself during the 1947 winter. She and another land girl had bought a partly furnished little cottage and they had sacrificed one piece after another when they were desperate for firing. She went on to say how one wild night she had gone to fetch her friend some brandy from the inn and, as she re-entered the cottage, she heard the church clock strike eight. Next day she found their lane blocked by a row of fallen elms. The innkeeper told her that they had come down like a row of ninepins just on eight o'clock. The villagers however regarded this happening as manna from heaven. The great trunks were hauled away with teams of horses by the local timber merchants, but the rest was attacked with choppers, saws, hatchets and bill hooks and loaded on every pram, truck and wheelbarrow in the village.

The great freeze up has now gone on for forty-two days. It is news. It is the worst in living memory. Starving pigeons have mobbed people carrying bread. A man has been charged with using icicles as offensive weapons; he has been clapped in jail and the icicles clapped in a refrigerator. Foxes in one place have attacked small boys who were sledging, and Angela tells me that the police have put a stop to children sledging down the steep dip in the middle of Kenilworth. They reckoned the children were reaching a speed of fifty miles an hour, and were afraid of fatalities.

A cutting from one American paper said that a New York doctor was advising husbands to forget all about chivalry, and let their wives clear the snow, for, he said, they were in better physical trim, thanks to housework, than their husbands. What a confession! I remember, a few years ago, a fuss in our papers about country children walking to school, as if it were a hardship. I forget whether it was the Minister of Transport or the Minister of Education. Anyway I thought he needed his head examining for one of the great joys of childhood *is* walking to school, meeting up with friends at certain junctions, making a fuss of the shire horses at the gate, balancing like a tight-rope walker along the parapet of the stream and other 'dares,' gathering the red campion and lady smock to stuff into the school jam jars. Then there are the secrets to be told and confidences to be shared, and the school songs to be whistled or sung in teacher's funny voice. There are the occasional scares, the quiet detours round sleeping tramps, a rare ride on a hay wagon and then the final wild race down the last hill as the church clock comes in sight — glorious exercise I think, ten times better than the ups and downs, knees bend and what-have-you in a heated drill room. These gymnasts are growing up into a race of motorists who drive out into the country in their biscuit tins, and then sit in them when they get there, with possibly one window open a chink to prevent asphyxiation. That gave me the chance to let that particular bee in my bonnet have a buzz around.

Now come with me across the snow. We'll leave the road by the first field gate, pass the gravel pits and cut up to the old Fox Cover. 'Whose footmarks are those?' you ask. 'They are Scampi's and mine' I reply. 'We have been this way a score of times since Christmas. The joyful Cairn tears on ahead, collapsing her front legs and ploughing her dear dark nose rapturously through the loose snow. Yes, these are her circling tracks made weeks ago; see we have followed the path made by the hares; see their great bounds, four feet apart and even five feet on the top meadow, that was where the Cairn surprised them, but she was an 'also ran.' The sun is warm on our backs, myriads of diamonds shine in the snow, the frost encrusted branches look like white coral against the blue sky; even the old stubble and broken teasle is bejewelled in beauty. Now we will turn right-handed, cross the Roman Road and take another look at the ponies. We are high above them and they are exercising themselves in the snow, circling in a figure eight when they hear us, or smell the hay we bring. They trot up to the gate, all except Possum. What is she up to? 'Possum! Possum!. She's got something cornered in the hedge, what a little devil she is. Ah! Now I can see what is there — a heron looking like an affronted little waiter. 'Come away Possum!' She comes in her own time. The heron runs free and spread its wings, flies above us and turns away.

71

LAST YEAR, my cabinet-maker retired to the south coast, where he is buying a boat or building one, I am not sure which. He is going to have the time of his life, if all goes well. His idea of bliss is to rise early and lie quietly off shore, fishing, watching the morning light spread across the sea, and meditating.

Another friend is helping me very well. He is a clever man from a clever family. He is 'retired' so not allowed to earn much and his charges are quite pre-war. I do not tell him this but try to make it up to him with quantities of home-cooking, which he appreciates, as he is a bachelor. The entries in my cash book look rather funny :—

Mr Appleyard. To help 15/- plus 7/6 (steak & trifle!)
Mr Appleyard. To help 12/6 plus 5/6 (casserole & cake)
Mr Appleyard. To help 17/6 plus 8/- (fudge & Chicken dinner!)

I expect him two days a week at 2 p.m., but he comes when the spirit moves him. When he arrives there is usually a large plateful of food steaming hot on top of a saucepan and he returns to his car with this, a knife & fork and the newspaper. Then on with the glue-pot, and an hour later we set to on various pieces of furniture — in the garden if weather permits. He replaces missing drawer runners, cuts and glues a piece of veneer, fixes a loose bracket and planes the top of a pine cupboard. Pause for a coffee break. Then he will give me a lift with a dresser and a settle from the store and then drill out three broken castors and replace with matching old ones from one of the countless boxes of bits and pieces. Now it is time for our tea-break, and a chat. While he has a hot bath, I put a couple of chairs by his car for restoration and tidy up.

Quite often he does not turn up at all. Once when I had given him up, he arrived when I had half eaten his dinner. He stood and watched me finish it. I did not know whether to laugh or cry, but *he* did not look like laughing, so I had to conjure up a mixed grill for him.

His heart is really in fruit-growing. He has a large orchard. Yesterday, he did not arrive until tea-time and said he had been scaring bull-finches. They were disporting themselves among his pear-tree buds, stripping them, not eating them. He caught one bull-finch, which is now flying round his house and sharing his crumbs, and he plans to release it in Oxford to-morrow. He used to keep poultry and, last time there was a fowl-pest scare in this district, he boarded out his last remaining ancient pet hen, a Rhode Island Red, for a few weeks with an understanding farmer's wife in a 'clear' zone. There she, the hen not the farmer's wife, perched quietly on an old towel-rack in an attic, until the scare was over. There was no fear of her cackling, as she had forgotten how to lay an egg years before.

❊❊ *72* ❊❊

I SHALL NOT FORGET to-day in a hurry. In fact I shall never forget it because of Mrs Mulligan! John had to drive into town and, as it was a closing day, I suddenly decided to travel with him. He dropped me off in the jewellery quarter, and I made my way to a little workshop where a man polishes and files the most beautiful reproduction brass furniture for antiques. He has told me that I am one of his favourite customers and to prove it he lets me open every dusty box on every dusty shelf. There I find engraved escutcheons, mirror finials, dresser knobs, brass eagle's feet and even incomplete sets of glorious French Chippendale handles which he has forgotten about himself. On the back of his work-bench to-day I discover a pair of exquisitely cast men angels, seraphs with hands uplifted. They appeared to have been supporting an alms dish or perhaps a Holy water vessel. Yes, he said, I might buy them, they had come in with some old brass scrap. He made me up a parcel and, after a wash at his little brown sink with the carbolic soap, I'm off again, weighed down nearly forty pounds on one side.

I pop into the little coffee house near by, and there is a lovely motherly face smiling at me from a corner table. It's Mrs Mulligan. I once sat next to her at a sale, and she told me about her childhood, her marriage and her big family. She is a widow now. I join her with my steaming cup of coffee, facing us at the same table is a Jewish gentleman, but he might not have been there as we were so glad to be together again, and off she started in her soft Irish voice,

'Have you ever been to Ireland?'

'No,' I replied, 'but I was looking at a poster only to-day extolling its beauty, and I thought to myself "I *must* go there before I die."'

'Yes, indeed you must,' she went on, 'It's the loveliest place

186

and there are the loveliest people there — the loveliest people! Just you go to Dublin and walk down Grafton Street. Oh the shops there! The beautiful jewellery and the wonderful things, you will see nothing so fine in all London. And as you go up Grafton Street, there's a little road off to the right, you must go up there and into St. Theresa's. It's so quiet and so beautiful. I cannot tell you what it is, whether it's the prayers that have been made there, or the beauty of it all, or the silence, but you feel it's in the Presence of God you are. Do you understand, my dear?'

Yes I did, and I tried to tell her about St. David's Cathedral, and the great congregations, and the Holy Communion Service when babies and toddlers were carried up to share in the blessings.

'Yes,' she said, 'That's how it should be, all together — one family. Then when you are in Dublin you must take a bus out to Dun Laoghaire, it's only about a shilling on the bus. Lovely people live in "Dunleary" and I have two sisters there. There is no pushing and shoving and 'mind out of my road;' the lovely people there have time to stop and talk and, when the sun shines, they say 'What a lovely morning! God bless it! They care about you there, they've got time, they don't keep looking at their watches and rushing off.'

'You've looked at the clock twice, Mrs Mulligan.'

'Yes, it's true I have. I'm on my way to Mass.'

At this the Jewish gentleman pushed back his chair and said he must go, and added,

'But I *have* enjoyed the sincerity of your conversation — and I am a Jew.'

An hour later at the auction room, a man vacated the chair next to mine, and a moment later Mrs Mulligan popped into it out of nowhere.

'Do you know who you are sitting next to?' I asked.

'Yes, it's you, and I've just lit a candle for you, my dear. Now you make a request to God and if it's pleasing to Him, it will be answered, Think now — it's burning for you.'

Comfort for a bereaved mother was my prayer.

'And it will be granted,' she whispered back, 'because it is not for yourself.'

My Godson came round this evening and helped me sweep

187

up some leaves. I told him a little about Mrs Mulligan, in my best imitation of her gentle Irish voice, and when I finished he said,

'Auntie, I havn't been here while you've been talking. I've been somewhere else.'

Perhaps he had been in Dun Laoghaire where the people are such lovely people, and where they have time to pause, and talk, and say,

'What a lovely morning! God bless it!'

❦{ 73 }❦

I WISH I HAD THE CHANCE of buying more oil paintings, as they sell themselves these days, portraits, still-life, interiors, landscapes, seascapes, flower-paintings, the lot. Even the empty frames and the frameless canvasses find ready buyers. I have had several oil paintings lately which have been ruined by attempts at restoration. Art dealers feel these amateurish efforts should be punishable by death, or at least by torture. If oil paintings are dirty, they can be safely wiped over with a sponge damped in liquid soap, but no pressure should be used; the soap should then be removed with a clean sponge and then do please STOP! The gilt frame can then be gently cleaned in the same way with a few spots of ammonia added to the liquid soap.

Among some pictures I bought the other day was an oil painting of a highly coloured sunset and on the back was a label bearing the words, 'Sunset in England 1883 following the volcanic erruption of Krakatao between Java and Sumatra. On the morning of August 27th 1883 a vast glowing cloud of incandescent pumice and ashes rose fifty miles into the air.' This was the first disaster I ever heard of. My Mother remembered the happening and told us how the top of the island had been blown off, and the dust from the explosion had travelled round the world and caused these superb sunsets for some weeks.

The first event of outstanding importance after my birth was the appearance of a very rare comet. My Father, astronomically inclined, carried me on his shoulders into the nearby fields to see it. I clung on to his tie and looked as instructed for 'a kite with a tail.' I saw nothing resembling my brother's paper kite with its tail of newspaper tufts and I fell asleep. The only disaster I remember in early childhood was the sinking of the Titanic. I remember the terrible newspaper picture of it upended, and my parents' horror.

The year is nearly at its end. To-morrow will only be another day, but when it is the beginning of a New Year, one stops to think and stock-take mentally.

Never in peacetime can I remember so many disasters in a single year. The hurricane Flora began it all with a toll of some ten thousand lives, and this was followed during the summer by the terrible earthquake at Skopje, followed swiftly by mine disasters, flood and dam disasters, a typhoid epidemic, fires, train accidents, and five air liner crashes in three weeks. Now at Christmas times comes the sinking of the pleasure liner Laconia, but nothing stunned the world more than the assassination of John Kennedy, the young President of America on that fateful November day.

My various buying expeditions lately have made me think of other Christmases as I have trodden familiar streets, past my old school at Warwick, under the East Gate, past the diamond latticed window of the cloakrooms, where we hung our black velours in winter, and our white panamas in summer, past the familiar little music room where Miss Springall despairing of my efforts after three years, had made a present of me to a younger mistress. I remember one day she had said 'Try singing, Anne,' hoping doubtless to find some music somewhere within me.

'Try singing "The Mountains of Mourne."' I hardly knew a note of it — only the last line in fact. Now, if I had been less shy, and had said 'May I sing Killarney?' she might have had a surprise. I used to sing it with my Mother, and *she* said I sang it like a blackbird.

The great ilex tree outside the Council School has gone.

189

Horror of horrors a little boy was decapitated by a tram there. We saw the blood and sawdust, and another day we saw a dripping covered handcart pushed from the river through St. Nicholas Field. 'Yes, she drowned herself, going to have a baby, 'drownded' herself,' said the voices. I could have wept, how sad, how sad, if *only* she had known she was going to have a baby I thought, how happy she would have been. Let's go home, come on, let's go home!

Past my old home I go, where there are still the bars at the nursery window. I wonder who lives there now? Past my great Aunt Jane's house. When she was away my Mother had the garden key and we used to play croquet there and gather syringa and heavy, old-fashioned scented roses.

There is Mrs Copsie's little bakehouse on the corner, but there is another name above the window. She used to call my Mother 'Lovey', which we children thought very funny. The little shop two doors away, the one with the bulging windows, has vanished. I used to be sent there with a turkey dinner on Christmas Day; the scarf tied over my head tickled my face, but the hot plate kept my hands warm. I would race home feeling wildly happy. It was Christmas Day! It all seems a long time ago, which it is, as it's nearly fifty years ago.

Yes, the year has nearly gone, the church bells will begin to ring any time now. The little niece who called my customers 'custymuds' was a bride in June. A first little great-niece has made her welcome appearance in the family. John has found his cottage on the Pembrokeshire coast and more new friends there have been added to the Christmas Card list. Our little grand-daughter really knows us now, and remembers us from one visit to the next. She welcomes us with shy smiles, her golden head down on one shoulder. Most engaging! Gordon wrote in the autumn that she had changed from a shy little flower into one of the hardier jungle animals. I can see what he means when that first shyness has passed. On our last visit, John was on tenterhooks each time she disappeared. The first time he found her standing in the kitchen sink squirting water from the tap, and the second time she was on the bathroom window sill sampling her fruit-flavoured toothpaste. 'The kiddies will love it' had boasted the T.V. advertisement, and it was true. Here I go, like a real old granny writing all this.

To neighbours and relations I send wishes for a Happy New Year, but to dealer friends and customers and myself I add the words 'and good hunting.'

74

IF A SHAGGY DOG STORY is one that goes on and on, I must record one here, told to me by Jane Tudor's husband, who keeps one going an unconscionably long time, but is less successful with his pipe, which fizzles out every few minutes :—

'Do you ever get a billiard table, Anne?' he enquired.

'Well, no, there aren't antique billiard tables, are there?'

'Perhaps not. Did I ever tell you about a fellow who had one made to his special requirements? No? I thought I hadn't. Well, this old chap had sold his farm well and had booked to go a world cruise but, before setting sail, he called on his local cabinet-maker, and inquired if he could have a billiard table made to his own specifications, and was answered 'Yes, certainly.' Well, first of all, I want it to have a centre pedestal, instead of a leg at each corner, and secondly I want the table to be circular.' 'Circular?' 'Yes, circular, and the baize to be navy blue instead of green. The pockets are to be ten inches apart and in the centre of the table I want a four-faced brass clock, mounted on a rod.'

'Good heavens!' I exclaimed, 'and what happened?'

'Well,' continued Jane Tudor's spouse, relighting his pipe, 'It's a sad story. The poor old boy died on the voyage and was buried at sea. So, Anne, if any of your customers want a circular billiard table, with a centre pedestal, in blue, complete with a clock, etc. I can put you in touch with someone, who has one going cheap.

Everyone knows that the price of goods and the cost of living has been going up since Income Tax started at 6d in the pound. Now one's really wealthy customers only retain 6d in the pound. The price of silver has risen about five times in the last

191

few years and antiques have perhaps doubled. I was reading an old book on antiques the other day, written in 1906, and the author wrote 'the price of antiques is steadily rising, and one may have to pay as much as eight pounds now for a good oak bureau.' An elderly antique dealer, in a large way of business, told me that before the war he often had half a dozen antique sofa tables in stock, which had cost him eight to ten pounds each, but now he has one in stock which has cost him eighty-five pounds.

I have jokingly said to my Cheltenham Uncle, who is a wizard with stocks and shares, that if he had commissioned me, in my student days, to buy him a few 'French Impressionists', he would be quite well off by now.

There is a saying that the young think the old are fools, and that the old *Know* the young ones are. But as I get older, I realise the truth of 'there's no fool like an old fool.' I proved it for myself in Oxford yesterday when I bought a firebasket (a dog-grate on legs) at the Oxfam Shop in Broad Street, and lugged it all round Oxford on my hip. As I staggered into Fullers for a coffee, an elegant young customer happened to follow me in and inquired,

'Isn't that terribly heavy Mrs Summers?'

'Yes.'

'Isn't it too much for you Mrs Summers?'

'Yes.'

'Are you feeling all right Mrs Summers?'

'No. I must be mad!'

One of my best buys at the Oxfam Shop was a vast collection of bone and ivory chessmen, priced at 1/- a piece, I began to sort a few out, when one of the helpers quietly said, 'If you are trying to make up a set, I'm afraid there isn't one. We have been through them.'

Many of them were so beautifully carved and of such fine quality, I felt I could not leave them, and they accepted my offer of twelve pounds for the great boxful. When I got home, I had a royal time sorting them out into battalions. There were forty-two castles for a start! I rang up a young dealer, who I remembered had been trying to complete a set, but he replied,

'No, I'm not needing them now, thank you. I have turned a couple of pieces myself and sold the set, and please don't mention Oxfam to me! I had a boxful of chessmen from them and when I got home I found they were all pawns!'

'What did you pay for them?' I enquired.

'Seven pounds,' he replied.

'Right,' came my answer, 'You've got a customer! I will give you seven pounds for them.'

'You *will*?'

'Yes, certainly, for there isn't one *pawn* in my lot.'

I made up thirteen harlequin sets and sold them quite quickly. I had to dye some of the white pieces scarlet and, to do this, it was necessary to remove all the grease out of them first by a good soaking in strong detergent, and I then left them for some hours immersed in cochineal. There were still scores of pieces left and I sold these, as a job lot, to a dealer who lives in Rye.

❈{ 75 }❈

I AM IN THE BUS on the way to see my Aunts. You will never guess what's in my basket for them to-day, so I'll tell you straight away. Three long twigs covered with rosy ripe peaches. They are off Angela's tree. She planted the stone on the top of her 'little mountain' when she was still at school. We think it was twelve years ago. Anyway, it has borne fruit for the last four years, first twelve huge ones, then thirty-six smaller ones, last year twenty when we had a late frost, and this year 120 when we didn't! Mr Appleyard, who understands these things, says we should have thinned them out to twelve inches apart, but he told us too late, and there they are in clusters of twos, threes and fours. Such a lovely velvety sight, and the blackbirds think the same!

The Aunts scold me whatever I take, so I feel I may as well be hanged for a sheep as a lamb, and fill my basket. When they scold me, I put a sob in my voice and say,

193

'Here I am working my fingers to the bone for you, and you are *cross.*'

One aunt laughs at this, the other turns away and thinks to herself,

'She always was a silly creature, not like her mother at all.'

I try to take them something different, at one shop I get some salty Welsh butter, at a special pieman's a couple of loin chops, or a dressed crab and at Kunzles a box of real cream cakes, meringues, and rum ba bas for the Aunt who hasn't signed the pledge. We call them drunkard's doughnuts.

As I turn down their little road, I always waft a prayer heavenwards, that I shall not say anything to upset them. The slightest thing can become so out of proportion, when chewed over in the dead of night if one is old and frail, I think. I also try to hoard up funny little things to tell them, and veer off controversial topics. One of them is very critical of the younger generation as her newspaper represents them, not as she finds them personally! Last time I said to them,

'I know you think the younger generation are a poor lot and I'm not taking sides, but let me read you this newspaper cutting about a member of the *older* generation,' and with a perfectly straight face I read as follows :—

'Old Mr. Will Cobley aged 92 of Upton Chadesby has handed in his resignation as postman. Although still hale and hearty, he says the eight mile round, tires him, especially in winter conditions.'

'There!' I exclaimed triumphantly 'throwing in the sponge! Is *that* a good example to the younger generation? It says he is 'still hale and hearty' — look, in black and white! You can read it for yourselves!'

While one Aunt makes tea the other says,

'It must cost you a lot to come to see us? It means eight buses, here and back?'

'Well I usually cover my expenses Aunt, all dealers do.'

'What do you mean?'

'Well to-day for instance, while I was waiting at the bus stop in the Bristol Road, I noticed that the old book shop was being demolished on the corner opposite. No bus was in sight, so I sped across the nearby Belisha crossing, found the foreman on the job, and bought a rather wonderful wrought iron sign still hanging on the corner of the building. It had entwined ivy leaves and lovely Victorian twiddley bits. I offered him a pound for it, he said 'Right, it will be down in a week' and I said I would get Pickfords to collect it. I was back at the bus stop in three and a half minutes. If I had had more time I might have found some old door-knockers too, and perhaps some ornate gas brackets upstairs and little 'maiden waist' fireplaces, but the stairs were suspended in mid-air, by cobwebs apparently, and I was wearing some gorgeous Italian shoes. That's what we call 'covering our expenses.' Now with a clear conscience I can put down to-day's travelling expenses in the column marked 'office expenses.'

Some farmer friends call occasionally with an antique dealer relative. He always starts off by saying that he must buy something to cover *his* expenses. His hostess once took me on one side, and said that she and Bob would be interested to know how much they were, as they met him at the station and dined him and wined him for a fortnight. He used the family stationery and phone, smoked Bob's Christmas cigars and begged his postage stamps off her.

I remember at one sale I went to, the things fetched such high prices I did not see how I could possibly cover *mine*. In the end I bought one magnificent cut glass vase for five pounds. A few days later a 'lady' dismounted from an enormous showman's caravan and gladly paid seven pounds for it. She explained that it was much nicer than the one she had in her opposite window, and that one had cost ten pounds. These people are always asking for Crown Derby china and will pay big prices for tea services which I never get, but they will also buy odd plates and any china if very rich and colourful.

One boyish old dealer I know, who sells old books and pictures, told me how he covered his expenses at a county sale on Tuesday. He belongs to the ring, so always has his share in the settlement afterwards. Towards the end of the sale, when the three good pieces had all been bought by the public, he bid one pound for a pile of junk which the other two dealers had not examined. In the settlement he told me he put another pound on it and the other two dealers thinking there must be something good there ran it up to seven pounds. My friend then let them have it and with two pounds to the good made his way to the local for a late luncheon and a drink.

≈{ *76* }≈

Somewhere, earlier in my journal, I wrote about shipping some despised Victorian furniture to Canada via Liverpool; it was at the time, when everybody here, wanted Regency furniture. Ten years after this, even the London dealers were asking for Victorian furniture, only calling it Victoriana, which makes it worth guineas perhaps instead of pounds.

Lately we have heard yet another word, Art Nouveau, called after a shop in Paris, L'Art Nouveau, which opened there at the end of the last century. This period covers about twenty years. from 1890–1910. Incidentally, both John and I must be art nouveau! Certainly our parents had among their wedding presents, vases and glassware from Liberty's of Regent Street, and in Italy this style of furnishing, for it covers fabrics and furniture too, is called Stile Liberty.

As is usual for the young, we thought it thoroughly old-fashioned and scorned the draped ladies in moulded pewter, supporting little ink-wells or fruit compotes, the Doulton vases with their Dickensian figures, the elaborate fabrics covered with designs of Persian poppies, honeysuckle and peacock feathers beloved of William Morris.

I well remember the first time an art nouveau object appeared at auction, as the auctioneer made fun of it too! Twin pewter ladies in windswept gowns, posed on tip-toe holding aloft a candelabra. When someone started the bidding at 'ten shillings,' the auctioneer called out,

'Hold him boys, don't let him get away!'

Now, even the London buyers, or perhaps I should say *only* the London buyers, are seeking it in our country shops. During this week I have bought two A.N. tables, one made of brass with little hoofs for feet and onyx insets; the other is of ma-

196

hogany with iron cabriolet legs and shaped top and under tier. But my pièce de résistance is a colossal pearwood carving, weighing quite forty pounds and costing decidedly more; it is of delightful babes, cherubs in fact complete with wings, and is a most beautiful colour and gleaming softly. If this is still in stock when I depart, it would make an idyllic tombstone. On the reverse side of the carving is written in pencil R. HOUGHTON PALACE YARD, WORCESTER. I must try to find out something more about this gentleman from one of the Worcester dealers.

One of this fraternity, young Mr David Bullock of Edgar Street, called to collect a pair of chairs last week. Angela and I love to get him talking about his work of interior decoration. He delights in pine panelled rooms and has lately completed a fabulous kitchen, all in pine for a wealthy London client. He is shortly leaving for Greece, where is he furnishing a house on a little island off the coast, and transporting himself there, by ferrying out the client's new sports car. He plans to use local stone and tiles for the floors and walls and make a selection of hand-made furniture from craftsmen on the mainland. Then later in the autumn when the workmen have finished, he will drive overland again, taking all the English bedding and fabrics and doubtless his sewing-machine for making the curtains and covers.

Angela and her husband have just driven up through France, and she is enthusing about the way antiques are displayed in country shops there.

'They look so *exciting*, Mummy' You just *have* to stop. The antiques overflow on to the footpaths and greens. All sorts of interesting furniture, cooking utensils, farm implements, chairs hang from hooks in the walls, bunches of baskets from overhead wires, and quantities of pottery everywhere. It's like Penny Priors used to be, with old people sitting on benches in the sunshine and horses abound.'

Well, the sun is shining here too. We'll show the Froggies. Out with some cart wheels against the road wall. Give me a hand with these staddlestones. I can tug out the tubs of begonias myself. Out with the old settle, it can live there. Let's plug a dresser rack on to the cottage wall, we'll drape it with harness and fill it with cheery old Ironstone. The sun won't hurt these hefty old 'wheelbacks.' Out with the spinning wheel and a couple of cradles, a three-legged stool and a muster of mahogany bed-posts for good measure. 'Why go abroad?' say the Railway Posters. Why indeed!

⪻ 77 ⪼

WELL THIS TIME NEXT WEEK the Election will be over. There is a funny story going around, told to me by the book-dealer by the bridges at Leamington. The Vicar was discussing the choice of hymns for the next Sunday with his organist.

'If the Conservatives get in again,' began the Vicar, 'I suggest we start with 'Now thank we all our God, if Labour gets in what do you suggest?'

'Let's have, 'O God our help in ages past,' replied the organist, 'and what do you suggest Vicar in the unlikely event of the Liberals getting in?'

'God moves in a mysterious way' would do very nicely I think,' replied the parson.

Our little granddaughter will be three this month and another little grandchild is on the way — Angela's. It will be a change to see a babe in her arms instead of a kitten, and a human face, instead of a horse's looking over her shoulder. She is so happy and gloriously well. History is repeating itself and like her Mother, her Grandmother and her Greatgrandmother she is expecting her firstborn in March.

It is October the twelfth to-day. I opened my shop twenty-four years ago to-day. So I am now embarked on my twenty-fifth year. Established a quarter of a century in fact. The Russians are celebrating for me; to-day they have launched yet another capsule into space, with three men in it this time. They are circling the world every ninety minutes, which is a bit quicker than Jules Verne's 'Round the World in 80 Days.' It must be more than four years since we walked up the Green, leant on the five-barred gate of the Great Meadow, and gazed at the moon, when it was first shot at by the Russians.

There have been other changes too. I snipped this little cutting out of a local paper to copy it into my diary:—

'The Landlord of the Swan Inn, Wilby, Suffolk, has retired after fifty-three years. When he took over, a customer could buy a pint of beer, a drop of gin, a hunk of bread and cheese, pickles, an ounce of tobacco, a clay pipe and a box of matches and still have a halfpenny change from a shilling.'

There are still adventures on earth though as well as in space, for below the above cutting is the following bit:—

'Peter Rainsworth (aged 31) a Briton with the spirit of Mark Twain, has arrived in New Orleans, after canoeing 2,052 miles from the source of the Mississippi to the mouth in 160 days.'

The garden is still full of flowers, Michaelmas daisies, dahlias, marigolds and roses. Mrs Clancey's mauve clematis is still a glory. I must be thinking of turning out the sheds for bonfire night. I always pretend I think the little black faced Guy in a push-chair is a dummy and pretend to be frightened when it blinks (it never speaks). I give it little prods in ticklish spots declaring, 'It can't be real!' 'It *is*!' 'It's my little brover, you know 'im!' comes the delighted rejoinder. But I remain doubting and go to look for some pennies.

At the moment there are fourteen houses for sale in Penny Priors. 'What's the matter with this village?' my customers keep asking, and one more outspoken than the rest said 'Has Penny Priors got the Plague?'

'I think there are really two reasons. A great many retired people think a cottage in the country is the ultimate, but after a few months they get lonely. They miss their old friends and neighbours, the shops, and often the husband is bored with retirement anyway. If they do grow roots and settle, perhaps after a few years one of them will die and the survivor will decide to move nearer a married son or daughter. Rather surprisingly almost all the newcomers start coming to Church, but within a few months the parson upsets them and they come no more.'

'How do you mean, upsets them?' the customer may ask.

'Well,' I reply, 'you know the two great commandments, "in which hang all the law," the one about loving God and

199

loving one's neighbour? Well, if we had a man like that, there would not be a happier village in all Stoneshire.' We feel like Warwickshire sheep without a Shepherd.

❧ *78* ❧

IF I HAD TO GIVE A LITTLE TALK on the evolution of the chair from the stool, I could do it quite well at the moment. I have in the shop an early three-legged round stool, a three-legged stool with a top like a half circle, a very early three legged Welsh chair, like a heavy stool with a back support, the sticks of which protrude below the heavy seat and above the top rail (or rather lump) and then I have a four-legged early comb-back Welsh chair with plain stool-like legs. The two early Welsh chairs arrived with a load of other old things at teatime on Friday. Three likeable Irish boys bounded as one into the shop and asked if I wanted some furniture. I *think* that they asked me that, I only could make out the last word. I pushed my purse into my pocket and went out on to the Green and watched them unload it all around me. Their van should have been called the Ark, for out came two rocking cradles, two brass lamps, two old tables and the aforesaid two chairs, and finally a high Welsh spinning wheel — in bits!

I tried to get them to say a price and vice versa. It was three to one, so I made a tentative offer of twelve pounds for the lot. This brought them out into the open and they said thirty-six pounds for the lot. Each time I raised my price by two pounds their leader would exclaim,

'No good, boys! Load on!' and I would quietly assist them. When it was loaded they would lower their price two pounds or so and start unloading. We repeated this charade three times, with no hard feelings on either side. They declared they only wanted to make two pounds on the lot. I think two pounds on each piece would have been nearer the mark. Anyway, we settled for twenty-two pounds finally, which meant that my price rose ten pounds and theirs came down fourteen. Was this a victory for me? I feel rather doubtful about this as they say they will bring me some more.

Now I must get the woodturner to make some more spokes for the spinning-wheel, the cabinet-maker to put new bottoms in the cradles, and I must set to with the injector, the scraper, the glue-pot and the polish.

Through the years I have bought many a little load of antiques in dear old Worcester. The heart of it, opposite the Cathedral, is now being torn out and scores of empty doomed shops line the High Street. No. 53 was once the home of 'Berrow's Worcester Journal,' the oldest Newspaper in the world; it is one of the weekly papers I take to discover Auction sales of antiques. In a recent article in this paper was one giving details of traders in the High Street one hundred years ago. There were cabinet-makers, upholsterers, sellers of harps, flutes and guitars, book shops, music shops, stockists of fire grates, iron balconies, weather vanes and verandahs. A shop for the needlewoman selling designs on canvas for petit point and Berlin wool-work, the tapestries could be mounted or framed on the premises. There were cloth merchants and silk merchants, sellers of brocades, damasks, taffeta and merino; dealers in lace, trimmings, cords, tassels and fringes, while others offered wallpapers of 'the most elegant quality.' At the silversmiths, the finest Sheffield cutlery was for sale, and tea pots and tea urns in silver, copper, brass and bronze; urns beloved of the Victorian age, and so sought after still, by our American cousins, for their original use, and by Englishwomen for imposing flower arrangements.

At the Oxford sale, where I bought the little journal with a hundred other books, was also a thin little volume privately published by an R. Mense Esquire which was titled 'The Narrative of Circumstances connected with the late Assault by Mr Shapland upon Mr Mense.' This sad little book describes the attack with a heavy stick by the Vicar of St. Peter's, upon the writer, in the High Street at Worcester in 1814, and all the events which led up to it.

It appears that the Vicar asked Mr Mense, who one imagines was a solicitor, to act as peacemaker between himself and his wife. When however the marriage broke down completely, the

Vicar blamed the writer, for Mr and Mrs Mense had taken in the distraught wife. On this April day in 1814 Mr Shapland met Mr Mense in the High Street and with tremendous fury and with shouts of 'malignant scoundrel, detestable scoundrel, etc.' aimed some heavy blows at him cutting through his coat and shirt.

One can imagine the gossip. First the separation, then the assault, to be followed only a few hours later by the death of the only child of the marriage who was still in her father's care. All the pathetic letters between the parties are published, and one feels that for thirteen years Mrs Shapland must have been the most patient woman in the world, bearing insults and blows in private, and sneers and scorn in public. But the distress of the husband and his unbalanced state makes the reader feel that he was the more wretched of the two. Mr Mense rather than go to court after the assault, decided to write and distribute his little book among his acquaintances, as the Vicar continued to blame him and, as a professional man, it would be necessary to clear his name.

79

YESTERDAY, coming back from Oxford, I was in a writing mood in the bus, but I had run out of writing paper. I dissected an envelope and after using every square inch of that, I defaced a letter from our family solicitor, that I had thought would be pleasant to have in my handbag, if I were run over. In it he had written, 'and I am not flattering you when I say that you are a very businesslike lady.' This letter was in answer to one of mine, giving a list of reasons, why I considered my rates should be reduced. Incidentally my appeal was successful, but the rates are still more than *double* what the rent and rates were *together*, before I owned the little place.

Next I turned my attention to my fellow-passengers and tried to imagine who they were, what they were, and where they would leave the bus. A beautiful young girl was reading a woman's magazine and concentrating on an article 'The Lovelier You.' I waited till I could see her left hand, and yes, she was wearing an engagement ring; her shoes were elegant, so I guessed she was going into town to the terminus. A tweedy lady, sitting immediately in front of me, was reading the New Statesman, open at the page about, 'The Position in Iraq.' She had no ring on her third finger but there had been one there for years. Was she too clever for him or what I wondered? She looked like a keen gardener, or a hockey player, with her strong useful hands. I suddenly knew that she would get off at the old beech tree, and that she would be met by a woman with a spaniel. Once or twice a year I know certain things like this. If I am alone I say it aloud or write it down, so as not to cheat. I do not think this can be thought transference, as it is about something that has not happened. It happened six times in a few weeks once. When I was half listening to horse racing on the Television, 'Golden Harvest will win,' I said aloud. I said two other winners. Another day, I said which horse would be second and another time that a certain horse would be placed. I just suddenly knew, when the names of the runners were being read. One of the first times when I *knew*, we were driving down to Tintagel with the radio on, and I told John which horse would win. He laughed, but when it did, he gave me a queer look and said,

'I must have married a witch!'

A queer thing that does puzzle me, is what I sometimes 'see' when I am dropping off to sleep, but still awake; not a bit what I should expect, as I am a lover of beautiful simple English things I see visionlike scenery in glorious colour, close up of mosaics, great drapes of elaborate fabrics in Eastern designs and mysterious patterns on everything. Once when I was still partly awake, a band of Asiatic type horsemen cantered past. Through the dust I could see their brown faces, coarse hair and embroidered headbands and all the fine details of their embossed saddles and harness, the weave in the rugs on their saddle-bows and the intricate designs on their daggers and spears.

80

JOHN HAD AN EXTRA HEAVY WEEK, so I persuaded him to have
the morning in bed yesterday, and went to Matins alone.
There was a choir each end of the Church. Eighteen well
scrubbed choir boys and girls at the east end, and unseen
feathered ones at the west end. The chancel was beamed with
February sunshine, and every time we sang, the birds sang,
even between the verses, as my little brother used to do. There
was certainly one robin, and there must have been several
starlings, who were standing in for blackbirds and linnets. The
volume of sound was wonderful, it rose in pulsing joy through
the Venite and continued through the Te Deum and Psalms! It
seemed a pity not to sing the Benedicte, for there was a verse of
their very own, 'Oh ye fowls of the Air, bless ye the Lord;
praise Him and magnify Him for ever.' They twittered to
silence during the lessons and prayers, burst into melody again
for the Sermon hymn, made remarks about the Text and then
slept or listened, I could not see which, during the Sermon.

'Well, what did you think of that?' asked old Mrs Glaston-
bury as we made our way up the green. 'I've walked miles, as a
girl, to hear the nightingales sing, but that beat the band!'

'Nobody would believe it unless they heard it.' I replied.
When I told John, he said that it must have been Penny Priors
Two Choirs Festival.

This morning we had long letters from both Gordon and
Joan. So good of them both to write. They know how we love
to hear their news, especially the latest bits about our little
darling. One of their neighbours related to them the latest funny
one about Fiona. She is now two years and four months old.
The other day she was playing with some older children when
the strains of martial music came over the radio,

'My Daddy was in the Guards once,' said one child.

'My Daddy was in the R.A.F. once,' said another.

'My Daddy was in the Army once,' said a third.

Then after a little pause Fiona piped up, 'And my Daddy was a man once.' 'So you see, Mum,' my son added, 'I've had my moments!'

To-day I had a really good working morning in the cottage, Hoovered upstairs and downstairs and then swept the yards, After lunch, still in a working mood, I set to on the shop, and it was looking like the wreck of the Hesperus when customers began to arrive. For the first time in my life I had four Doctors in at once, so I didn't have to remember names! It was 'Yes, Doctor,' 'No, Doctor,' 'Ten guineas, Doctor' and so on. While I was wrapping up a Rockingham tea-pot I overheard one say to another, 'I believe his name is Beecham, but no relation to the Pill.' This started a train of thought, so here are some of the bits I've overheard, and smiled about. Men are the worst gossips. One man customer to another,

'Did you know our new parson came from your village?'

'Yes, I knew,' said the other ominously, 'we've been trying to get rid of him for seventeen years!'

Another gentleman patron said,

'She is *second* wife, you know.'

'Yes, I did know, but the first one died properly,' replied his companion.

Two lady customers, trapped in the back of the shop, were discussing me, when one said in a stage whisper,

'Do you think she can possibly make a living?'

I must have been selling too many bargains, and I had proof of it another day. A parent, with a school-boy son, told me he took him into another local shop, and when the boy enquired the price of a writing desk and was told three guineas, he exclaimed,

'Gosh! it would be about seven and six at Mrs Summers''

As I get older I find names harder and harder to remember. I suppose I must know thousands now and all the little pigeon holes are full. I have Herrings, Whitings, Mackerell and Trout. I have Englands, Englishes, Scots, Irelands and Brittons, I have Blacks, Whites, Greys and Browns, and Norths, Souths, Easts and Wests as well as Goodes, Toogoods, Goodenoughs and I feel that *is* enough!

After the sudden invasion of customers, I finished tidying the shop and have made a good clear space at the front for a little load which is coming in the morning. An architect friend had taken me to see 'a bit of stuff,' at an old mill, which he thought might interest me. The house alongside the river as one might expect had been allowed to go to rack and ruin. The antique wall-papers were peeling off, the floor-boards were rotting, and the whole place over-grown and uncared for. 'Would you like to give fifty pounds for the contents?' 'No, but I would be pleased to give fifty pounds for a chest-of-drawers, two tables and the set of chairs.' I could hardly believe my eyes when I saw the chairs. They were pure Regency. There were five in the dining-room, one in the larder and two tied to a window hasp upstairs as a burglar trap. Eight exquisite Regency chairs! They would have to go to the cabinet-maker for expert restoration, then I would clean them off with methylated spirit and steel wool, polish them back to beauty with Penny Priors beeswax and turpentine, and finally re-upholster them with striped iceblue brocade. They would be worthy of a Manor House.

As I explored the old mill with my friend, I said sadly, 'They must have been desperately poor.'

'That's what everybody thought,' he replied, 'neighbours used to try to help, one kind soul was allowed to come in. She loved the old place, and knew where every bird nested in the wilderness that had been a garden. The old man who outlived his wife, left the property to her, plus what was in the bank — sixty-eight thousand pounds to whit!' I'm surprised you did not read about it in the local press.'

81

WE ARE DOWN AT THE Welsh cottage again. It is November. This afternoon John and I braved the north wind and, in wintry sunshine, strolled along our favourite beach with only myriad sea-birds for company. John teases me when we go beach-combing, and asks me what antiques he is expected to find; he reminds me that 'we are on the wrong side for King John's jewels,' so I settle for a carved figure-head or a lump of amber-gris. What treasures the old grey widow-maker must enfold. We find a dead seal and a few stranded jelly fish. I fill a pocket with little ramshorn shells. When we turn for home, we gather flotsam and spear a ball of pitch for a fire-lighter. We are sitting by the great fire now, a piece of broken mast still bearing some torn green canvas burns with bright blue flames. If it had tongues, this kindling could tell as many tales as my old furniture. The ball of pitch is melting now and, as strings of sapphires, it streams into the wood ash below.

To-morrow we must take the bow-saw down to the beach for a silvery trunk, denuded of bark, lies at the foot of the stones. Perhaps it has made its own miniature Kon-tiki Expedition from Ireland.

I am not cooking to-night. It is Starvation Supper in the Church Hall and we sit on pine benches on either side of a long scrubbed table and are served with either bread and soup, or bread and cheese. There is a pudding basin on the table which is a collecting bowl for the hungry. The Rector is our genial, beloved host. The meal may last an hour or more, and the company and the laughter make it a feast.

Last time, someone enquired if I had a pair of globes to sell, a celestial and terrestrial one. I said that I had never had a pair, and that they were rare and costly. The only celestial object I have at the moment is a telescope and this prompted my neighbour to say that he had once bought one in Haverfordwest Market. He thought that if it magnified the stars, he would get a wonderful 'close-up' of the passing ships but, to his dismay, they appeared upside down.

'You could stand on your head' suggested John.

'And I would have done it too, in my younger days,' came the reply, 'but that was before I lost my thatch!'

Yesterday we tracked down an ex-customer who deals a little herself. I came away without my address book, and the name of her village was both unspellable and unpronounceable to me. However, by calling at several garages and asking for 'the new Irish Lady with the boxer-dogs' we finally found her and what a lovely welcome we received.

She is renting a small holding. Her favourite mare has moved with her and was grazing contentedly on the valley side. The property includes a splendid dry stone barn used as an antique store. I bought some country Hepplewhite chairs and a very fine beaded Victorian one.

The piece I liked most was in her home but was not for sale. It was a gem of an early yew tree table with drop-leaves. She had bought it for fifty shillings from a junk man. It had been covered in white paint and the vendor had done his best to dissuade her from buying it, and to have one with a plastic top. I also admired a really lovely French clock; she had just had it cleaned and the jeweller had offered her £35 for it; her grandfather had paid 2/6d for it some eighty years ago, and had not been very pleased about it at the time, as he had not bid for it. He had been riding his baby son on his shoulders, at a country sale, and the auctioneer had mistaken the child's waving arms as a bid.

John says that I have earned my keep this little holiday, as I have covered several arm chairs, including his big wing one, with some rather glorious deep red brocade. The only thing is that they make the carpet look shabby. It is so strange and so delightful to have no interruptions, and to begin a job and finish it in one fell swoop — no tradespeople, no 'custymuds' at the door, and no neighbours until the day's work is done. The silence is complete, except for the occasional racketing of a tractor down the lane with its noisy outriders of farm dogs who some hours later may give a repeat performance up the lane. I have remembered two other sounds, both of which we love. Sometimes we hear gales of laughter from the nearby barn when the children school their ponies there and, at night, we sometimes hear the soft murmur of the sea, when the wind is in the West.

82

I HAVE BEEN A DEALER for twenty-five years. A quarter of a century! Some of my customers with children were not born, when I opened my shop.

When I was newly married, a gypsy selling lace at the door, rattled off my future, 'You've a lucky face, lady! A very lucky face! You'll have a son and a daughter. You'll be lucky and happy! You will keep your husband's love, indeed it's a lucky face you have, lady!' She was puzzled by my palm, however, 'You are going to spend a great deal of money, a great deal of money, but I cannot tell you how.' I can for I suppose I have spent a hundred thousand pounds since that day.

This antique business is really like a germ, a fever for which there is no cure. Even if I go out for the day, on the Women's Institute Outing, I always manage to cover my expenses. One year at Worcester, I found a £12 outsize Regency sideboard in the Shambles. The dealer delivered it free and I made ten pounds on it. Another year at Hereford, I only left the party for fifteen minutes, but in that time I wrote a cheque for a set of my favourite country Chippendale chairs, which were waiting for me down a side street. Gordon brought them on his next visit to Penny Priors. My friends could tell, by my face, that I had found something, when I rejoined them at the bus, 'What is it this time, Anne? A grand piano? Or an early mangle?'

Last W.I. Outing was to Lichfield, where I found myself attached to a group of new members, otherwise I might have got them to hump a pretty conversation piece from near the Cathedral to the parked coach. They did however volunteer to carry some tall vases and pitchers. We wandered back to the bus, like a group of Rebeccas, looking for a well.

In the spring we did a Day Trip to the Ideal Home Exhibition in London, and Angela came too. On arriving at Olympia, we took a taxi off to the Hornsey Road, where we had heard of a dealer who specialises in selling to the trade. There he was, bearded and genial, sitting among his French clocks, stuffed pike, cricket cages, humming birds, figurines, Welsh hats, spoon warmers, jade trees and stars of David. We filled a quantity of boxes with our purchases, settled with cheques and arranged their collection.

We hared back to Olympia by underground, and found that four hours had sped by. At one of the stands, we revived ourselves with saucers full of shrimps disporting themselves in a famous mayonnaise, and then made for the Section of Craftsmen at work. We hurried past the Stands of modern sprayed furniture, standing on garish carpets, all so alike, until the Sanderson Stand pulled us up in our tracks. This firm was displaying its beautiful wall-papers as a background to antique furniture, mostly pine pieces. How each enhanced the other!

We spent the next hour watching the carpet-makers at their looms, and the lace-makers at the pillows — what wonderful things human hands can do. In the Hong Kong Section we bought a box of imitation singing birds. We bought these to put in Victorian brass birdcages and to perch on the boughs of almond blossom in the shop.

On the coach home, we quietly studied the Programme of the Exhibition, and realised we had missed many stands of interest to us both. I decided to stop talking for the whole journey, as I often feel I am rather much for my quiet girl. Bless her heart!

I TRY TO LEAVE THE WEATHER out of my diary. I said somewhere that I liked this climate! It is certainly always breaking records, which is not surprising, as records have not been kept for long. The only cheerful thing about the weather this last ten days has been this little rhyme I found. It comes from Oxfordshire and describes the situation to a T.

Fust it rained and then it blew,
Then it frez and then it snew,
Then it cum a shower o' rain,
Then it frez and snew again!

We all know that the prices have been rising all our lives, but when I look round my shop, there is still not a single piece there which could be *made* for the price and that would exclude the materials. Almost daily one reads in the press of the rise in prices; a Georgian Silver Chocolate Pot which in 1949 made £300 under the hammer was resold in 1965 for £2,600. Five years ago I could buy very large circular Rosewood Victorian dining tables for about six pounds each — three in one afternoon was my record. Now they are hard to find at twelve pounds, but a cabinet maker would not copy one for fifty pounds!

Pine furniture is very popular at the moment. This is made of Canadian yellow pine, which in 1900 was eight pounds a standard, and is now £250. Fashion is a funny thing — take brass bedsteads for instance, I saw a new one the other day, a four-poster all complete with mattress and frills for £85. At Blenheim Palace at Woodstock in Oxfordshire one can see the one in which Sir Winston Churchill was born. My own parents had a rather grander one in turquoise blue enamel and brass. We children liked to unwind the knobs and wind them on again, it was not a four-poster but had a high head and high side arms to support the curtains. The first one I saw in a Manor House locally was particularly beautiful. They had just had the lovely ornate head piece, with its garlands of brass flowers, pegged to the wall and the double divan-bed on Shepherds' casters was pushed up close to it and was footless. The bedspread was ice blue silk and over it was flung a ruched white spotted muslin cover. It looked a dream. The other furniture in the room was all French Provençale, which is solid walnut French country furniture, often garlanded too. The pièce de résistance in the room was an immense wardrobe with its great panelled doors hung on iron hinges and adorned with great iron escutcheons, quite fifteen inches long.

This furniture is most decorative. There are chairs, stools, console tables and a lovely walnut wardrobe in this furniture from Brittany, to be seen in an exclusive gown shop just by the Royal Shakespeare Theatre, at Stratford-upon-Avon.

When my customers ask for Flemish or French Provençale furniture this is what they mean. When they ask for French furniture, they usually mean very fine painted or gilded pine furniture. Chairs would have tapered fluted legs and the seats and chair arms would almost certainly be upholstered in real silk brocade; tables would probably have similar legs, console tables might have marble tops and so could the commodes, which in French means cupboard or chest-of-drawers. Our English word commodious, meaning to hold or contain, comes from the same root of course. Other Flemish chests-of-drawer may be described as bombe, similar to embonpoint in a human, but twice as pretty. Angela once bought a very fine bombe Flemish bureau and regretted selling it. I bought only two French chairs last year, one from a dealer friend at the door. Before I had a chance to carry this chair inside, a Penny Priors lady had snapped it up. The second one I bought in Swansea, from a dealer there. This also was quickly snapped up too and the profit on it covered my expenses to Wales and home again. The same day, which I shall not forget because it rained non-stop, I bought the most superb pair of chamber pots I ever had. They were on top of a high cupboard in a dealer's shop, but a ladder was fetched and they were handed to me. Could they be Swansea? There were the roses and the lavish gold decoration, — eight pounds ten shillings. I must be mad, and madder still to take them with me. They got heavier, or I got weaker, as the day wore on, handbag dangling from my left elbow, umbrella above my head, woven fish bag containing the two 'gussunders' in my right hand, plus a sodden paper carrier-bag that threatened to miscarry its lobster child. I caught sight of myself in a dark beteared shop-window. I looked down on my luck.

The chamber pots were right. I had thought they were not, as I was unable to see a light shining through them, and thought they could not be porcelain. 'No,' said the purchaser, as he cheerfully wrote his cheque, 'not when porcelain is as thick as that.'

'HAVE YOU ANY old prints or engravings?'

'Yes, I've quantities. Let me put the portfolios on this large table, and here is a comfy chair. Would you like to look through them quietly, or shall I help you?'

'Well, I am really a dog-breeder,' may come the rather surprising reply, 'and I am interested in any old prints showing King Charles spaniels, or mastiffs.'

Another customer may say,

'I've got all day to look at them. So perhaps you would like to leave me to it? I'm a collector of antique dolls and children's toys, so I buy any old prints that include them. Some customers want sporting prints, others ask for coloured prints of fashions, horse-drawn vehicles, flowers, birds or fish.

The finest bird prints I have ever had were by Gould, and were bought in a second-hand shop during the war. I suppose they had been pulled out of one of his famous books on birds. I wished afterwards that I had persevered and really tried to track it down.

A few years ago, a superb book of flowers engraving was sold at a village sale near by. The London buyers heard about it and it made £530. Each engraving was about sixteen inches by twelve inches and exquisitely coloured by hand with water colours, a sheet of tissue paper between each page. A single specimen of one plant in bloom, say a spotted orchid, would be in the foreground, with a magnificent background of mountains and sky to illustrate its habitat. For once I attended the View Day and had time to feast my eyes.

To-day has been a historic one for fine art dealers and auctioneers for there has been the first Transatlantic Auction Sale on Television. Let me put down the date, May 27th, 1965. Messrs. Sotheby's of New Bond Street held the Sale in London, with an audience there, and with another audience in New York.

It was a most suitable Première, as most of the pictures were engravings from the drawings of the famous artist-naturalist John James Audubon. The man is world-renowned for his Studies of the Birds of America.

He was the Haiti-born son of a French naval officer and at eighteen, in the year 1804, was sent from France to live and work on a property of his father's called Mill Grove, on Perkiomen Creek in Philadelphia. His father had hoped he would develop the property, for it contained a lead mine, which seemed a good investment. The young man fell instantly and deeply in love with the earthly paradise in which he found himself. He ranged the countryside with his gun and dogs, finding empty nests everywhere. As the snows melted the birds returned. The pewees, small olive green birds were the first, followed swiftly by countless other varieties all unknown to him. He began to sketch and paint these birds with unbounded delight. To add to his joys, at their first meeting he fell deeply and lastingly in love with Lucy Bakewell, the fifteen year old daughter of an English landowner on an adjoining estate. She once said 'I have a rival in every bird.'

Quickly young John James became an expert taxidermist and devised a way of wiring specimens on to flowering boughs or seedheads and rushes, thus being able to faithfully and exquisitely complete his drawings. As his studies increased, so his business decreased. But his joy was unbounded and he once remarked 'not a ball, a skating match or riding party took place without me.'

The elder Audubon felt that his son was wasting his time and his allowance was stopped. The young man immediately returned to the family home near Nantes, and convinced his people of his sincere love and devotion for Lucy and promised to try to be a successful businessman for her sake. He returned with a young friend as a partner, Each time this friend suggested new areas for commerce, John James welcomed the idea as new opportunities of seeing other birdlife and natural wonders. In 1808, when he was 23 and Lucy 20, they married, and the following day she left her sheltered life. The honeymoon was a sample of what was to come. They travelled by coach over rough roads and then journeyed over a thousand miles down the Ohio River by flat-boat. It was a naturalist's paradise and she welcomed her new life with open arms. They knew poverty, hardship, many separations and deepest grief — their two sons lived, but both little daughters died. They often lived like pioneers, he wrote afterwards to her 'the pleasures I felt under the roof of that log cabin can never be effaced from my heart.'

Finally his business failed. The creditors closed in and he was left with nothing but his clothes, his gun and the folios of *The Birds of America*, worth a king's ransom, but which nobody wanted. Lucy helped support the home by running a little school and he helped by teaching the pupils French, drawing and music. He scraped some money together, working as a taxidermist and painting portraits at five dollars a time. He tried in vain to get the Art World interested in his life's work and was advised to try his fortune in our old country, where fine engravings could be made. Lucy urged him to go and helped with money. His Exhibition in Liverpool in 1826 met with instant success and he travelled all over England and Scotland with his work. Crowds thronged to see his unparalleled studies, and also the delightful and interesting man himself, who seemed to bring the freshness and beauty of the wilds with him. In one of his love letters from England to his wife he wrote :- 'I need not tell thee, I long for thee every hour I am absent from thee. If I fail, America will still be my country and thou, I still feel, my friend.'

But it was success at last, for John James, sponsors quickly came forward to have his work engraved and printed. The first of the many were prints of the Wild Turkey, which these days command four figures. So after fourteen months it was home again, success and fourtune and the end of their monetary trials.

Before I write about an old print I have in the back of the shop, I must enter in my journal that an oil painting hf Sir Winston Churchill's was sold at this first Transatlantic Auction, It was the first to be offered since his death and made the record price of 14,000 guineas!

Now about this other print, I have it still. It is of the child marriage of little Ann Mobray. You have probably read this year of the discovery of this eight-year-old's body in its little lead coffin, when excavations were being made on a building site in London.

I am going to try to do a little drawing from this print for my journal. The two sturdy children in the foreground stand on a little step, the Bishop kneels beside them, and bejewelled figures stand behind them. The child bride holds a ribboned lead to her spaniel puppy, who scratches his ear. The ring, which is being placed on the chubby finger appears to be a rosette of diamonds, not a plain band. The words below the picture are as follows :— The Marriage of Richard Duke of York, Brother to Edward the Fifth on the 15th January 1477 with Lady Ann Mowbray, Daughter & Sole Heir of John Lord Mowbray, Duke of Norfolk. Painted by J. Northcote Esq. R.A. London Published Feb. 1. 1826 by W. Sams, Book & Print Sellers to the Royal Family. No. 1. St. James's Street, opposite the Palace, Engraved by W. Say engraver to T.R.H. the Duke & Duchesse of Gloucester. Vide Sandfords Genealogy of the Kings of England.

THIS MORNING, I went by bus to a sale thirty miles away. The piece I coveted was Lot 64, described in the catalogue as a Flemish walnut dresser, but it turned out to be a natural coloured oak Edwardian sideboard. I had seen it several times before. I mentioned this to a dealer friend and he muttered,

"Arf the stuff been offered before — I wonder some of it don't jump up on the table and hoffer itself.'

Some twelve years ago I was at a farm sale near Banbury and the auctioneer had a job to get a single bid for a wonderful old four-wheeled farm wagon. It was knocked down for 22/6. The local scrap metal dealer was standing next to me and remarked 'Folks will pay fifty pounds for them in years to come. Just the job to put in the grounds of a big house.' I remembered his words last week, when I read in the Daily Telegraph that Bernard Miles was trying to find one for 'The Hay Wagon' which he is putting on at the Mermaid Theatre.

I have been offered some wagon wheels this week, by another scrap metal man. He didn't say 'wagon' exactly, he used another word. Perhaps they are painted red. I shall certainly have a look at them, as he has some old panelling and some brass bedsteads too. He said, 'Call any time, before the boozers open.' I heard of one lady who had a great wagon wheel laid down flat in her garden and grew herbs, — a different variety between each spoke. I am wondering if it would be possible to put one down flat, with a rod through the hub, to use as a children's playwheel in the garden. I have seen piles of them being burnt, just to retrieve the iron rims. It seems all wrong.

A dear Cornish friend, whom I used to visit long ago, told me how, as children, they used to gather by the little stream in their village to watch the smith fix red hot iron rims on the wheels and toss them hissing into the water to cool and contract. Even greater excitement was experienced when gipsies came to the village, to collect a new caravan which had been built for them in the local wheelwright's shop. The gipsy king would take a meal with the family. My friend, as a little girl, would watch him put little piles of sovereigns, in settlement, in front of his plate on the old refectory table.

It was in this old Cornish house, that I first saw butter being made by hand; tasted saffron cake; saw pasties being made properly with raw meat and thinly sliced raw potatoes, onions and herbs; consumed bacon and egg pie; and learnt what they mean by 'thunder and lightning' for tea. That meant home-made white bread, spread generously with Cornish cream and zig zagged with running honey, — scrumptious!

Customers often ask me what books or novels I can recommend them to read about the antique trade. I think Mr Vachell's 'Quinneys' was probably the first novel. Later a film was made of this book and filmed in Chipping Campden in Gloucestershire. One of my customers, an antique collector, lives in the beautiful stone house which was the hotel in the picture.

I sometimes make a little list for customers, like this :—
'Quinneys,' by A. H. Vachell.
'Quality Chase' by M. H. Tiltman.
'Make me an Offer' by Wolf Mankowitz.
'Knock or Ring' by Michael Nelson.

'Looking in Junk Shops,' and 'More Looking in Junk Shops,'
  by John Bedford.
'Antique Dealing' by the Staff of the Antiques Year Book.
'A Shop in the High Street,' by S. Leek.
'Antique Dealer's Diary,' by R. P. Way.
and of course, the 'Antique Year Books.'

'Antique Dealing' is rather delightfully dedicated to dealers
in the following words, 'Dedicated to the Much-Maligned
Dealer, without whom so much Beauty would be Dust.'

Before I forget, I will pop a bit in here about a film, a
historical film, that was made at one of the great houses in this
district, shortly after the war. I believe it was called 'The
Black Orchid,' but I am not sure. Anyway, it was summer time,
and conveniently holiday time for the children; a little gang
of them would go off on their bicycles each day to watch.
Gordon thought it was wonderful, and was full of it one day at
tea-time; Angela, however, was quiet and thoughtful.
'What did you think of it, Pet?' I enquired.
'Oh, it was all right.'
'When you say "all right" like that, it sounds "all wrong"?'
'Well Mummy, do you think it is right to pretend?'
'How do you mean Pet?'
'Well Mummy, they dug a trench and put a fence down in it,
and then the hero jumped it on his horse and the cameraman lay
on the grass, to make it look brave.' I looked appropriately
shocked and said it was cheating.
'Yes, I think so too, and it was such an easy fence. Any of the
girls at Pony Club could have jumped it, Mummy.'

❧ 86 ❧

Now that i am older, I open my shop only one day a week. This gives me more time to get out and find the goods and time for working on my stock. I am lucky enough to have some splendid part-time helpers. I have written somewhere else about Mr Appleyard. A polishing lady comes two mornings a week; a retired friend in the village rubs down and paints all my iron garden furniture, while another who has a tank of caustic soda strips all my pine pieces for me. Most Thursdays, the upholsterer delivers and collects various chairs and stools and then I set to and put on their final coverings of velvet or brocade.

I must not forget my youngest helper, my elder grandson. He is now two and a half, the same age as his mother was when I opened my little shop. It is hard to say yet, if he is going to be interested in the trade. He certainly enjoys sticking my little self-adhesive labels on the brass knobs of the dresser and everywhere else imaginable. He pulls out my bureau slides and 'posts' his biscuits into the slots. He is fascinated by clocks and watches so perhaps he is a budding horologist! He is certainly observant, a great asset to any dealer. Last week, when he went to tea with a family who own a Manx cat, he made numerous close inspections of its posterior and was baffled. The solitaire board with its glass marbles is a great favourite of his and, like his Mother, he loves to join in and help with everything.

When visiting the Arboretum near Badminton in Gloucestershire last summer, we discovered that our many-trunked evergreen trees are called Lawson Cupressi and next summer we are planning to make a little tree house for him and fix it in one of these obliging trees, just a few feet from the ground.

Somewhere in my diary I wrote about Angela's peach tree, which grows alongside the Cupressi. Although it receives no care, it always blooms and usually bears, whereas our wisteria which we have tended, pruned, nurtured, watered, coaxed, manured and cajoled for twenty-four years has only bloomed once — the year we had two grandsons.

A POOR OLD WOMAN aged 88 was cremated in Oxford to-day. Years ago she and her husband used to deliver bread and coal round these villages, both from the same vehicle! This little two wheeled cart was pulled by a donkey. The coal sacks were under the driver's seat and the great baskets of cottage loaves on the tail board. Now follows one of Mr Bede's stories about them. They were delivering coal one day to one of his cronies. A small village boy was proudly holding the donkey's head, but his pleasure was shortlived. Suddenly there were screams for help and cries of 'The moke's up, The moke's up,' and they all rushed out. Sure enough the removal of the coal had upset the balance and the load of bread had caused the contraption to rear its shafts, taking the steed and its little attendant aloft. I tell Mr Bede that he should submit some of his stories to a matchbox firm. He just chuckles and says, 'Did I ever tell you about the old bounder who lives up there in that cottage on the hill Mrs S? Well, one day I was delivering him a few seed potatoes and he said, "You might take that gun, and take a pot shot at those two blooming pigeons in the oak tree. They are getting all my peas".'

Mr Bede obliged and there was a double funeral. 'But why.' he asked, 'didn't you shoot them yourself?'

'Not likely.' he replied, 'I thought the blooming gun might bust.'

By Mr Bede's back door is a little statue of a maiden, minus a few fingers and toes. We always used to call her Psyche until one of his regular taxi customers tried to buy her. 'How much do you want for your little Frisky?' he asked, — he must have seen the name written somewhere. Quite rightly Mr Bede wouldn't part with her, and when he enquires after my health and the family's. I return the compliment by asking after his and Little Frisky's.

Isn't it funny how some little jokes get funnier? When Angela and I were out in our little van, and perhaps had met a sheep-dog padding along the grass verge, one of us would say something quite silly, like 'He's late for his appointment,' or 'He usually raises his hat,' or 'He didn't recognise us. Must have something on his mind.' Just because we were out buying, and happy together, it seemed very funny and we would shake with laughter.

This isn't an antique dealer's diary at all to-day, it's just scribble. But as in a book, I am trying to wind it up, and summarise a little. For instance, Mrs Clancey's heart is still ticking away, bless it, and no one even has to take her pulse these days. Both my God-daughters are married. Of course all the older dears have departed this life and lie in a neat row in the Churchyard, with two young warriors between them and a little drowned boy. I have not sold my tombstone yet. But I have found some words I like for it by Francis Thompson, 'Look for me in the nurseries of Heaven.'

THE LOVELY old shire horses are no more. For some strange reason all the Wellingtonia trees in the village have died. Perhaps they were all planted at the same time and had run their natural span, or could it be because of the sinking of new wells? Mr Bede is just as kind and helpful and hasn't used up all his funny stories yet. He has fulfilled a life-long ambition in getting a robin to feed off his hand.

About the Tudors; you may remember, I helped them when they moved farms, and Jane was very sad about it all? Well, the move was a wise one. Slowly they made their new home and garden even more beautiful than the last. 'New' is not at all the word, as the old house is Elizabethan, with its original fine staircase. In the grounds are the remains of an old maze we think. Several times they have dug up Roman coins, and once the head-stone of a priest's grave. The big house had been empty for some years, and the foxes took short cuts through the garden and were much too friendly. But the nightingales were friendly too, and one never-to-be-forgotten June evening, they sang to Jane's accompaniment on her grand piano.

Some years later, another little daughter was born to them. She was the most beautiful girl-child I ever saw. The children have grown up, the years slip by, one daughter is married and one at college, but three things remain the same there. The house is full of music still, the scent of wood fires still fills the rooms, and oh, those welcomes!

More than thirty years ago, I heard for the first time my son saying, or rather practising, the word 'Mummy' as he lay alone in his nursery. Now I have heard the next sweetest word, 'Gwanny,' and it seems right that it should have a 'w' in it, for the beloved little granddaughter now lives in Wales. Her home is on the side of a steep valley, with a stream in the garden. Several little girls come to play with her each day when they get home from school. They have soft gentle voices and sweet names strange to us, such as Bethen, Blodwen and Mara. Life is unhurried there. They fetch the milk from the farm as we used to do. Neighbours stop and talk and exchange recipes and sittings of eggs. They give car-less people lifts into town or to Church, and rally round and share each other's joys and sorrows. Gordon is always singing praises of their thoughtfulness and their generosity. The last time I returned by coach from Wales I had a little illustration of this. The bus driver glanced back once or twice at a young fellow struggling with a large map in the front seat and shortly afterwards he halted his bus in a lay-by. Getting up, he went and sat by the passenger and quietly refolding his map for him, must have shown him our route. Then beaming at us, he remarked in his musical Welsh voice,

'We have to look after our overseas friends, don't we, ladies and gents? Can't have them getting lost, can we?'

Angela and Dave have not moved away after all. Sometimes we take care of their boy in an evening. I bath him too, an child easier or jollier could not be imagined. Bathing our grand-

daughter for the first time was a different experience. She shot
from one end of the big bath to the other, thrashing the water
like a hooked salmon, 'Gwanny' in hot pursuit, on her praying
bones, trying to keep the little mouth above water. Somehow, I
landed her, alive!

John has not forgotten my Swedish customer and sometimes
says, 'Have you got a kiss for your old horse-pond?' So what
the gyspy said came true.

We now have three grandchildren. Let me finish to-day with
two joyful verses from the Psalms :—

'Yea, thou shalt see thy children's children.'

'Then was our mouth filled with laughter and our tongue
with singing.'